Talyllyn Pioneers

The team that changed the
world of preserved steam railways forever

The original conspirators pose in front of *Dolgoch*: In the cab is David Curwen (Chief Engineer). On the ground from left to right are Bill Trinder (Chairman), Pat Whitehouse (Secretary), Tom Rolt (General Manager) and Pat Garland (Treasurer) on Whit Monday, 14th May, 1951. *(Photo: The Times)*

Talyllyn Pioneers

by

Michael Whitehouse

Wilderness Enterprises Limited

2015

Contents

FRONT COVER: A timeless scene: The 'Old Lady' *Dolgoch* heads towards Cynfal with a mixed train on Saturday 18th April, 2015 *(Photo: Barbara Fuller)*

BACK COVER: Top: Whit Monday, 1951 and the first public passenger train in the history of the TRPS is ready to leave for its historic journey to Rhydyronen. *Dolgoch* simmers in the station at Towyn Wharf and Bill Trinder, the Society Chairman, cuts the white ceremonial tape *(Photo: Pat Whitehouse)*.
Bottom: *Edward Thomas* hauls a heavy summer train up the Afon Fathew Valley. The engine has been fitted with the ugly flat Giesl ejector and every coach has been pressed into service, including some yet unfinished by the carriage workshops *(Photo: Jim Jarvis, Kidderminster Railway Museum collection)*

© Michael Whitehouse and Wilderness Enterprises Limited.
First published in 2015 by Wilderness Enterprises Limited, Worcestershire.

ISBN 978-0-9933974-0-0

Writtten by Michael Whitehouse

Designed by Ian Blaza

Printed and bound in Great Britain

(Photo: Brian Goodchild)

The Road to Adventure

This is a story of human endeavour and success from the 1950s and at a time when the world at large was slowly beginning to return to life after a terrible war fought to secure freedom for individuals and nations. A group of enthusiasts formed a 'Big Society', took over a railway by-way which became their own and rebuilt it so that many thousands of people could enjoy it. This is their story, largely told by them and in their own words.

'The Talyllyn Railway is one of the very few lines which have not been made straight or bulldozed off the map. Some may say it has become a worn out anachronism in this age of the jet plane and the atom bomb into which it has strayed. Surely, then, so much time, money and energy could have been expended to some better purpose? To this I would reply with another question: What other and more fruitful fields has the planned state left open for individual initiative and creative enterprise? With every year that passes there is less fertile ground left and it is a dreary, ill-nourished crop which sprouts in state owned fields. False quantitative standards of equality and uniformity imposed in the name of democracy; the false equation of mere size with efficiency which assumes that the larger the organization the better it must be; these things run counter to the grain of human nature and lead to damnation and the dark night of the spirit.

It is, of course, arguable that when economic or social change threatens any institution with extinction it should be left to die because attempts to preserve it, however well intentioned, are but nostalgic kickings against the pricks of change and can only succeed in embalming a corpse from which the spirit has flown. There is so much truth in this argument that in any other age but this it would be unassailable. But we are moving rapidly towards a new Dark Age where evils of unprecedented power threaten the whole world. And when the house is afire the instinct to save something of value from the blaze is too strong to be denied.

It may be thought that I am seeking to magnify out of all true proportion the significance of our efforts to preserve one small railway in a remote valley in the Welsh mountains. But the Talyllyn Railway is not simply an engineering museum piece; it is a local institution and as such it has become a part of Wales and of Welsh life. There is no finer tonic in this atomic age than a visit to Towyn with a volunteer working party. For the Talyllyn Railway bears eloquent witness to the fact that man can build as well as destroy.

In this ancient kingdom of Gwynedd, under the shadow of Cader Idris we have striven against odds not merely to preserve a railway but to keep alive a spark of that fine tradition which flourished so richly when the Talyllyn line was born. Is it not worth cherishing? Certainly in the last two years the Talyllyn Railway has given pleasure to thousands, a new sense of purpose to those who have joined our Society, and to me good companions and an adventure which I shall remember all my days.[1]

1. Railway Adventure by L.T.C. Rolt 1953

The Talyllyn Railway as part of our lives

I t was barely dark when I used to go to bed about 6.30pm in Aberdovey on our family Whitsun holidays in Wales. I was then only six years old. I used to lie in bed listening to the curlews circling over the Dovey estuary and the sound of the small tidal waves lapping over the small shingle beach outside our village cottage while I waited to hear the sound of the steam train across the water as a prelude to enjoying a mix of green liveried narrow and standard gauge steam engines on holiday in this delightful part of Wales. Both types of railway were to become significant parts of our lives, but then we were to influence their futures too in preservation.

My patience in listening to the sounds over the Dovey estuary was rewarded by the far away sound of a Great Western Railway 'Manor' pulling three or maybe four coaches from Machynlleth to Aberystwyth along the other side of the estuary. I would lie in bed and listen to the distant but regular beat of the two cylinder small 4-6-0 as she took her train down the opposite coastline, her exhaust sometimes as clear as a bell across the water and sometimes disappearing for a short while as the train's passage was hidden by a rocky bluff. If I sat up in bed, pulled back the curtain and looked out of the window across the water in the gloaming I could see the white exhaust of the train as it made its way down the shore line and then disappear after turning south at Ynyslas. I would then sleep content in the knowledge that the next day would bring even more interesting sights: a small prairie 45XX tank engine huffing and winding round the sharp estuary coastline through Aberdovey and on to Towyn, dwarfed by a large *Cambrian Coast Express* headboard on the top of its smokebox and then the delightful small narrow gauge tank engines of the Talyllyn Railway, often double headed, fussing with heavy trains of tourists

riding in a cosmopolitan collection of carriages up to see waterfalls in the foothills of the Cader Idris mountain range.

I knew my father would be amenable to a child who wanted to go to Towyn and see these small green steam engines pulling quaint red coaches on the Talyllyn Railway. He would let me pretend to drive the hugely different range of static engines in the Museum at Wharf station whilst he was having many long discussions with grown ups about how the railway was to be run and what was to be done next. Then, as a family and with friends, we would all travel up on the 2'3" narrow gauge line to Abergynolwyn, hopefully in one of the open coaches or in the newly restored Corris coach behind either *Edward Thomas* or *Douglas* or both double heading together. All these experiences: holidays in Wales, listening to the Aberystwyth bound train across the estuary and riding the Talyllyn Railway were to prove life enhancing for myself, my family through three generations and then also for many thousands of people countrywide as our family interests turned to actions over the years setting the scene for railway preservation as we have come to know it now.

On our frequent journeys on the Talyllyn, there were many highlights to look out for: the immediate thrill of running through the long bridge after Wharf station, the glimpse of engines through the windows inside Pendre shed, listening to the engine labouring up the sharp gradient from Rhydyronen, leaning out eagerly at Brynglas to see the down train coming in the other direction passing us and tugging Mummy's sleeve, when we reached Abergynolwyn, in the hope and expectation of an ice cream while we watched the small engine run round the train ready for the journey back to the sea. We would often walk up the 'extension', always to the Winding House and sometimes even up into the quarries where I

All these experiences: holidays in Wales and riding the Talyllyn Railway were to prove life enhancing for myself, my family through three generations, and also for many thousands of people countrywide as our family interests turned to actions over the years setting the scene for railway preservation as we have come to know it now

Top Left: A child's holiday memory taken with his Brownie Cresta box camera: "As a family and with friends we would all travel up to Abergynolwyn, in the restored Corris coach behind Edward Thomas and Douglas double heading together." Both engines in standard TR green stand nearly under the enlarged Neptune Rd overbridge at Wharf with a heavy summer train in 1962

Top right: Herbert Jones on *Talyllyn* and Bill Faulkner on his beloved *Edward Thomas* (for which he gave £25 so the TR could buy it from BR) after arrival at Abergynolwyn with another fully loaded 1962 summer holiday train

The Whitehouse family and children wait somewhat impatiently for a train on the TR at Rhydyronen station about 1907

would marvel at the 'sleeping beauty' of the track on the extension which had not yet been relaid and so remained exactly as it was before the TRPS came into being. We would visit this railway many times over for several years and enjoy ourselves at picnics with friends and other families by the lineside, chasing dragonflies by the streams and floating 'Pooh' sticks under bridges over babbling brooks. The Talyllyn Railway was part of our lives and summer holidays centered around it for our family and many friends as it had always done over the hundred years before with many generations of families on holidays from the industrial Midlands.

The Talyllyn Railway as part of our lives

Many of our holidays when I was a child were in Wales and they have continued to be so even as a grown up and now the fourth generation of Whitehouses also enjoys the small narrow gauge steam railways which proliferate particularly in Wales, due in no small measure to a band of men who gathered together in the Birmingham Imperial Hotel on 11th October, 1950, shortly after the second World War and decided to rescue the Talyllyn Railway from oblivion as they sought adventure whilst everything around them was being nationalised. It did not matter that the railway was then an insignificant byway with little purpose left than to entertain us holiday makers. The railway was available as a gift and this was enough to motivate volunteers to give it their all

One of the B. Whitehouse & Sons lorries with a rebuilt Glyn Valley Railway coach body being taken to Towyn Wharf station. Much behind the scenes largesse came from Midands industry to help the fledgling TRPS get off the ground. The station sign in the background, and indeed all the early new signs, were made and painted in the carpentry and paint shops at the Whitehouse construction firm

and rebuild it so that it could run for their benefit and also the enjoyment of their families and many thousands of holiday makers who flocked to the area before the jet age of Flybe was invented. The Talyllyn Railway became part of us and we became part of it. Even my toybox had a picture of *Dolgoch* on it taken from an *Airfix* magazine front cover. I was curious to see this engine which I had been told was now worn out and had gone to be mended at the works of Tom Hunt, the man we always saw when we visited the Sutton Miniature

Railway on weekend day trips from our Harborne home.

We lived at 344 Lordswood Road, Harborne which was at the very edge of Birmingham as the Black Country started just across the road. No.344 was (and still is) a 1920s brick built suburban detached house with front bay windows and a separate garage. Our home was always full of railways, even in the 1950s. On the walls in the hall were several brass L&NWR engine nameplates with magic names such as *Queen of the Belgians* and *Lady of the Lake*, which had been acquired for the princely sum of 10/6d and the family 'Works' had them mounted them on beautiful wooden boards. The bookcase in the hall was brimful of railway books written by people who became involved in the TR. We had a steady flow of railway minded visitors too: O.S. Nock, L.T.C. Rolt, John Snell, W.A. Camwell, Bill Faulkner, Lord Northesk, Viscount Garnock and the artist Terence Cuneo. The roofspace was full of model railways: a scale 4mm model made by Dad in eighteen point one millimetre gauge featuring the local L&NWR Harborne suburban terminus station, surrounded by a double track main line over which roared trains of all L&NW and GW descriptions hauled by engines built by now famous modellers: a Guy Williams built 'Claughton' would canter along the back straight with an express train of coaches

Left The Whitehouse family children, Cecil (father to PBW), Percy (uncle) and Kathleen (aunt) digging a trench for the sea water in time honoured traditions on Towyn beach in about 1905

Pat Whitehouse
(1922-1993)

Born in Warwick into a family with construction and shipping line antecedents. Became Squadron Leader in the RAF during the second world war, navigating 'Lancaster' bombers over Germany and then with 'Dakotas' in the middle east on transport service, where he became the only survivor after his plane was shot down over the Mediterranean. Returning to civilian life he married Thelma and had two children, Michael and Maggy, and ran the family construction firm B. Whitehouse & Sons, merging it with Cubitts in the 1960s. In addition to his work as Secretary of the TRPS, he became founder Chairman of the Dart Valley Railway plc and the Birmingham Railway Museum at Tyseley (now Vintage Trains) and one of the early pioneers of main line steam running. He was a keen photographer and traveller and renoun for his work with John Adams on the BBC TV *Railway Roundabout* series

PBW in his element with Bolex 16mm cine camera during a *Railway Roundabout* BBC TV film shoot sporting his TRPS tie made by Dad and pass a G2 0-8-0, exquisitely crafted by Rex Rose, labouring in the opposite direction with a long goods train. I was allowed to watch and, under supervision, drive. Many people came to run the railway with us: Ken Cope, Pat Garland and Eric Russell being just some of them, all of whom served on the first Talyllyn Railway Preservation Society Committee. They would come to have dinner at home and then wake me up by climbing the stepladder into the roof and run trains round the model railway circuit for hours while they chatted. They were all members of the Birmingham Loco Club and the Midlands Area of the Stephenson Locomotive Society. They were chatting about the Talyllyn Railway. As Dad was the Secretary it was always being discussed at home, many letters fell through our letter box addressed to it and, when we went there, Dad was always engaged interminably in conversations with other men about it. It seemed that all of Birmingham and the Black Country businesses were also involved with the TR; certainly they spent much time and effort providing materials in its rebuilding.

Mostly, the engines I saw working on the TR in those early years of my life were the newly acquired *Edward Thomas* and *Douglas*, but I was always curious to see *Talyllyn* which had been shunted off the railway and sat in a barn at Pendre station where the engine shed and workshop were. I could not understand why *Talyllyn* was not also working as it looked complete to me, but Dad said there was something seriously wrong with its firebox. I simply retorted that it should be mended then, but things did not initially seem as easy as that for some reason.

We went for many rides up the line, hopefully in the open coaches if the sun was out, and ate a picnic in the farmer's field near Rhydyronen station with the Adams family by their caravan there. Dad and John Adams were in partnership as *Colourviews* making and selling films and pictures together; this developed into the famous nationally known BBC TV *Railway Roundabout* team making films on the rapidly changing railway scene and broadcasting them live directly from the BBC studio in Birmingham. From the Adams caravan at Rhydyronen I would watch *Edward Thomas* pass by and learn that, here, the line ran downhill a little but otherwise the journey was uphill all the way. Sometimes, we stayed with Mrs. Jones at her small hotel by the Dolgoch falls and there I watched the little train cross the tall red brick arched viaduct and then ran up the steps to the station to see the engine take water in the beautiful station surrounded by rhododendron bushes.

One exciting day, we were taken up the line in an open coach behind *Midlander*, the small diesel engine, which was most unusual. Dad was taking

PJG carefully constructing his 4mm scale GWR model railway, complete with signal bell instruments before he was drawn into a world of "Talyllynitis"

Terence Cuneo to look for places where he might make a painting of the train. Dolgoch station was chosen of course and Cuneo readily agreed to Dad's suggestion of *Talyllyn* (which I was pleased to see had by then been mended at last and was running again with both a brass ring round her chimney and a lovely brass dome), the Corris coach, one of the Glyn Valley coaches and open coaches heading up the train. We spent the day with Terence Cuneo whilst he started the painting at Dolgoch station and I was amazed to watch *Talyllyn* appear on the canvas as if by magic; three strokes of a black paintbrush and the chimney appeared! It took a long time to make the painting, so *Talyllyn* had to run up to Abergynolwyn and also back down to Brynglas to get out of the way of the service train. I was allowed to press the shutter of PBW's Rolleiflex camera to capture a shot of *Talyllyn* on Dolgoch viaduct; I was 'instructed' to squeeze the shutter so the picture came out sharp and it did.

PBW's 'EM' model railway in the roof at 344 Lordswood Rd, Harborne, where much conversation took place between the pioneers over evening operating sessions. In the shed yard stand two exquisite models by Rex Rose: the LNWR 'G2' and GWR "*Tre Pol and Pen*"; Rex made two models of the latter – one for each of the Pats

One year *Edward Thomas* had a new chimney; an ugly flat triangular shaped chimney, which did not suit it at all. But, by this time I knew all about these chimneys as a Dr. Giesl had been to our house for lunch and shown us pictures of Austrian engines fitted with them; they looked ugly too. John Snell, who was an early volunteer on the TR, seemed to know about these sorts of things and, as he usually stayed with us over Christmas, showed us lots of pictures he had taken of Eastern European engines, some of which wore these ejectors. He was of the view that the funny chimney was only necessary in that part of the world as the boiler designs there were not as good as ours and so putting one on No.4 was simply a publicity stunt.

By now, I had my Brownie Cresta box camera and so busied myself taking pictures of the four working TR engines within my allowance of twelve exposures on one film: *Talyllyn, Edward Thomas, Douglas* and *Midlander*. *Talyllyn* was my firm favourite simply because it looked so nice; I had never seen another engine with a copper ring round its chimney before and its appearance was one of elegance which is all that mattered to a small boy, even if the TR engine crew struggled with its performance. The summer holiday trains were very very busy at this time and, so, many of the trains were double headed, which gave me the excuse to ask for more film! Some trains were even banked up to Rhydyronen and, one day, I was allowed to have a footplate ride on *Talyllyn* whilst working this duty and driven by Herbert Jones. The picture I took at Rhydyronen of Talyllyn before she rolled back to Towyn was good enough to appear in a childrens' newspaper, even though it was taken with my Brownie. Like many other

children who rode the TR, I was learning about railways, how steam engines worked and how to take better photographs – all as well as having a lovely holiday – such were the subliminal benefits of a railway as a preserved tourist attraction, kept and run purely for enjoyment.

I kept asking when *Dolgoch* was coming back from being repaired as she had been away for a very long time. I was eventually rewarded by being present at Wharf when the low loader arrived bringing her back and so I took so many pictures of her being unloaded and towed up to Pendre by *Talyllyn*. Dad rationed my film for the rest of the holiday and would only allow me to have contact prints made of the pictures I had taken which I was cross about as they were far too small.

By now, it had been explained to me that the Talyllyn Railway was the first preserved railway to be owned and run by volunteers and that all the many people who came to see us at 344 were the people who ran it. Most of them were Birmingham people and we often went to see them in their homes and play with their model trains. Pat Garland, the Treasurer, had a GWR 'EM' gauge railway in his garage and 'Uncle' Eric Russell, the Auditor, had a French narrow gauge railway in his attic. John Adams, the Photographer, lived out near Bromsgrove by the famous Lickey Bank so we used to picnic there and watch the express trains toil up the bank shoved by several tank engines and a 9F with a headlight and the long goods trains have their brakes pinned down at Blackwell by the guard before descending.

Dad had steadily been making a 16mm colour film of the TR and, by now, I knew the story by heart and had thumbed through all the various books and magazines about the TR and many other railways. We had been up to see Alan Garraway at the Festiniog Railway one very wet Whitsun and also travelled over the Vale of Rheidol Railway from Aberystwyth. We had been to Fairbourne very many times ostensibly to ride behind *Count Louis* (or more often the petrol engine, *Dingo*) but actually for Dad to have interminable conversations with John Wilkins who provided a key lifeline helping the TR out financially supporting the railway from his *Servis* washing machine business. We would also go over to Sutton Park on the outskirts of Birmingham where there was a superb 15″ gauge miniature railway running round in a balloon loop by the Pat Collins' fairground. Dad's conversations with the owner, Tom Hunt, went on for so long that I was able to have multiple free rides behind both the red and blue Atlantics *Sutton Belle* and *Sutton Flyer*!

Of course, all these conversations and meetings had a purpose: the saving and rebuilding of the Talyllyn Railway as the World's first preserved railway, more often than not using the varied and useful resources of their own firms. Our family firm was B.Whitehouse & Sons Limited, building contractors, who were part of the tribal Birmingham 'mafia' of business men. A surprising number of them were interested in railways and were willing to use their businesses, then largely their own personal fiefdoms, to the Talyllyn Railway's advantage. All these men knew each other well and, often, they were also interested in railways and had met either through their memberships of the SLS or the Birmingham Loco Club or through their business dealings as owners

All these men knew each other well and they were all in a position to provide help and resources for the Talyllyn Railway through their business dealings as owners and leaders of companies and family firms in Birmingham and the Black Country

ABOVE: **Michael and Maggy Whitehouse, children of Pat and Thelma, pose slightly awkwardly in front of *Talyllyn* for the family album during the Cuneo painting sessions at Dolgoch**

LEFT: **Terence Cuneo painting *Talyllyn* and train at Dolgoch**

and leaders of companies and family firms in Birmingham and the Black Country. They were all in a position to provide help and resources for the Talyllyn Railway, in the form of building materials, paint, wood, metal castings, machining work, general engineering and office administration. And, if they did not personally have what the TR required within their own firm or works, they knew people who did and who could be 'lent on' to help out. Often the white painted lorries from our family building firm would groan slowly over the Cambrian mountains carrying castings from Hunt Bros. at Oldbury, wooden station nameboards new from the family 'Works' carpenters' shop and even a whole coach body when Hunts and Whitehouses had rebuilt one of the Glyn Valley four wheeled coaches. The offices of the Birmingham based Talyllyn committee members became devoted to

John Wilkins tending to *Count Louis* on his Fairbourne Railway just up the coast from the TR. Technically, this was the first preserved railway as John bought it in 1947 but he ran it as his own hobby railway rather than as a 'Big Society' with voluntary support. It was his interest in the Fairbourne which led him to give considerable financial support to the Talyllyn, without which the TR revival simply would not have got off the ground

administration, secretarial support and financial bookkeeping to keep the developing show on the road. The team was tight knit. To ensure success, for failure was not ever contemplated, there was only one way ahead: for half a dozen people to say that is what they were going to do and do it; the revival would never have got off the ground otherwise.

Midlands families routinely took holidays in Wales over the generations. In our family album we have photographs of the Whitehouse family taken in the early 1900s at Rhydyronen station on the TR, digging sandcastles on the beach with B. Whitehouse & Sons builders' spades and Dad also wrote about his boyhood 1930s adventures taking a circular tour by train over the Cambrian, Festiniog and Welsh Highland Railways and even cadging a footplate ride on their single Fairlie *Moel Tryfan* through the stygian gloom of the mile long Moelwyn tunnel. Wartime split families for a while – and sometimes for ever. My grandfather fought in the army in the first world war and was retired injured in the back by a bullet in the battle of the Somme. He recovered to lead the family construction firm through the second

> To ensure success there was only on way ahead; for half a dozen people to say that is what they were going to do and do it

world war, contributing many public and other buildings to the Birmingham skyline such as the University library and the Alexandra theatre. My father followed in his footsteps.

In the early 1950s, after demobilisation from the Second World War, Dad and all his friends used to meet up regularly for railway film shows and model railway operating evenings, extended to days out on the Sutton Miniature Railway and to see and photograph many standard gauge railways as they started to close and chase down engine classes which were beginning to be withdrawn in droves. Arthur Camwell was the Manager of the Midland Bank in Handsworth Wood, but he was also the Secretary to the Midland Area of the SLS and organised many special steam trains which were run from Birmingham to mark the closure of a line, the end of a particular class of engine and also the annual trip to Swindon Works. These trips were also great fun for me to tag along on and so I was fortunate to see many last engines of their class and travel on several last trains: Midland 0-6-0s on the Harborne branch, double headed L&NWR G2 0-8-0s, visit Tyseley shed to see the last Star *Princess Margaret*, footplate

(and even drive!) the last B12 when she ran out of Stratford to Leamington in the pouring rain and cadge many cab rides on the GWR 'small prairie' No.4555 owned jointly by Dad and Pat Garland. Little did I know then and, indeed, little did even Dad realise what seeds were being sown in relation to standard gauge railway preservation during all these jaunts; but that is another story and, for now, we must confine ourselves to the Talyllyn Railway. 'Garland and Whitehouse Railways' (GWR) were to come along later!

So it should not really have been any great surprise when Tom Rolt convened a meeting at the Imperial Hotel in Birmingham in 1950 to discuss the plight and possible saving of the Talyllyn Railway, that all these men should turn up together and largely become the first committee and driving force to save the railway, following Bill Trinder, Tom Rolt and Jim Russell's initiative and encouragement. Although Bill Trinder and Tom Rolt received most of the credit for convening and holding the meeting, Jim Russell's contribution in drawing many of the attendees there should not be underestimated. He was a keen GWR 4mm scale railway modeller and so knew Pat Garland who was of the same persuasion. Pat knew Dad through railway modelling and the SLS club and, indeed, Pat Garland was my father's best man at my parents' wedding! The TR has a lot to thank 4mm scale modelling in EM gauge for!

Also, the whole idea of a preservation society must be credited to Owen Prosser who instilled the concept in Tom Rolt's mind, as well as keeping the original 2'3" gauge rather than converting the railway to a miniature line as Tom had originally thought of doing, following the approach successfully taken with the Ravenglass & Eskdale Railway in the Lake District. These concepts proved to be spot on as they encouraged people to volunteer their time to work on the railway without pay: a concept hitherto unheard of at the time and the forerunner of today's 'Big Society'. These ideas have stood the test of time for, as Edward Thomas, the long time manager of the Talyllyn Railway before preservation, said: "People come to ride on the railway because they like to see the train in its original form" – it was still running as originally built, then some 85 years earlier!

Right from the beginning, the Midlands TRPS Committee men held rather different views to Tom Rolt who ran the railway on the spot on a day to day basis for the first two years. Generally speaking the view of the Midlands men prevailed, because they were used to being leaders in their respective fields and not used to any other form of

Above: PBW's TRPS Life Membership card

Below: Conversation piece at Abergynolwyn with the original train: Tom Rolt chats with Thelma Whitehouse as Pat look on

Perhaps the start of 'Garland & Whitehouse Railways'. No.7827 *Lydham Manor* and the two Pat's very own No.4555 double head the annual TRPS Special train into Morfa Mawddach (Barmouth Junction) station on their way back to Towyn to pick up the Society members for their journey back to the Midlands and London on 26th September, 1964. Both these engines ended up on the Dart Valley Railway in Devon, which was the two Pat's 'follow on' venture after giving their all to help the TR get established. *(Photo: Mike Pope)* The purchase of this engine resulted in a cartoon being published in The Talyllyn News showing No.4555 regauged and sitting outside Pendre shed!

management other than 'top down.' Whilst the TR was being rescued and rebuilt, its management and direction was largely centered on Midlands men and this situation prevailed until the early 1960s when management moved to Wales largely led by Bill Faulkner as unpaid managing director, who had been heavily involved on the railway since the very earliest days. There was a migration of Committee meetings from Birmingham to Towyn and the establishment of various sub committees dealing with the various walks of Talyllyn life as the railway began to come up for air after ten years of intensive rebuilding. However, whilst there may have been occasional friction between those running the day to day at Towyn and those people providing things from further afield, in the early development days both were necessary and one could not have succeeded in its work without the other.

This then is the story of the pioneer preservation of the Talyllyn Railway as viewed by those who rescued it, largely told in their own words and from the viewpoint of one of the families who were, and still are, at the forefront of railway preservation. This book tells in contemporary accounts how they felt about the pioneering, what they did and how they transformed the TR from an almost forgotten and completely dilapidated anachronistic byway into a thriving community run railway burgeoning with success and with passenger journeys rising over ninety thousand by the railway's centenary in 1965.

Michael Whitehouse
Worcestershire
2015 – the 150th anniversary year of
The Talyllyn Railway

Reviving the Talyllyn Railway has
given a sense of purpose to the lives of
a great many people from all sectors of
the community, who have contributed
according to their circumstances
— *John Bate*

CHAPTER 1

Discovering the Talyllyn Railway

Tom Rolt

"There is no finer sight in Wales than this suddenly revealed vision of the lake of Talyllyn sparkling in the setting of its encircling mountains. In the crystalline atmosphere of this evening of sunshine after storm the contrasts of light and shadow on these mountains were almost unbelievably vivid"

It was on a fine evening after a day of heavy rain that I came over the pass from Dolgelley and, looking down between the crags which tower above that narrow defile, saw the valley for the first time. There is no finer sight in Wales than this suddenly revealed vision of the lake of Talyllyn sparking in the setting of its encircling mountains. In the crystalline atmosphere of this evening of sunshine after storm the contrasts of light and shadow on these mountains were almost unbelievably vivid; the majestic face of Craig Goch on the southern shore so golden in sunlight; the slopes of Cader opposite so deep in shadow that night seemed already to have fallen there. After a day's downpour, torrents were everywhere thundering off the mountains in milk-white cascades that glittered like vertical veins of quartz on the dark rocks of cwm or precipice. The reverberations of this falling water filled the evening stillness with a sound like that of a wind in the treetops. Yet in the valley there was sheltered calm. Only on the high skyline of Cader where the streams were leaping into the invisible bowl of Llyn Cae was a wind whipping their spray into the air like plumes of steam.

I resolved to renew and enlarge my experience of the narrow gauge, so I journeyed into Towyn by bus on the Wednesday morning with the object of travelling back as far as Abergynolwyn on the afternoon train and then walking the remainder of the way back to Talyllyn. Unfortunately, however,

Railway Adventure by L.T.C. Rolt, 1953, Chapter 2

the walking part of this programme was fated to prove much longer than I anticipated. For when I strolled down to the Wharf station after lunch my hopes were dashed by a small hand written notice which had been pinned on the board by the station gate. NO TRAIN TO-DAY it stated laconically in characters slightly smudged by haste and rain. So that was that. There was no sign of life. The little red brick office building was locked up and a wet wind from the sea was whipping across the deserted yard.

I set off under the Wharf road bridge and through the long water-logged cutting in the direction of Pendre. Here, where the track fanned out into loop and shed roads, I saw for the first time the ancient four wheeled coaches. They were at rest in a long narrow open sided shed which fitted them so nicely. Just beyond this was the locomotive shed, and here I discovered signs of life and at the same time an explanation for the absence of any animation anywhere. An engine was standing in the shed, and beneath her in the gloom of the pit between the rails, my eye caught the flickering light of a tallow candle. The sound of a heavy hammer striking unyielding metal was followed by a spate of rapid Welsh. Much as I should have liked to do so, I deemed it tactful not to enter the shed. At any rate the mystery of the missing train was now solved. So I left them to it, walking on past the little

> **Ahead, the distant peak of Cader Idris played hide-and –seek with its clouds and foothills, now lost, now clear and majestic against the blue**

station platform and shelter, over the gated level crossing and away up the grass grown track which, with high hedges on either hand, was more like a country lane than a railway. I came to Rhydyronen station, sheltering in a group of pine trees. It did not take me long to reach Brynglas once I had passed the ivy covered bridge at Rhydyronen, for the two stations are comparatively close together. But then followed a long two miles to Dolgoch. There was a

"Ahead, the distant peak of Cader Idris played hide-and-seek with its clouds and foothills, now lost, now clear and majestic against the blue"

CADER IDRIS & THE AFON MAWDDACH
GWR **WALES** GWR

"Just beyond the long narrow open sided carriage shed was the locomotive shed, and here I discovered signs of life and at the same time an explanation for the absence of any animation any-where. An engine was standing in the shed, and beneath her in the gloom of the pit between the rails, my eye caught the flicker-ing light of a tallow candle. The sound of a heavy hammer striking unyielding metal was followed by a spate of rapid Welsh." (Photo: John Snell)

"I walked on up the grass grown track which, with high hedges on either hand, was more like a country lane than a railway"

considerable cutting and an overbridge beyond Brynglas and then the character of the line changed. For the broader levels near Towyn had been left behind now and instead of a country lane the little railway had become a mountain track, a narrow shelf cut in the lower southern slopes of the valley of the Afon Fathew. Between bushes of thorn and hazel I looked down to the little stream meandering through its marshlands and beyond it to the grey farms and the steeply-tilted patchwork of small fields on the opposite slope of the valley. In places dark bushes of gorse grew so closely beside the wavering line of metals that they threatened to overwhelm them. Beyond the hedge on my right were the steeper bracken covered slopes of the open mountain which swept upward to a bare crown where a buzzard was soaring on motionless wings, borne up like a kite upon ascending air currents. Ahead, the distant peak of Cader Idris played hide-and-seek with its clouds and foothills, now lost, now clear and majestic against the blue. At the approach to Dolgoch there were rock cuttings and oak trees whose branches arched over the track to make a tunnel of green shade. Then suddenly, as though I must needs be reminded that this was no mere mountain trackway but a railway, the line emerged from a cutting and strode proudly over the Dolgoch ravine on its lofty three-span viaduct.

"Then the character of the line changed. Instead of a country lane, the little railway had become a mountain track, a narrow shelf cut in the lower slopes of the valley of the Afon Fathew"

Below, the stream tore down its rocky channel and to my right, invisible behind a dense screen of trees, I could hear the thunder of the falls. Once across the viaduct another rock cutting, this time on a sharp curve, led me to Dolgoch station where the platform and the little slate-built shelter were almost buried in the great bushes of rhododendron which flourished in that peaty soil. Here, too, stood a leaky wooden tank on a slate column for supplying engines with water. Now on the last lap of the way, the track took me out of the shelter of the trees and past a quarry siding. Having now lost the waters of the Dolgoch stream, the valley below soon became waterless while its slopes were higher and steeper. On my right they rose to a sky-line no longer even but jagged with outcropping rocks which had scarred the slopes below with small screes. Here the road bed was completely covered by a close carpet of short mountain turf which left only the line of the worn and rusty rails visible, and straying mountain sheep bounded ahead of me along the line. When I reached the little terminus at Abergynolwyn I struck off down the track to the valley road and the village.

John Snell was rather luckier when he first visited the TR:

John Snell

I had broken my journey at Towyn and I was delighted to see a small handwritten notice in the window at Wharf station promising a service of three trains on Easter Monday. It seemed very unlikely. The railway looked dead. The station was locked and deserted, with cobwebs in the windows; the yard was empty and the rusty track, curving out of sight, also looked as if nothing had moved on it for months. But when the day came, everything was different.

I turned up in good time for the afternoon train. Edward Thomas, the General Manager of the railway for most of his life, was in the ticket office selling tickets to some twenty passengers and for a bicycle. Three four wheeled wagons stood primly in the puddles outside, loaded with slates brought down by the morning train from the quarries at Bryn Eglwys. After a few minutes there was a steamy shriek and an engine rumbled backwards under the bridge and splashed towards us.

The journey was like an anthology of old jokes. There was indeed an encounter with a cow, from which we were rescued by a farmer with a pitchfork. We really did chase sheep and were ourselves pursued by maddened sheepdogs. We

"Then suddenly, as though I must needs be reminded that this is no mere mountain trackway but a railway, the line emerged from a cutting and strode proudly over the Dolgoch ravine on its lofty three-span viaduct. Below the stream tore down its rocky channel and to my right, invisible behind a dense screen of trees, I could hear the thunder of the falls"

Dolgoch Upper Falls

thumped our way along a muddy footpath, all scenery quite invisible behind the rank hedges, a sort of rural tube railway. Brambles and gorse scratched along the footboards and nodded in at the windows. We were moving at about ten miles an hour and, even at that speed, the ride was appalling. From time to time the coach lurched drunkenly to one side, listing for what seemed an age before it recovered. More often we crashed down into a pothole and bounced out again, coach and occupants alike sore and creaking. All the time, we rattled and shook as the flat spots in the tired old wheels slapped round and round. The seats were bare boards, there was no leg room, it felt as if we were in a Wild West stagecoach being

The 'Old Lady' *Dolgoch* and a short mixed train ready to leave Wharf for another journey up the line probably in 1947 and taken on the same visit as PBW first started his TRPS publicity film

pursued across country by outlaws. It was all rather enjoyable.

When we eventually got back to Towyn, I asked permission to visit the works at Pendre. The engine shed was like an alchemist's murky dungeon, littered with mechanical debris and black with soot to the rafters. It reminded me of Merlin's den in "The Sword and the Stone". I looked upwards for the traditional wizard's trophy, a stuffed crocodile hanging from the roof, but it wasn't there. In the workshop stood *Talyllyn* and the famous brake-van-cum-booking-office, both hopefully awaiting

repairs. In one corner stood a Ruston single-cylinder diesel engine coupled to belts and line shafting which might still be coaxed into driving a lathe and a drill press. Various other equipment lay around, all covered with dust and cobwebs. The only signs of life were two hens scratching on the dirt floor, and a kettle boiling on the old blacksmith's forge.

The Talyllyn Railway had opened in 1866, and practically all its possessions were delivered then or shortly afterwards. For eighty-five years no new capital equipment had been purchased, apart from a new frame, but little else.

Latterly they had been kept going by desperate expedients. *Dolgoch* had been overhauled at Shrewsbury in 1946, but *Talyllyn* was still as she had been when last run in that year. One side of the smokebox had been patched with a large flattened Ovaltine tin brazed on, the printing still legible. Moving the reversing lever produced a distant subterranean clanking and jangling, like chained and weary prisoners tramping around some ancestral dungeon. But worse could be seen inside the firebox. A number of stays had snapped, and one side of the box had bulged inwards under pressure.

The only repair attempted had been to plug the stayholes with bungs. *Talyllyn* was no longer a locomotive: she was a self-propelled steam bomb. To protect her from further demons, and to symbolize retirement, somebody had found an old Victorian cast iron fender and laid it on her footplate in front of the firedoor. All she now lacked were slippers, an armchair, and a toasting fork for muffins. Plus, of course, a fire.

> **The journey was like an anthology of old jokes. There was indeed an encounter with a cow, from which we were rescued by a farmer with a pitchfork. We really did chase sheep and were ourselves pursued by maddened sheepdogs**

Dolgoch, the engine that still went, was not really in much better shape. Having been given a new firebox in 1939 by the Britannia Foundry in Portmadoc, she was reasonably steam tight, to outward appearance at least. The elderly plates of her boiler were getting thin, as one realised when one listened beside her as she stood quiet, and heard the bubbling of water round the firebox. But she still contrived to satisfy the boiler inspector. She was pretty rough mechanically, with quite a lot of slop in all ways and bearings, and her handbrake shoes were visibly worn beyond the limit of the brake screw's travel; but there was always the reversing lever to stop with. Worst of all, but not visible, was the weakness at the rear end. The eight fitted bolts securing the four volute spring hangers to the frames, which carried the whole weight of the back of the engine, had stripped their threads. Unless they were driven home again after each day's running – an operation which took several hours as it involved jacking up the locomotive and

"We thumped our way along a muddy footpath, all scenery quite invisible behind the rank hedges, a sort of rural tube railway. We were moving at about ten miles an hour and, even at that speed, the ride was appalling." *(Photo: John Snell taken at the foot of Cynfal bank on a 1951 works train)*

that Ruston stationary engine and a few hundred yards of second hand fifty pound rail in 1938. The four four-wheeled coaches and the brake van were still the originals. The two locomotives had hardly been altered either, except by the process of decay. Each had had a new firebox, and *Talyllyn* had had

"The track was
unspeakable"
*(Photo: John
Adams)*

Below: *Edward
Thomas* rolling
along the track
between the high
hedges with a down
train for Towyn in
the early TRPS
years

"*Talyllyn* was still as she had been when last run in that year. One side of the smokebox had been patched with a large flattened Ovaltine tin brazed on, the printing still legible. Moving the reversing lever produced a distant subterranean clanking and jangling, like chained and weary prisoners tramping around some ancestral dungeon. But worse could be seen inside the firebox. A number of stays had snapped, and one side of the box had bulged inwards under pressure. The only repair attempted had been to plug the stayholes with bungs. *Talyllyn* was no longer a locomotive: she was a self-propelled steam bomb. To protect her from further demons, and to symbolize retirement, somebody had found an old Victorian cast iron fender and laid it on her footplate in front of the firedoor. All she now lacked were slippers, an armchair, and a toasting fork for muffins. Plus, of course, a fire"

removing part of the cab floor – *Dolgoch* subsided onto her rear axleboxes. The strains resulting from this chore being neglected in 1949 caused both sides of the frame to break clean through. The railway had to close down for most of that season while repairs were carried out, but the root of the trouble was left untouched.

The track was unspeakable. By the late 1940s new sleepers, other than those obtained by chopping down lineside trees, were more or less non existent. When the staff, that is two men who acted as driver and fireman on train days and fitters or platelayers at other times (except during harvest), were moved to attempt to cure some particularly horrible abscess in the track, they had first to walk down to Sir Haydn's office above the ironmonger's shop in the High Street, where if they were lucky they would be issued with a pair of new dogspikes from a sack kept beneath the great man's desk. By 1950 derailments averaged one a week.

CHAPTER 2

150 Years of a Welsh Hill Railway

A very early picture of Talyllyn most probably in original livery scheme at Kings (later renamed Wharf), Towyn. *(Photo: Talyllyn Railway Archive)*

The lonely, lovely valleys that fall to the western seaboard from the forbidding mountain massif of North Wales were the cradle of the narrow gauge railway. It was after their successful birth in the wilds of Snowdonia that the slender metals went forward to conquer the mountain regions of the world from Switzerland to the Himalayas. In England many engineers, notably Isambard Brunel the champion of the 7 foot gauge, held that even our 'standard' gauge and 4 feet 8 ½ inches was too narrow and dismissed it contemptuously as the 'coal wagon gauge.' Even so staunch a supporter of the standard gauge as Robert Stephenson believed that steam haulage on a much narrower gauge was not a practical proposition. It was left to enterprise in Wales to

> **The lonely, lovely valleys that fall to the western seaboard from the forbidding mountain massif of North Wales were the cradle of the narrow gauge railway**

prove him wrong.

In this instance, necessity which is always the mother of invention was to find some economic means of transporting slate from inaccessible mountain quarries to the coast for shipment. The rapid growth of the industrial towns in England created an enormous demand for roofing slate which the Welsh quarries could not meet so long as their output had to be carried on the backs of ponies to Aberdovey, Portmadog or to the shores of the Menai. To construct standard gauge railways through such country would have been enormously costly, if not impossible, but the Spooner family of Portmadog solved the problem. In 1836 James Spooner connected the quarries of Blaenau Ffestiniog with Portmadog by a horse tramway on a 1 foot 11 ½ inch gauge which, in fourteen

L.T.C.Rolt – an amalgam of text from Railway Adventure and other essays

torturous miles, conquered the mountain barrier of the Moelwyns. Climbing continuously from sea level, the narrow track eventually invaded the buzzard-haunted sheep walks of the open mountain, occupying a dizzy rock shelf high above the Vale of the Ffestiniog. Imagine then the consternation and scepticism which prevailed amongst Victorian engineers when James Spooner's son Charles proposed to rebuild this tramway as a steam railway of the same diminutive gauge. But in 1863 the conversion was completed with great success and in the following years the Festiniog Railway became an object of pilgrimage for railway engineers from all over the world.

This pioneer railway and the other little Welsh lines which were built as a result of their success not only carried a prodigious tonnage of slate but also brought a welcome means of passenger transport to areas hitherto as isolated as anywhere in Britain. In their toy like carriages the inhabitants of remote sheep farms or quarry villages were able to travel down to their market town or to the nearest standard gauge railhead. And, as the years went by and North Wales became increasingly popular as a holiday area, they carried a great tourist traffic during the summer months. Doing so they endeared themselves to successive generations of English visitors. The enraptured small boy would return

George W. Cuthbertson

"My mother often told us of the time when at the cessation of hostilities in 1918, the 'train bech' blew its whistle all the way up from Towyn to Abergynolwyn, and this was the way that the locals knew there was something had happened."

years after to take his children for their first journey on 'the little railway.' The white plume of steam appearing so improbably high up on mountainside, the shrill whistle echoing across the deep valleys, the fascinating Lilliputian train clattering so self-importantly into the lonely station, these things became as familiar and well loved a part of the Welsh mountain landscape as its waterfalls, sheep farms or trackways.

But, alas, after the first world war the fortunes of the railways began to decline The palmy days of the slate trade were over. Machine made tiles were taking the place of Welsh slate on English roofs and a younger generation no longer relished the hard, ill-paid and hazardous occupation of the

The earliest known picture of the Talyllyn Railway showing *Talyllyn* posed on Dolgoch viaduct before the trees all grew up to obscure such a view. The engine still has an open cab as when delivered new, a cab weatherboard, a horizontally hinged smokebox door and tool box over the cylinder. Unusually, the brake van is at the head end of the train. *(Photo: John Owen, Newtown c.1867, collection The National Library of Wales)*

slate quarryman. Buses, charabancs and cars invaded the valleys in steadily increasing numbers, all drawing precious revenue away from the narrow gauge lines. So their life gradually ebbed away until the second world war gave them the *coup de grace*. Welsh Highland, Glyn Valley, Ffestiniog, Corris disappeared from Bradshaw one by one until, by the time the railway system was nationalised, only one independent Welsh narrow gauge railway line survived – the Talyllyn.

The Talyllyn Railway was born 150 years ago, the child of an unfulfilled dream of mineral wealth. In 1847, a Welshman named John Pughe began quarrying for slate at Bryneglwys, a lonely and inaccessible place high in the mountains of Merioneth, not far from Cader Idris and eight miles from the coast of Cardigan Bay. Pughe found good slate, but it had to be carried by packhorse over the mountains to the little port of Aberdovey for shipment and this limited the scale of his operations.

In 1864, a group of Manchester cotton magnates, headed by the brothers William and Thomas McConnel, formed the Aberdovey Slate Company with a capital of £75,000, later increased to £112,500, to lease and work the Bryneglwys quarry. Why should these hard headed Lancashire businessmen suddenly decide to so much money in this remote place? There were two reasons.

Above: Loading parcels into No.5 van at Pendre. Spot the difference between 1865, 1935 and 2015!

Right: Quarrymen sitting in slate wagon on their way to work, pause at Dolgoch station whilst their train engine takes water. Or are they?

Left: *Dolgoch* brings a goods train up past Ty-Dwr on the mineral extension with freight for Abergynolwyn, Hendrewallog and Beudyn-newedd. Or does it?

Below: 'Savoy Café' carved into the doorway lintel of the Lower Mill. *(Photo: Talyllyn Railway Archive)*

First, the outbreak of the American Civil War in 1861 had adversely affected the cotton trade and they were anxious to diversify their interests. Second, they hoped to find not only slate, but also gold at Bryneglwys. This hope was by no means so far fetched as one might think. In 1860, the Clogau mine, near Dolgellau, had struck a vein so rich that in three years it yielded £43,783 worth of gold, paying £22,575 in dividends on the company's small capital in five years. John Pughe insisted, perhaps to his advantage, that there was gold at Bryneglwys.

Improved transport to the coast was essential to the development of the quarry, so the McConnels engaged an engineer, James Swinton Spooner, the elder brother of Charles who had brought innovative little steam engines to the Festiniog Railway a few miles further north, to survey a line of railway. Whereas similar projects elsewhere were built simply as mineral lines under wayleave agreements, the McConnels decided that theirs should be a passenger carrying railway and they therefore sought Parliamentary powers, with the effect that the Talyllyn Railway Company received the Royal Assent on 5th July, 1865. It could so easily have been built as a mineral line by way-leave agreements, but this did not suit the McConnels. They had to have a real railway which had been

> I am convinced that the Talyllyn Railway owes its existence to the belief that there was gold to be found

Quarrymen gather for a photograph together with one of the quarry shunting horses in Bryn Eglwys quarry slate sorting yard by the Lower Mill at the top of the Cantybredd incline. *(Photo: Talyllyn Railway Archive)*

A gauge of 2 ft. 3 in, was chosen, no doubt because the trams of this gauge were already in use in the quarry. A fine three arch viaduct had to be built to span a deep ravine at Dolgoch but, apart from this, the line was terraced along the slopes of the valley leading down to the sea at Towyn and the construction proceeded fast. *Talyllyn*, the first of two locomotives ordered from the firm of Fletcher, Jennings of Whitehaven, was delivered by sea to Aberdovey in the autumn of 1865; and, although the line was not passed for passenger traffic by the Board of Trade until a year later, it was in use well before this.

Alas, the rosy dream of mineral wealth soon faded. There was no gold and slate of good quality proved increasingly difficult to get. The whole concern was put up for auction in 1879, but found no takers. The original mining company was wound up and the McConnel family carried on the company on a more modest scale until 1911, when they sold out to a local man, Mr (later Sir) Henry Hadyn Jones, who was for many years MP for Merioneth. Abergynolwyn, in the valley below the quarry, had become a sizeable mining village, so closure would have been a local disaster. Although many of the underground levels in the mine had become dangerous, the local inspector of mines turned a blind eye and allowed quarrying to go on upon a diminishing scale until 1947, by which time labour had drifted away to other employments, mainly in forestry.

blessed by Parliament. Also, this was the first time a quarry railway had been laid down other than to a port, as it proved unnecessary to go further than Towyn to connect with the standard gauge Cambrian Railway. Additionally, the line served as a common carrier from the outset and its village incline and branches at Abergynolwyn reached almost every dwelling in the village, so offering a 'door to door' service, perhaps the only railway ever to do so.

Naomi Royde-Smith

The toy train was the smallest and, to us, the greatest train of all. The toy train ran from sea level six miles up to slate quarry in the mountains. There was only one carriage and it had no second-class carriage. A simple upholstered first class compartment, usually locked, and, so far as I ever knew it, reserved for moths and bluebottle flies, formed a section of one of its two coaches; the rest consisted of third class wooden carriages and a van which was also a booking office. The toy railway possessed a dozen large, stout, pink cardboard tickets. These were issued, collected and resold until they wore out. In July and August, when there was a glut of summer visitors, Jacob – he was guard, porter, stationmaster, booking clerk and signalman in one–would collect our tickets before the train started and resell them to latecomers. Nobody ever missed the toy train. When we set out to climb Cader Idris and took the 7 am. up to the terminus, we explained to Jacob that we might be late for the 6.30 pm. down and he agreed not to let it start without us.

Top: This picture shows *Dolgoch* renamed as *Pretoria* in 1903 standing at Abergynolwyn with William Lewis, fireman, and a young lad with a play hoop posing for the photographer. It is one of the earliest known pictures of *Dolgoch* and many people have used this image as justification for saying the engine was red, but there is no evidence for this. The image came from a collection of outstanding pictures of the London Brighton & South Coast Railway and so may well have been taken on a summer holiday.

Bottom: *Talyllyn* has brought down some loaded slate wagons from the quarry and left them at the head of the passing loop at Abergynolwyn station, while the engine runs round the passenger coaches in the platform and the wagons are allowed to gravitate to be coupled to the back of the train. *(Photo: Martin Fuller collection)*

Public Meeting at Towyn in 1910

A well attended public meeting was held at the Market hall on Wednesday evening to consider what steps should be taken in view of the probable suspension of the Talyllyn Railway. The Council had called the meeting thinking the ratepayers would like to discuss the matter. The quarries had already been closed and it was only a matter of time before the railway would follow suit. The railway was a great convenience for Towyn, Llanfihangel and Talyllyn. For the last forty years it had conveyed thousands of visitors, and during the season there was no doubt that myriads of people had been delighted with the scenery. If a committee were formed to take over the railway, they could not expect a big profit; in fact, they might run it at a loss unless some industry were opened. It might be to the advantage of Towyn to continue the railway, for it might pay, in an indirect way, as residents were dependent on visitors who made frequent excursions by this railway. Mr Bennet, clerk to the Council, believed it was the duty of the town to provide the means of locomotion to convey people to the beautiful scenery at Dolgoch which was bequeathed as a most valuable asset to the natural attractions of the district.

The meeting was assured that Mr. McConnell would let or sell the concern at the most reasonable price possible, as he was extremely anxious to keep the line open, but he would only do so if guaranteed from actual loss.

It was proposed by Mr. J.C.Edwards, seconded by Mr. Garland, that the meeting express the opinion that in the interests of Towyn and its residents the railway should be kept open. This was carried unanimously.

Aberystwyth Observer, 13th October, 1910

NOTE

It is extraordinary how similar this meeting seemed to be to the one held at the Imperial Hotel, Birmingham in 1951 as we shall see later. There was even a Mr. Garland at both meetings. But, after this 1910 meeting, it was Haydn Jones who rescued the railway. Maybe he was really the preservation pioneer. Just maybe also his wife remembered this when the Talyllyn Railway Preservation Society suggested a similar outcome some forty years later?

Records through the years[2]

In the TR's first year of operation, 11,564 passengers were carried; this grew steadily to a peak of 23,502 in 1878. An all time peak of 30,918 was reached in 1898, after which there was a general decline to 20,719 in 1910, followed by a slight rise in 1911 and a sudden jump to 28,166 in 1912. The first post war years produced very similar traffic figures, but from then onwards it is a story of rapidly accelerating decline.

In 1926 only 19,128 passengers were carried and in 1930 traffic fell below 10,000 for the first time to 8,807. The reduction of winter services to three days a week in 1934/5 brought a further drop to 6,110 in 1934, to 4,615 in 1935. In 1938 only 3,904 passengers were carried.

Turning to the financial side, the Annual Returns made to the Board of Trade confirm that the Talyllyn Railway never declared a dividend. However, there was an operating surplus in some years: 1869, 1871 and every year from 1875 to 1884 and then only in 1894, 1903 and 1906. The highest operating surplus was £545 in 1880 and the lowest £7 in 1903. The highest operating deficit was £525 in 1891, but in 1905 it was only £1. After the first

> **The Talyllyn Railway never declared a dividend**

world war, the deficit was less than £100 on only two occasion: the worst year was 1926 with £404. Though these figures would not seem very high nowadays, they take on a very different aspect when compared with receipts and expenditure.

Total receipts only exceeded £2,000 in two years: 1873 and 1874. The worst year was 1911, when total receipts were only £602; however, this was also the year in which expenditure was the lowest at £790.

Generally speaking, goods traffic always brought in more than passengers – often twice as much and in one year, 1883, three times as much. Only in two very poor years of 1911 and 1912 and a few years in the late twenties and thirties did passengers bring in more income than freight and, by 1938, freight was once again twice as important. After the war, receipts did not fall below £1,000 until 1929; the worst year was 1935 with only £409.

Goods consignments, other than slate traffic, were recorded in heavy leather bound ledgers or which the most recent, begun on 11th November, 1938, survives in the Wharf office. Even in the early forties goods traffic was remarkably extensive and of bewildering variety, though probably hardly profitable. What excitement would be produced nowadays by a parcel from St. Pancras to Cynfal?

Talyllyn waits with passenger train at Abergynolwyn with staff and passengers posing for the photographer in the 1920s

[2] *E.K. Stretch*

What would volunteer guards make of 'two small pigs' or even 'one duck'? One wonders, too, whether a bicycle wheel was really of any great use to the inhabitants of Beudy-newydd, a house near the foot of the third upward incline.

Opening the book at random we find 23rd April, 1939 a fairly typical day. Goods traffic comprised one washstand, one marble top, one table, a bookcase, one tin case, and one carton, all from Abingdon to Abergynolwyn; fish from Grimsby to Abergynolwyn; 2 cwt. Potatoes; 3 cwt. 'Uveco' and one bag of oats, Towyn to Brynglas; one box of tiles from Towyn to Rhydyronen; and five parcels to various destinations, all transferred from the G.W.R. The next lot of goods, three days later, consisted of '4 kilderkins of ale' and one case of spirits from Wolverhampton to Abergynolwyn; one case, one tin, one bucket and one bag from Glasgow to Abergynolwyn; one tin from Towyn to Brynglas; five cases of jam from Gloucester to Abergynolwyn; and one case and one box to Bryneglwys.

The fish from Grimsby and beer from Wolverhampton were regular consignments, usually one a week; equally regular but not quite so frequent were cases of boots from Northampton. Quite a large amount of coal, sometimes two or three tons on one train, was carried to various places up the line. Local traffic as distinct from tranship traffic from the G.W.R., reflected the needs of an agricultural community, sacks of fertilizer, poultry food and the like. Very occasionally there was some 'down' traffic, for example 'eleven sheets of wool', Hendrewallog to Portmadog. (Hendrewallog is a house roughly opposite the summit at Cantrybedd incline, across Nant Gwernol).

The total of goods traffic for 1939 was 120 tons 14 cwts. 21 lbs. bringing a revenue of £48 6/-. Actually, the tonnage figures are not completely accurate, for parcels, unless very large, did not have their weights recorded, and neither did many single items such as cart wheels, agricultural implements etc. As the years passed more and more items were unweighed, and nearly everything rounded up to the nearest quarter, or occasionally the nearest stone. Finally, after about 1947, no one bothered to add up the weights at the end of the year, as they really only represented about half the traffic.

These was a sharp drop in 1940 to 88 tons 5 cwt. 27 lbs. (£34 13/2d), but in 1941 the full rigours of petrol rationing seem to have brought about an increase to 296 tons 9 cwt. 3qr. 8 lbs. (£97 12/3d). Then there was a sharp decline to 58 tons 5 cwt.

3 qr. 2 lbs. (£22 14/4d) in 1942. The following year saw immense quantities of sand, cement, brick and pipes, and even a concrete mixer, all conveyed to Fach Goch and all consigned to Sir Lindsay) presumably Sir Lindsay Parkinson, the engineering contractors). This brought the 1943 total to 236 tons 4 cwt. 17 lbs. (£61 7/4d). But after this burst of activity comes a steady decline:

1944 41 tons 18 cwt. 1 qr. 23 lbs. (£13 7/6d)
1945 21 tons 7 cwt. (£7 1/10d)
1946 20 tons 4 cwt. 2 qr. 14 lbs. (£8 5/7d)

From the spring of 1945 to April 1946 traffic was infrequent, *Dolgoch* was being overhauled at Shrewsbury and a decrepit *Talyllyn* struggled with the goods and mineral traffic. About this time, naturally the regular traffic in beer and fish seems to have deserted the railway. In 1947 traffic was down to 9 tons 16 cwt. 3 qr. 14 lbs. (£4 16/4d) and in 1948 to £2 6/11d – very few weights were recorded after July. The first complete gap in traffic, representing the end of the winter running, comes from 8th October, 1948 to 15th June, 1949, and is repeated every year thereafter. In 1949 goods traffic produced only 11/1d, but in the final year of the old regime this rose to £1 6/7d.

The last two consignments destined for anywhere beyond Abergynolwyn village on the mineral extension were three cwts. of coal to Hendrewallog on 15th June, 1949 and three bags, contents unspecified, to Beudy-newydd on 16th August, 1950. It appears unlikely that Alltwyllt and Cantrybedd inclines were worked specifically for these two loads, particularly as there would be nothing coming down to balance the loaded wagons going up, and it is presumed that they were merely sent down the village incline to be collected by the consignees.

The village of Abergynolwyn was built largely to house workers in the quarry and when that closed down the lives of most of the people in that village were disrupted. Wales is not a large country but it possesses a language and a culture of its own, which is sometimes overlooked by Englishmen. The decline of the slate industry and lack of opportunity for normally ambitious young Welshmen has caused many of them to emigrate to England. As one might expect, this tendency has hit the village of Abergynolwyn particularly hard. Before the advent of the motor lorry nearly everything which was consumed in this once prosperous and still interesting village, including beer for the Railway Inn, was transported there by our Railway and lowered down the Village Incline. At the foot of the incline there was a small network of rails which extended to all parts of the

The oft reported statement by Sir Haydn that the TR cost him £5 per week was already true in 1938

1. COACHING IN SYCHNANT PASS, PENMAEN MAWR 102

SUMMIT OF CADER IDRIS

3. Dolgoch Station (Tal-y-Llyn Railway)

village. The main branch ran across the main road adjacent to the Railway Inn, and in a track or lane between the backs of the houses in Water Street and Llanegryn Street ending at the rear of the Methodist Chapel at the north end of the village. There was another branch which ran at the back of the houses in Tanybryn Street. In the old days, supplies were brought to the very doors of the houses by this means. The goods traffic supplying the needs of the inhabitants adjoining the railway, like the passenger traffic was, however, subsidiary to the main purpose of the railway, which was to carry slate.

1. A coach and four in Sychnant Pass, Penmaen Mawr. Whilst further north than the TR, this would have been similar to the round trip offered by the Talyllyn & Corris Railways via Talyllyn lake

2. A Valentine's Series commercial postcard of an early climbing party on the summit of Cader Idris. Maybe they first took the train to Abergynolwyn and walked from there?

3. *Talyllyn* pauses at Dolgoch station for water whilst passengers pose for their photograph

Station stop at Brynglas to unload some goods whilst several slate wagons at the back of the train are full of happy passengers riding up to see the falls at Dolgoch *(Photo: Talyllyn Railway Archive)*

Dolgoch waits at the station of the same name, probably in the 1920s as the train's well dressed passengers look on

The TR in 1920

Every day we went up the railway and, of course, when we travelled with the brother of the owner, we never paid any fare. There was an old guard on the train known to us as Jacob. We always travelled in the guard's van, sitting on the floor and letting our legs dangle outside through the openings of the large sliding door. One end of this vehicle was separated off into a little ticket office complete with ticket racks and a date stamping machine and a little window from which Jacob issued tickets at intermediate stations; in those days there was no bus service up the valley and the railway was much used by the local inhabitants.

Sometimes we watched the passengers leave the train at Abergynolwyn and would see the coaches shunted into the siding; then a dozen empty slate trucks would be picked up by the locomotive and transported to the Bryn Eglwys slate quarries, about one mile further on and (great pride to us children compared with ordinary passengers) we were allowed to travel in trucks as far as the foot of the great incline that led to the quarry.

Sir Haydn Jones, when he went up to the quarry on the train, also travelled in the guards man and sat on the outside edge as we children did, but he was probably long enough in the leg to have his feet resting on the running board. He wore a black morning coat and carefully spread the coat tails at backwards over the dusty floor of the van. We children would cautiously step on these tails (and leave a footprint) the feeling that you have put your foot on the tail of a knight's coat was a very daring feat.

The highlight of a day on the railway was the fact that if my father gave Jacob half a crown, he would leave an empty slate truck at Abergynolwyn or at any intermediate station as the last train went down to Towyn.

We could spend as long as we liked on the hills and then come back to the named station when all of us piled into the truck; the only danger was that of starting too early; we might have

A family coast down the line after the last train in two slate wagons hired from the ticket office.
(Photo: Talyllyn Railway Archive)

caught up with the train! We piled into the truck, gave one push and set off for Towyn by gravity, as indeed the original loads of slate did.

The trucks had no springs and the traffic was rough but we were young and did not notice these discomforts. Each truck had an individual brake and there was one point where the gradient was extra steep and the brake had to be used while there was another stretch which was so level that one or two of us would have to get out and push to maintain progress.

So we made homeward, always having to stop at the level crossing at Pendre station in order to open the level crossing gates; we left of the truck in a siding at Pendre and went back, highly content with the doings of the day.

A.C. Waine

Summer passenger train waiting to leave Wharf in the 1930s with five slate wagons loaded with passengers

Miss Enid Williams

The highlight of our year was the English Presbyterian Sunday school outing. The Minister, the Rev. George M. Davis, known affectionately as "Georgie Giraffe," because of his height and commanding figure, would appear elegant and beaming, clad in knickerbocker suit, bow tie and Panama hat. He would arrive with the rest of us at Wharf station en route at the Lein Fach to Dolgoch.

"Georgie Giraffe" and his youngsters (myself included) would assemble by the lineside eagerly watching the curve bring the train from the engine sheds at Pendre. With a shriek of the whistle the engine would hove in sight, steam and smoke belching from the toy funnel, rattling and clanging like a friendly dragon, carriages behind the engine and the open slate trucks in a string behind. The staid adults made for the carriages, while we youngsters (and "Georgie") piled into the trucks. Then the fun would start. As the engine got underway, each truck in turn would give a convulsive jerk, sending its occupants into a heap on the floor.

With the shining sea behind us and the luscious green valley ahead, we were on our way to Samarkand. At Pendre a few more passengers joined

Towyn. Off by the Toy Railway

Guard Jacob Rowlands, on the van step, anxiously watches the antics of a party of holidaymakers in well filled slate wagons at the rear of a train as it leaves Pendre level crossing and heads for Ty Mawr bank

us and gawping sightseers peered through the bars of the level crossing gates, while Mr. Rowlands' chickens fled squawking in terror.

The mountains gradually closed in on us, the scenery grew wilder. Rhydyronen, Brynglas, sheep scattering in panic, the steady pull making our dragon snort in a metal frenzy.

Foaming waterfalls leapt to meet us, black glistening canyons almost spanning the twisty mossy track. Dripping shoulders of naked rock framed in vivid green fernery watched our triumphant passing.

Over what seemed a flimsy trestle bridge, then the sweating monster pulled itself up to a trembling exhausted stop. We were there! Fairyland, the Never-Never Land, the Delectable Mountains from which there was no return, or so we hoped!

But it was not to be. In the cool of the evening we returned exhausted but happy down the Lein Fach, back towards the shining crashing sea, where the golden sunset had already laid a shimmering pathway across the gleaming yellow and to the Isle of the Blessed – Bardsey.

Tourists came during the summer months to visit the waterfalls at Dolgoch and to walk from Abergynolwyn towards the foot of the great Cader Idris.

About the turn of the century, a horse drawn coach service ran from Abergynolwyn to Talyllyn Lake and then to the upper terminus of the Corris Railway. This round trip operated on many occasions as an excursion organised by the Cambrian Railways.

The passenger trains would tow behind them a string of empty slate wagons on their upward journey and, during the summer months, these were most popular as open coaches. Indeed, it was quite in order to hire a wagon for a day for a modest sum, arrange for it to be attached to an up train and detached at Dolgoch or some other remote beauty spot, where the party would picnic in the woods or by the waterfalls, returning at its convenience by gravity power.

Tickets for the journey were purchased at the Wharf booking office, with its printed notices forbidding passengers to smoke or walk on the roofs of the carriages and where, above the manager's desk, there was a glorious colour poster of an Atlantic paddle steamer operated by the White Star Line.

For passengers joining en route, tickets could be obtained from the small window of the unique travelling Booking Office built into the Company's one and only brake van.

Graham Teasdill

In the 1940s, the guard used to carry a gun if he saw rabbits for his tea and I remember the engine driver stopping the train to collect some eggs that had been laid out at the side of the track.

James Boyd takes a ride in 1943

A ride on the Talyllyn Railway, so much more ethereal and unbelievably out-of-this-world in a country at war.

Dolgoch is in a sorry state. Seventy nine year's fair wear and tear have brought the valve gear to near ruination. The pins from which the expansion links are hung are so worn that they allow an extravagant amount of side play and the die blocks, expansion links and eccentric straps are so ill fitting that at each wheel revolution the reversing shaft receives a hefty clout which completely precludes any chance the driver may have of putting his reversing lever either into full forward or full backward gear. A water tank is fitted at the back of the cab but its capacity is small. Its filler projects through the rear sheet as does the filler of a petrol tank in a car. There is an injector and, atop the boiler, a stop valve, which once connected to a vertical engine in the repair shop, as was used as required. The hand brake has lost one of its shoes and the reversing gear is used to assist stopping — an emergency stop would be out of the question. The regulator, of the push pull type, gives very little control between dead stop and flat out, and requires a degree of tact to handle. The water gauge glass shows the presence of some coffee-like fluid in its short length; one of the two try-cocks was used to fill the platelayer's billy can. Ugh! On the shelf above the firehole door stand two large coloured tea pots. Other impedimentia include a shovel, with a 9-inch handle, for firing, a bent crow bar and a box of assorted tools. Cab accommodation is very cramped. A large wooden door is hinged on one side and drawn to in inclement weather. The weight of the engine falls short of ten tons and, together with the long wheelbase, is harsh on the track.

On the occasion of my visit, Friday found the morning edition of the two days per week service train, with *Dolgoch* at its head, standing in Wharf station, surrounded by a large sheet of water. The passenger accommodation consisted of a four wheeled, four compartment first class coach, painted scarlet and very clean, with open back seats. In the rear was an empty slate wagon, later filled with sacks of coal, an iron wagon loaded with sacks of flour, and a truck filled with track repairing material. It was obvious that I was to be the only passenger that morning, so after a word with the crew – a lad of about fourteen and a driver-fitter – we made a steaming exit and headed for the town station. My attention was immediately drawn, by the plunging and bucking of the coach, to the state of the track, which had got into deplorable condition. At the town station, the locomotive shed, carriage shelter and repair shops are passed. There were no passengers here either so we set off across the open country behind the town heading slowly for the valley entrance, just visible as a gap in the hills ahead. It was a glorious morning and after an overnight journey from the north I settled down to a breakfast of austerity sausage. There is a continuous rise of about 1 in 60 by my estimation, and *Dolgoch* was making heavy weather of it, running with an appalling clatter and lugging the coach as if it were an obstinate mule. Speed was constant, about 10 mph.

It was obvious that I was to be the only passenger that morning

The coach was lightly upholstered and had doors on one side only; platforms are all on the left hand after leaving Towyn. A transfer notice informed me bluntly that spitting is frowned upon in these parts. Within ten minutes we had reached

Rhydyronen where we picked up the permanent way gentleman who loaded more missiles into the rear wagon. *Dolgoch* was very short of breath and pressure down to 20 lbs., so we waited a few minutes before proceeding. Then, with the whole of the company's servants on the footplate, we wound our way to Brynglas, each stop being heralded by a shrieking whistle. Here we deposited some sacks of coal, followed again by a wait for steam and passengers (the latter not being forthcoming) and further on we stopped en route to drop the pw gentleman, who unhitched his wagon and rode it downgrade to effect some repairs until our return.

Our next stop should have been Dolgoch but owing to the presence of some pigs on the line our fireman was despatched armed with a fire iron to run some hundreds of yards and chase them off the line. Just round the next bend we nearly killed two stubborn cows who waited until the last minute before leaving the track.

Dolgoch – no passengers here. The journey continued, the driver making several impromptu stops to show the first class passenger the beauty spots. The country is very wild and there is quite a magnificent viaduct with three arches, just before reaching Dolgoch, while the waterfall above it was in spate. The autumn tints had lingered and with the bare slopes of Cader Idris across the valley the little train, almost as changeless as its surroundings might have been running through 1873 instead of 1943. Here indeed was that element of the steel byway in all its elusive picturesqueness.

Abergynolwyn at last. The hand point should be called foot points for the fireman ran ahead and kicked the blades over. The coach was uncoupled and the wee lad drove the engine round the coach to pick up the wagons and propel them to the quarry funicular. The coach was locked up and left behind, to be picked up on our return. On the way beyond Abergynolwyn we passed underneath an old winding-house which once hauled goods up a funicular from the village below. On a visit three years later my impression that this incline was disused was proved wrong when we watched three wagon loads of bricks descend the incline at break neck speed. We had turned down an offer to ride in them.

Before the war there were 180 men working in the quarries and three trains of ten loaded wagons were brought down the railway daily. Today there are 8 men working there and their output is about four wagons per week. The foot of the funicular is situated on a high ledge above the river and the

> **Just round the next bend we nearly killed two stubborn cows who waited until the last minute before leaving the track**

In 1938, *Talyllyn* brings an up train into Pendre, the main station for Towyn and the engineering and operating headquarters of the railway. The engine shed and house is shown to the left of the train and was just big enough to house the two engines. *(Photo: Talyllyn Railway Archive)*

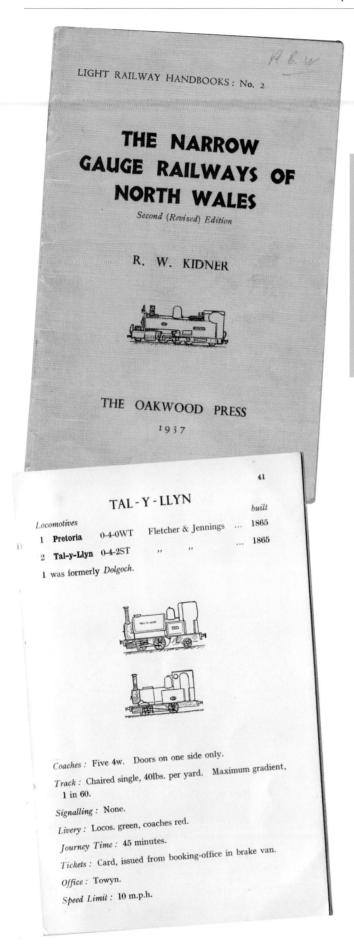

LIGHT RAILWAY HANDBOOKS : No. 2

THE NARROW GAUGE RAILWAYS OF NORTH WALES

Second (Revised) Edition

R. W. KIDNER

THE OAKWOOD PRESS
1937

41

TAL - Y - LLYN

Locomotives   *built*
1 **Pretoria**   0-4-0WT   Fletcher & Jennings   ...   1865
2 **Tal-y-Llyn** 0-4-2ST   ,,   ,,   ...   1865

1 was formerly *Dolgoch*.

Coaches : Five 4w. Doors on one side only.

Track : Chaired single, 40lbs. per yard. Maximum gradient,
1 in 60.

Signalling : None.

Livery : Locos. green, coaches red.

Journey Time : 45 minutes.

Tickets : Card, issued from booking-office in brake van.

Office : Towyn.

Speed Limit : 10 m.p.h.

Kidner's Narrow gauge Railways of Wales: front cover and somewhat childish sketches of the two original engines

line curves sharply to meet it. The engine pushed two wagons to the foot and the cable was hooked onto them. They rose and shortly afterwards tow loaded sate wagons descended on the other side. Many feet, in the river bed below, the four wagons full of slate. I was told that the cable breaks often,

With the loaded wagons, we returned to the coach

> The original locomotives and passenger coaches – even the original rails -were still in use. All were in deplorable condition

and I was invited to try my virtuosity at the regulator. The gradient, state of track and lack of brake power make this no easy testing ground for a novice. We stopped to take water from an overhead trough supported on slab piers. At the receiving end a moveable trough is thrust into a convenient stream and there is a down spout overhanging the track at the other. Another moveable section of trough, with its own down spout, is placed with its open end just out of reach of the cascading spout end. Then, from behind the very necessary shelter of his cab, the driver pushes it under the cascade with the aid of a poker. The water enters the aforementioned filler pipe in the rear tank. The whole of the rear of the engine is engulfed under this flood, most of which is spilled.

Eventually we reached and ran round the coach, and I attempted to back up gently. Contact! But the coach slips slyly away. Again...contact! Missed it! The driver kindly leans against the far end, I adopted my finest technique, the little lad dropped the link at the crucial moment and mind triumphed over matter once more. And we had a passenger.

There was some careful driving to follow. The track is very bad and in parts too near the cliff edge to be healthy. However once through Dolgoch (four more passengers here) and over a wicked piece of line where the running is over corrugated iron, we opened up a bit. I was just judging the slop in the regulator handle to a nicety when we caught up with the cows of earlier acquaintance. This time they had made up their minds. Whistling, steam jets, coal throwing, none was of avail. The driver jumped down and chased them for nearly a mile, but they finally became nasty, reversed and charged down on him and the engine. I slammed the quadrant lever into forward and assisted the fireman with all the strength we and the one brake block could muster. We slithered to a stand and the two brutes stood panting and glaring at us. I yanked the regulator hard open and the beasts leaped one each side to left and right; lower down we took aboard a breathless driver. By the time Towyn was reached, the new driver had knocked three minutes off the timetable and we had a coach full of passengers.

At the town station, Pendre, all the passengers left us so the driver took me to examine *Talyllyn* in the engine shed. The fascinating booking office van is also in the shops as the wheel treads on one side have worn very thin. On days when there are no trains, the running staff maintain the stock or unload slate into the G.W.R's wagons.

Early publications

One of the earliest publications featuring the Talyllyn Railway was R.W.Kidner's little booklet *The Narrow Gauge Railways of North Wales* published by The Oakwood Press in 1937. A delightful slim volume with minimal information and childish engine drawings encouraged the curious to find out more.

More detail about the railway was provided in a small booklet by Lewis Cozens published in 1948 for 2/9d. This included sketch maps of the line and the quarries, extracts from the Act of Incorporation, a commentary on the early days and subsequent history with a description of the line for passengers including the mineral extension, some specimen timetables and general details about the engines and rolling stock. Its conclusion ended with a prophetic wish:

"May we hope that it may be found possible for many years to come to operate at least a summer passenger service, to the delight of tourists bound for the Dolgoch Falls and the grandeur of Tal-y-llyn Lake and Cader Idris."

Sir Haydn had proclaimed that the Talyllyn Railway should continue to run as long as he lived and, thanks to his second in command, Edward Thomas, who had served the line for fifty years, run it did, albeit precariously. Between them they managed to keep the railway running during the summer months for tourist traffic, but run on a shoe string and, when Sir Haydn died in 1950, it was in such a state of dilapidation that it seemed certain to share the fate of the quarry that had brought it to birth. That the line could live to see its hundred and fiftieth anniversary seemed impossible. Because of the failure of the quarry to fulfill expectations, there had been no incentive to modernise or improve the railway; the original locomotives and passenger coaches - even the original rails - were still in use. All were in deplorable condition.

It seemed certain that, at the end of that summer season, the railway would close for ever. The last train under the Haydn Jones regime ran on Friday 6th October, 1950 and clearly some passengers came simply because it could well have been the very last opportunity to travel on the line. Seven returns to Abergynolwyn, three returns to Dolgoch, seven half-singles from Wharf to Rhydyronen, three and two half returns from Pendre to Dolgoch and three returns from each of Rhydyronen, Cynfal and Fach Goch to Towyn were recorded for the day. Receipts for the day totalled £4. 1/2d!

> **It seemed certain that, at the end of that summer season, the railway would close for ever**

The 'Old Lady' and the original train return to Wharf having reached the end of their working lives, or so everyone thought

A young lad acting as fireman fills the oil cups on the front of Dolgoch while the engine takes water at Ty Dwr on the mineral extension above Abergynolwyn

CHAPTER 3

Tom Rolt uncovers the opportunity

Tom Rolt was fired by an understanding of the beauty and importance of preserving ancient and historic machinery still fulfilling its intended purpose. But more than that, he sought to keep alive the tradition of the old railway companies in their local independence and pride, their attitude to service, self discipline and respect. At that time Britain's main line railways had just been nationalised, and the last vestiges of company independence were being scraped away. It was clear that they were going to be replaced by the narrow and defeatist Treasury attitudes that we have seen since. A very few privately owned railways survived, as if they had simply been overlooked. Surely, one should be rescued and maintained in memory of past glories. (John Snell)

Tom Rolt begins the story[1]:

---

1. Landscape with figures by L.T.C.Rolt, 1992

Tom Rolt

I leafed through the pages of the Transport Bill which was to nationalise Britain's transport and I found myself turning to the section dealing with railways where I came upon a list of companies, additional to the 'big four', which would be taken over. The list was extremely comprehensive, indeed I could think of only one statutory railway company – the Talyllyn – which had been omitted.

A few days before this, I had been listening to a party political broadcast during which a Labour party spokesman had assured me how wonderful it would be when I, as one of the citizens of Britain, owned the railway system instead of a bunch of acquisitive capitalists. How different it would be when railways were run for the benefit of all! Because I was old enough to remember the pride

What a fine thing it would be if at least one independent railway could survive to perpetuate the pride and glory of the old companies. Why not the Talyllyn?

and efficiency of the old pre-grouping companies, the spit-and-polish of their locomotives and rolling stock which spoke so eloquently of that tremendous *spirit de corps* that existed throughout the railway service, I doubted the truth of this socialist dogma. Instead of 'our railways' it seemed to me that they were far more likely to become nobody's railways under nationalisation. They would fall into neglect and decay just because they had become political pawns about which nobody felt responsible and nobody cared. It was with such gloomy thoughts in mind that I reflected what a fine thing it would be if at least one independent railway could survive to perpetuate, if only upon a small scale, the pride and the glory of the old companies. Why not the Talyllyn? Why not indeed? But then I thought of that seven miles of worn out track…as a romantic it seemed a brave notion, but as a practical engineer it seemed madness to attempt to reanimate a railway so run down that it had become so much scrap metal. Then a compromise occurred to me. Conversion to a miniature gauge might prove to be a cheaper, quicker and more economical solution than any attempt to restore the worn out railway to its original state. The old track could be sold for scrap and replaced by new rail. I reckoned that scaled down versions of narrow gauge locomotives running on the slim gauge of 10 ¼" should be capable of hauling as many passengers as the original Talyllyn locomotives had done in their prime. I did not envisage scrapping the original Talyllyn locomotives and coaches. They could form the nucleus of a narrow gauge railway museum at Towyn and become 'operable relics', running over a length of original track laid between the two stations at Towyn. The whole project would be manned by volunteers recruited from the ranks of railway enthusiasts. I argued that railway enthusiasts had, hitherto, been denied any practical creative outlet other than model making and would, therefore, be only too glad of the opportunity to assist in the construction, maintenance and day to day running of a public railway; the more so as most of them were condemned by the age to wholly uncreative jobs in normal life.

Tom Rolt was obliged to discuss his thinking about how the railway might be reconstructed with Owen Prosser who was in frequent correspondence with Rolt. Tom explains:

"My friends and I had not intended launching the idea on the public until we had detailed plans and figures worked out, but when an article appeared in *The Birmingham Post* I felt that we should respond.

"We have been occupied with the problem of the survival of the railway for two years now, and during that time we have, I assure you, investigated every possibility including your suggestion of importing the 'Tattoo' from the Corris. I have a sentimental interest in the 'Tattoo' having served my apprenticeship at Kerr Stuarts but, like other similar schemes it just is not a financial proposition. Whatever is done, the railway can never become a 'goldmine' nor do

At that time, the idea of a voluntary society of enthusiasts taking over and operating a statutory railway company was entirely novel and majority opinion held that it was foredoomed to failure

Scenes on the 2 ft. 3 in. gauge Tal-y-llyn Railway: The incline to the quarries; the inclined plane from Abergynolwyn village to the main line; and, right, booking office in brake van

The three foot gauge Ravenglass & Eskdale Railway in Cumbria closed when its granite traffic succumbed. However, Wenham Bassett Lowke and his business colleagues took over the railway and regauged to to 15" so that they could run on it equipment they already had for a tourist railway. It was this conversion which inspired Rolt to consider the same fate for the Talyllyn but, fortunately, he was dissuaded; his discussions about a potential conversion led him to meet David Curwen, a miniature railway engineer, who then spent a year of his time ensuring *Dolgoch* survived the first season of operation by the Preservation Society

I consider it from this aspect, but unless we can show that the railway would show at least a small return on capital expenditure it is useless to call for funds. We have made exhaustive enquiries into the possibilities of re-opening the Bryn Eglwys Quarries but, though there is one faint possibility to pursue, this seems very unlikely. This means that we can rely for revenue solely on holiday pleasure traffic during a relatively short season. The present track is completely worn out and so are the locomotives while the rolling stock is inadequate. Therefore the cost of restoring the line in its present form could never be justified in receipts.

"I originally envisaged conversion to 15" gauge as was done on the Eskdale, but this was in anticipation of quarry traffic. Without such traffic even this would not be justified. We are now convinced that the only practical solution is to relay in 10 ¼" gauge. In this form we believe

that the line would pay its way and earn a small return on capital. We have not yet found out whether the Company could realise on the scrap value of the current rails or whether their value would not justify the labour cost of taking them up. If not, then it has been suggested that we leave the old rails in situ, ballast up between them and lay the 10 ¼" track (which comes in pre-assembled lengths on steel sleepers) on the new ballast. In this way the old rails would retain the new road bed. We await an estimate from the track makers, but the cost is expected to work out at approximately £1,000 per mile. At the outset 5 miles of line from Towyn Wharf to Dolgoch would have to be relaid (Dolgoch Falls being the chief attraction on the line) with eventual extension for two miles to a new station and café at Abergynolwyn situated at the foot of the first quarry incline. Running would commence with one steam locomotive and train with the addition, as soon as funds permitted of a diesel (based on the GWR railcar) for standby and off-season duty. If the working comes up to expectations the locomotive stud would, of course, be increased by at least one. In practice there is little to choose between Atlantic and Pacific types for haulage capacity and the line is easily graded. Mr. Curwen who has inspected the line with me, guarantees that his Atlantic would haul a minimum of 50 passengers up to Abergynolwyn and probably more. This compares very favorably

'A sight we hope to see again', Tom with *Dolgoch* at Nant Gwernol on a trip in the 1940s *(Collection: Tim Rolt)*

STRIKE? NOT ON OUR PUFFING BILLY!

WHAT does it take to keep a railway running?

A band of enthusiasts who call themselves the Talyllyn Railway Preservation Society would give you the answer in one word DEVOTION.

They are men who have never outgrown the urge to be engine drivers.

Today the urge calls men of all stations to an out-of-the-way corner of Wales to see that a quart-sized "puffing Billy" railway maintains its service: ALL STATIONS FROM TOWYN TO ABERGYNOLWYN.

Duty—free

Their leader and T.R.P.S. president is 52-year-old Lord Northesk (left) never happier and seldom grubbier than when he is dressed for duty in the cabin of the Edward Thomas engine wielding an oilcan, stoking up the 1921 loco and driving it along its 6½ miles of 27in. gauge track.

There's a Birmingham accountant who comes down and "does" the company's books — free and for joy; a university student who'll be ticket-collector, guard, cleaner, fireman or whatever task may be urged a retired G.W.R. away.

Sometimes the volunteers have to do "lodging-turns." the shift which is causing the Sunday rail strike threats. But would the T.R.P.S. men strike? Only for more work!

This is one of the "Puffing Billies"

with the present train's seating capacity of 75 when economy and ease of working are born in mind. I need hardly add that the superficial appearance of these locomotives can be varied as desired and that we are not envisaging the American appearance! Something more appropriate to the Welsh scene is obviously desirable.

"Scale details, a signaling system, crossing places, improvements to stations and works are envisaged eventually if all goes well, but initially all one can hope for is the initial minimum of one train on five miles of track. I am afraid this may not appeal to some enthusiasts who have written to me and who probably envisage the preservation of the railway in its present form, but I am afraid that simply is not possible. In its present state it is very doubtful whether the line will run another season and it has only continued so long because the owner Sir Haydn Jones has been prepared to run at a loss. In the event of conversion on the lines we suggest, we envisage that one of the locomotives and at least one of the coaches would be preserved either at Towyn (vide the Wantage Tramway loco at Wantage Road station) or in the Railway Museum."

This explanation of his thinking is remarkable and a complete antithesis of his original thinking to preserve the last independent railway which escaped nationalisation. Fortunately, Owen Prosser talked him out of this view as did Edward Thomas who took the correct view that passengers come to see the train in its original form. Even Edward Thomas had discounted the possibility of buying a diesel engine because that "would mean coupling something new to something old."

Owen Prosser was a junior civil servant and, soon after the end of the second world war and the advent of nationalisation, he became particularly interested in the Talyllyn Railway, fearing for the future survival of rural lines.

It was Owen Prosser who first suggested not only the name but the very idea of a preservation society using its members' volunteer labour to maintain and operate the railway. He even offered to purchase the railway himself and had a meeting with Edward Thomas to that effect when Sir

Haydn died: a tremendous gesture, which in the event was not necessary, arising from his affection for the railway developed on family holidays in the 1940s. When he read Tom Rolt's letter in *The Birmingham Post*, he wrote to Tom suggesting the idea of a public meeting to consider how the railway might be saved. He explains his idea:

"I was first involved in advocating the kind of arrangements which have since created what may best be termed the railway restoration movement, the trend for lines that had not covered their costs on a normal commercial basis to be revived by the mustering of community effort in the task. We all know that this process has since achieved resounding success, with applications spreading to many parts of the world, and in Great Britain alone, well over two million passengers and some thousands of tons of freight carried annually.

Trinder and Rolt climbed the incline to the quarry where they saw the very last wagon of slate being loaded by two old men. *(Photos: Talyllyn Railway Archive)*

"When I sought the reactions of the Ministry of Transport to this idea, it led to a reply dismissing the possibility. But in striking contrast to that, warm praise for what we began on the Talyllyn voiced by the same department in their 1977 White Paper on transport policy commending our work as showing "imagination and ingenuity.""

"I did not think that the kind of folk we should look to for help would seek a return on capital, but would rather be prepared to make donations to what they would see as a good cause. For what I had in mind was an assembly of people of goodwill. In fact, I suggested the title of the kind of organisation which seemed best fitted for the job; *The Talyllyn Railway Preservation Society*"

Rolt continues: "As an amenity body, the Society was at that time unique. No one had ever thought of trying to preserve a public passenger carrying railway before and there was a great deal of head shaking."

"But could this lone survivor of private enterprise manage to live on into this new era? As the old railway companies which I had known and loved were finally dissolved before my eyes I found myself becoming more and more keenly interested in the future of Talyllyn and talked the question over endlessly with two railway-minded friends in Banbury, Bill Trinder and Jim Russell."

Tom Rolt was an author of industrial and transport subjects who also had an engineering background at Kerr, Stuart & Co. Not much liking the repetitiveness of the shop floor, he dropped out and took to a nomadic life on the canal waterways whilst he eeked out a living writing and enjoyed vintage cars. Even more so than with the railways, the canal system was regarded as slow, outmoded and so falling out of use. He was a joint founder of the Inland Waterways Association established to promote the canals but fell foul of the internal politics which sought to preserve every mile of the canal system whereas Rolt considered that it was only practical to retain a few routes. He was expelled from the Association for his views which, as always, were firmly held. It was during this period that Bill Trinder got to know Rolt during the many periods when Rolt's narrow boat, *Cressy,* was at Tooley's boat yard in Banbury. Trinder kept an electrical shop in the town where Rolt bought batteries for his radio after meeting when Rolt had brought his radio in for repairs. Trinder was a former GWR employee.

Trinder had a genius for instant friendships and the two very soon had a regular coffee date each morning at Butler's Café opposite 'Trinder's Radio' at 84 High St. One morning, when chatting over coffee in the autumn of 1947 about the grim prospect of railway nationalisation, Rolt remarked that only one independent railway would survive– the Talyllyn. This aroused Trinder's interest in the Welsh narrow gauge, and he bought some of Kidner's potted histories of minor railways and introduced Rolt to Jim Russell who was a professional photographer and also a former GWR employee.

In March 1948, Trinder set off by car with Rolt and Russell to visit the Talyllyn and they reached the Tyn-y-Cornel Hotel after dark in stormy weather. Next day dawned bright and clear, and they parked the car in Abergynolwyn. Russell went off alone, so Trinder and Rolt climbed the inclines to the quarry where they saw the very last wagon of slate being loaded by two old men (it was apparently taken down the line by *Dolgoch* on the following day). After taking some pictures they walked the line through to Wharf where they met and became became acquainted with Edward Thomas, then Traffic Manager. During 1948 Trinder went to Towyn several times, getting to know Edward Thomas so well that he was asked to preach sermons in the Methodist Church there. Trinder was a Methodist local preacher and secretary of the Banbury Liberal Association, attributes that were to prove most helpful when the time came to meet Sir Haydn, who had been Liberal MP for Merioneth from 1911 until the Labour landslide of 1945. Both men were direct and upright and would have recognised the qualities in each other.

Rolt was not very active in this period as he was moving around the country in *Cressy*. Trinder kept him fully informed, however, by visiting *Cressy* wherever she was moored. All the time, Edward Thomas was pressing for action of some kind, although nobody had any clear any idea as to the form this might take.

By Whit Monday 1949, Edward Thomas had put Trinder in touch with a Mr. Jonathan who kept the Cambrian Stores opposite Sir Haydn's office over the post office and was Chairman of Towyn UDC. With extreme reluctance, Jonathan agreed to introduce Trinder and Rolt to Sir Haydn a few days later. On the appointed day, at 2 pm., Jonathan took Trinder across the road and up to

> **If you've got some scheme to save it, I'll give you all the help I can**

Sir Haydn's office.

Jonathan knocked on the door, shouted Trinder's name through the panels, and fled!

Trinder played his Methodist Liberal cards judiciously, as well as claiming a couple of common acquaintanceships.

After three quarters of an hour's conversation, Trinder asked Sir Haydn "What's to happen to the railway?" "Trinder", Sir Haydn replied, "If you've got some scheme to save it I'll give you all the help I can". Edward Thomas was thrilled when he heard about this.

Before long Trinder was back in Sir Haydn's office with Rolt discussing ways in which the railway might be kept going. Messages were exchanged between Trinder and Sir Haydn which confirmed the old man's wish that every effort should be made to keep the railway open.

Rolt continues:

Sir Haydn spoke without sentiment and to the point. He was losing money on the railway, but so long as he lived he would continue to run a summer service. He would welcome any suggestion which might help to ensure the future life of the line but he did not see that anything could be done short of the expenditure of a large sum of money with little prospect of any commensurate return. Ever since he had acquired control in 1911, Sir Haydn had delegated the responsibility of running the railway entirely to Mr. Edward Thomas, placing the practical management of the line in his extremely capable hands.

Edward Thomas' job during the summer running

The Banbury building which used to house Bill Trinder's radio shop – where it all began (Photo: David Mitchell)

season was no easy sinecure. He was secretary, accountant, booking clerk, station master and guard all rolled into one. When I first saw him, clad in the neat grey tweed suit he always effects, he was busily selling tickets for the afternoon train at Towyn Wharf station. When the last passenger had been booked in he clapped on his trilby hat, locked up the office and walked briskly towards the waiting train with the cash takings in a linen bag tightly clasped by the neck. Before hopping nimbly into the brake van it was his invariable custom to signal the 'right away' by a quick, peremptory flick of the wrist of his free hand, as though he were shoo-ing the train away like some disobedient dog.

At Trinder and Russell's suggestion, following up my miniature railway scheme, we consulted Messrs Fuller and Franklin of Basset Lowke Ltd of Northampton (who had acquired and miniaturised the Ravenglass & Eskdale Railway in the Lake District) who were the best people to advise us

initiative at the present time that we so often grumble and say: "Why don't *they* do something about it?" and so seldom pause to consider whether we might not be doing something about it ourselves." Then without going into details, I went on to say that a scheme was afoot to ensure the future of the railway and would anyone interested please write to me.

In the meantime, Jim Russell, who was more closely in touch with Birmingham railway enthusiasts then either Bill Trinder or myself, told us that it was their considered opinion that the idea of the conversion of the railway was most unlikely to attract support and that only a plan to preserve the existing railway would prove sufficiently popular. Against my own judgment I allowed myself to be persuaded by this argument, though no one knew better than I what an immense gamble we were taking.

I was working *Cressy* through one of the locks on the Oxford canal in 1950 when I received verbally

> Surely it is a sorry symptom of the decline of individual initiative at the present time that we so often grumble and say "Why don't *they* do something about it?" and so seldom pause to consider whether we might not be doing something about it ourselves

about the feasibility and cost of converting the Talyllyn. They told us that an engineer named David Curwen was the best person in England to help us, so we drove down to Baydon in the Wiltshire Downs where we found David building miniature steam locomotives in a small workshop down a rough track near the village. He estimated that conversion would cost around £10,000, which seemed a very large sum at that time, but was probably only a fraction of the expense of restoring the existing line to perfect order. I was at once very impressed with David both as an engineer and as a person. I think we took an immediate mutual liking to each other and he proved to be one of the very few intimate friends I made as a result of this railway venture. Our friendship was later cemented when, although I played no part in bringing them together, David married my cousin Barbara Willans.

In 1949, to my surprise, a nostalgic article on the Talyllyn Railway appeared in *The Birmingham Post* newspaper. The writer acknowledged the beauties of a railway which, he said, was obviously on its last legs and ended with a plea to Government or British railways to do something about it. This seemed much too good an opportunity to miss, so I replied with a letter in which I said: "Surely it is a sorry symptom of the decline of individual

the news that Sir Haydn was dead. It was now or never. As soon as we moored that evening at Twyford Wharf, just south of Banbury, I typed a letter to Mr. Arthur of Machynlleth, the solicitor to the Haydn Jones estate, outlining our new proposals for the Talyllyn Railway which were that a society should be formed to preserve the railway for a trial period of three years and that the railway should be administered by a joint board consisting of directors nominated by the society and the executors. I urged that the directors should come to no irrevocable decision before I had time to organise a meeting in Birmingham to discuss the formation of such a society. Whilst I was at Market Harborough I received a very satisfactory reply confirming that no decision would be made pending the outcome of the Birmingham meeting.

Such ready acquiescence was entirely due to the advice given by Edward Thomas. Having first joined the railway in 1897 as a seventeen year old assistant clerk to his father, Hugh, who was then manager, Edward Thomas succeeded his father after the railway had been acquired by Sir Haydn and he subsequently became one of the two representatives of the executors on the board. From my first visit with Bill Trinder and Jim Russell in 1948 it became clear to us that, in our efforts to save the railway, Edward Thomas was

H. M. ARTHUR,
SOLICITOR
AND
COMMISSIONER FOR OATHS

A/H.

Machynlleth

TELEPHONE "MACHYNLLETH 35"

27th July, 1950

L.T.C. Rolt, Esq.,
The Cottage,
Stanley Pontlarge,
Gretton,
Nr. Cheltenham, Glos.

Dear Sir,

Sir H. Haydn Jones decd.
re Talyllyn Railway.

        I thank you for your letter of the 20th inst. and confirm that I am acting for Lady Haydn Jones, widow of the late Sir H. Haydn Jones, the sole executrix and beneficiary of his estate. She appreciates the interest taken by you and your friends in the Talyllyn Railway and it would be her personal wish to continue the running of the Railway if this were at all possible but all you say in your letter as to the position is unfortunately only too true, apart from the added complication arising from death duties on the late Sir Haydn's estate. In these circumstances I have already had to advise Lady Haydn tentatively that the line should be closed permanently at the end of this summer season in order to avoid any further financial sacrifices due to a sentimental regard for the railway itself and for the faithful employees concerned.

        As you have already been in touch with the late Sir Haydn Jones, Lady Haydn instructs me to state that she authorises me to continue such discussions on her behalf.

        The final decision to close down will be deferred for the time being so as to give you an opportunity of formulating any definite proposals you may find yourself able to make in the light of any definite undertakings you may be able to obtain for financial support to your project of "rescuing" the line.

        I appreciate your offer to travel to Wales to see me, but possibly this is premature at the moment as I have not as yet had sufficient time to do more than make a cursory investigation of the position.

Yours faithfully,

H M Arthur

wholeheartedly on our side. So, when it came to winning over Lady Haydn and her solicitor to what must have seemed to them- as it did to many others – a completely crack brained idea, his advocacy proved far more effective than any Englishman's could conceivably have been. Sir Haydn's widow, Lady Gwendolyn, had in her possession letters making it clear her husband's wishes regarding the railway. If a scheme for continued operation could be devised, she would put the railway in as her contribution.

I drafted a circular calling for a public meeting on 11th October, 1950 at the Imperial Hotel, Birmingham, a copy of which was sent to all those who had already written to me about the railway and to all the railway minded acquaintances we could muster.

Mobilising the team to save the railway

Tom Rolt

The 'Old Lady' *Dolgoch* sits at the buffer stops at Wharf station on 15th August, 1953. *(Photo: Jim Jarvis, Kidderminster Railway Museum Collection)*

The meeting at the Imperial Hotel was a great success and the large room we had hired for the purpose was full. Bill Trinder chaired the meeting very ably and was supported on the platform by Mr. Edward Thomas, Jim Russell and myself. Edward Thomas, particularly, impressed us all by the way he spoke and by his obviously sincere concern that our efforts would prove successful and enable the railway to continue. He needed no second bidding to make the long journey to Birmingham where his eloquent speech on behalf of the railway undoubtedly influenced the decision to form a Talyllyn Railway Preservation Society, there and then.

I drafted out a set of rules and constitution for the Society for approval at the first meeting of the newly formed committee. I produced a democratic document which I believed to be proof against

> **Edward Thomas impressed us all by the way he spoke**

take overs and so it has proved. The Society really does own and run the railway. But as the railway and the Society flourished and grew over the years and the amount of business increased, so the defects of this democratic system became more apparent. In order to satisfy Society members that their wishes were truly represented we had to have a huge and unwieldy Council and a plethora of committees. As a result, decision making became exasperatingly slow and difficult. Even so, when a decision was reached, it was often bitterly contested by the membership who would claim that the Council were out of touch and unrepresentative. Sometimes, things would reach a farcical pitch that the impossible course of holding a plebiscite of the whole membership seemed the only way of reaching an acceptable decision.

Pat Garland and Pat Whitehouse, both key members of the original Birmingham based

The meeting convened to consider the future of the Talyllyn Railway was held at the Imperial Hotel, Temple Street, Birmingham

7.15pm on the 11th October, 1950

Mr. W.G. Trinder of Banbury being the Chairman.

In addition to the many railway enthusiasts present, the meeting welcomed Mrs. Mathias, the only daughter of the late Sir Haydn Jones, Owner and Manager of the Railway, and Mr. Edward Thomas, who for many years has been responsible for the practical administration of the line.

In his opening address, the Chairman explained his long-standing interest in the future of the railway and his concern that it should continue in operation. To this end he and his immediate associates, Mr. J.M. Russell and Mr. L.T.C. Rolt had discussed ways and means, had visited the railway on several occasions and had interviewed Sir Henry Haydn Jones; Mr. Thomas; a representative of the Towyn Council; and the present MP for Merioneth.

The line was very popular with holiday makers and the Chairman stressed its great possibilities, but at the same time he emphasised the hard facts, which Sir Haydn had himself pointed out to him, that the line was losing money, that the track needed renewals and locomotives extensive repairs. In conclusion, the Chairman pointed out that the death of Sir Haydn last July had lent urgency to the situation, for unless external help in some form was forthcoming, it was extremely unlikely that the line would reopen next year.

Supporting the Chairman, Mr. Rolt said he hoped the meeting would lead to the formation of a strong working committee to investigate to possible lines of approach: (1) acquisition of the railway;(2) formation of a supporting society which would keep the line running under present ownership. On the practical side the Committee should consider the first two priorities (1) track improvements (2) provision of additional locomotive power to enable the line to work six days a week instead of three as at present. In connexion with the first requirement, Mr. Rolt suggested introducing rails from the Corris with the assistance of voluntary labour for relaying.

Mr Edward Thomas then spoke. He confirmed the bad state of the track but added that they already had in hand 10 tons of rails purchased from the Corris Railway which had not been laid, also 400 sleepers most of which had been put down. He then stated that 1950 had been a record season, passenger receipts being £400 8/-, representing 5,235 passengers. He estimated that this figure might have been increased to 8,000 if accommodation had been adequate, but as it was passengers had often been left behind.

Mr Fuller, Birmingham, then rose to say that no information had been given on the vital question of the financial position of the undertaking and he went on to ask a number of pertinent questions in this connexion. Replying, Mr. Trinder and Mr. Rolt pointed out that up till now, as individual enthusiasts, they had no justification or standing to enable them to carry out financial investigations but that if a Committee was formed this would be their first task. At the moment the object was to discover whether the interest and enthusiasm was sufficient to warrant the setting up of a Committee.

Mr. Thomas was then asked whether the line would in fact close if no help was for forthcoming, the speaker pointing out that the staff were being kept on at the moment. Mr. Thomas replied that the staff were being with retained pending the result of the meeting.

Mr. Gray then suggested the possibility of leasing the line for a season or two as a trial and said that this might be arranged at a nominal figure if the owners of the line were thereby relieved of any deficit on working. He added that on three occasions he had travelled on the line recently he had had to struggle for seat, and from what had been said he considered the possibilities far greater than he had imagined.

Mr. Roberts stressed the importance of reopening next year but was not in favour of purchase. He thought any sum raised should be devoted to improving rolling stock and track. To this the Chairman added that he felt confident that if handling facilities were adequate, passenger traffic could be increased from 50% to 70%.

Mr. Cope suggested that the line might be kept going next year by guaranteeing any loss that might be incurred. He was prepared to contribute and thought the time had come for a proposal to be made. After further discussion Mr. Oakley suggested that they might get some indication from people at the meeting how much they were prepared to put down. To this Mr. Rolt replied that this question must be subject to the financial position of the line being investigated and considered satisfactory.

PAGE 1

PAGE 2

A member of the audience then asked whether, if the line was purchased by a private individual, the Committee, if formed, would give their support. To this the Chairman replied that the purchaser would have the wholehearted approval, not merely of a Committee but the railway enthusiasts all over the country.

Mr. Oliver said he lived at Towyn and had examined the track. He considered bad sleepers and lack of ballast worse faults than the rails themselves. He suggested that an adjacent quarry could provide suitable ballast and that rails could be used from the disused funiculars to the quarries.

The value of publicity was then mentioned by two speakers, but it was pointed out that this must await the outcome of financial investigations. If these showed that continued working was practicable then wide publicity should be sought to rally public support.

Mr. Garland said there must be many enthusiasts who would be prepared to do something practical to assist in maintenance and repair of the line in their spare time, while Mr. Prosser said he could transfer to Towyn and devote every evening during the summer months. He was willing to work the train and would contemplate purchase if funds allowed.

Volunteers to serve on the proposed Committee were called for and the formal motion that the Committee be set up was proposed by Mr. Oakley, seconded by Mr. Reading, and carried unanimously. The committee consists of Mr. Trinder, Mr. Rolt, Mr. Russell, Mr. Fuller, Mr. Oliver, Mr. Whitehouse, Mr. Garland, Mr. Tonks, Mr. Cope, Mr. Clifford, Mr. Grey, Mr. Walker, Mr. Prosser, Mr. Smith and Mr. Tippetts.

Mr. Garland and then kindly offered the use of his office for committee meetings and this was accepted. It was then arranged that the Committee should hold its first meeting and elect its officers on Monday, October 23 at 6:30 pm. After further general discussion the meeting then terminated.

Committee made a material contribution to facilitating the success of the preservation effort using their respective Birmingham and Black Country business contacts and working with their friends John Wilkins, Tom Hunt and Bill Faulkner in particular, each using the good offices of their firms and their business acumen.

Pat Whitehouse

Bill Faulkner in particular was magnificent. He did so much for the railway. Without Bill the railway would probably never have got off the ground. He put an enormous amount of time and effort into it. He and I knew each other simply because he was in the railway transfer business and I was a railway enthusiast collecting railway transfers. We talked about the railway and he suddenly said to me one day that

Bill Faulkner

Tom Rolt designed a carefully crafted constitution for us and then found, to his dismay, that it could prove a serious handicap to decisive action. At the time "democracy", for many, was a "buzz" word carrying undertones of "No more Big Brother", "No more rules", and a comforting feeling that we now had our very own railway and could do what we liked with it *(Harold Vickers)*

he thought he would like to go down and have a look at it. So I took him down and when we came back he said he was interested but he was not going to do anything at all unless he was properly involved. Once he got himself involved, it was his life, initially working from Birmingham but he soon relocated himself and his family to Wales and became unpaid Managing Director on the ground.

Peggy Faulkner and Dorothy Boyd, wives of two of the earliest TR volunteers, buy tickets from No.5 van as a publicity photo. *(Photo: John Adams)*

Bill was in on the action from the very start and by constantly ensuring that the right people, the right advice, the right materials and, most of all, he himself were there when needed, he made himself indispensable to the new railway in its critical years.

Bill was the crisis man par excellence. If the ideal manager is defined as the one who ensures that the job continues as smoothly in his absence as when he is there, then that was not Bill's way. He preferred to have all his options open and then play his cards as he saw fit when the occasion rose.

Inevitably as the organisation matured and everyone gained experience, with track and rolling stock coming up to scratch, crises became less frequent and Bill's role as a crisis manager diminished. The part that he cherished most was probably that of sole volunteer driver on No.4. By the time that even this distinction disappeared in 1969 when volunteers were at last recognized as competent drivers, Bill's place in history was secure.

In a way, his role, although the circumstances were very different, was comparable with Edward Thomas before him. They had both been in the right place at the right time. It was Bill's identification with the TR, his single determination that every single passenger desiring to travel should be able to do so, come what may, that became perhaps the most important single contribution to our survival through these critical years.

(Harold Vickers)

Because Bill was Bill he threw himself wholeheartedly into the work and in those early days with a small team it was essential to have someone of his calibre who acted so much as a catalyst. Bill never had any thoughts beyond those which were right for the railway and I know that he was an invaluable source of inspiration to me at times when things could, and sometimes did, get on top of me as Secretary; indeed, there are times when he kept us all going.

Ian Faulkner writes about his father:
My father was born on the 17 June 1912 in Kings Norton and served in the RAF during the second World War. He worked for many years as Managing Director at Tearne & Sons, a transfer manufacturer in Birmingham. In the middle 1950's he designed and produced for the T.R. a neat garter transfer, based on originals found on some of the old company's literature, it is still used as the Railway's Logo and can been seen on the locomotives. Bill loved the T.R. and his world revolved around the fortunes of the line. In my memory he was always doing something for the railway and as a child I was often roped into help with tasks related to the T.R. I recall one particularly tedious job that I was given: Bill as usual had been 'scrounging' around the Midlands and had been given sacks of reject nuts, bolts and washers. My job was to sort out the good from

the useless. Some washers had no holes, screws with no slot in the head, nuts and bolts without threads, but there was a fair quantity of usable material once the sorting had been done.

Most of our week-ends would be spent on the T.R. doing such jobs as sawing sleepers for lighting up with a two man cross cut saw, quite exhausting! In 1964 Bill gave up his job in Birmingham and we moved to Towyn to be able to spend even more time on the Railway, later we moved to Aberdovey. I have very fond memories of firing for him on No.4 in the 60's; I very quickly learnt that letting the engine blow off was most definitely frowned upon! But what a wonderful warm feeling it was to be on the receiving end of a smile and a few words of encouragement, "Easy isn't it" was a great complement that I was on the receiving end of at the end of a long hard day of firing for him. Running back down Cynfal bank at the end of a long hot day with cool air flowing through the cab, just looking across and him giving a smile and a wink was all that was needed.

I also remember how happy he was the day that the train crew was Bill Faulkner (driver), Ian Faulkner (fireman), Diana Faulkner (assistant guard) and John Brown (guard).

Bill passed away Jan 18th 1982 just a few weeks after his last driving trip on the 30th December 1981, just as he was leaving home to go to Pendre...

These people became driving forces of the Talyllyn Railway in the early years and their approach was somewhat different to that of Tom Rolt which caused some friction during the early years when the railway was effectively directed from Birmingham by the Committee but run on a day to day basis from Towyn by Tom. Indeed, Tom Rolt comments on this himself which is worth quoting up front so the reader can bear these thoughts in mind as the story unfolds[1]:

When I look back on my eighteen years of association with the Talyllyn Railway, despite the fact that they yielded more frustration and pain than reward where I was concerned, I would not have changed the set up even if I could. For it seems that my experiences of the two organisations, the Inland Waterways Association and the Talyllyn Railway Preservation Society, typifies in a microcosm the perennial, unsolved dilemma that besets all human government. Impatient of the inefficiencies, the compromises and delays inseparable from the cumbersome democratic machine, there is the understandable tendency to streamline and simplify the machine

---

1. *Landscape with Figures* by L.T.C Rolt

PJG stands by *Dolgoch* with John Snell on left, David Curwen in the cab and PBW in his white ex BW&S painter's coat. *(Talyllyn Railway Archive)*

in an attempt to make its action speedier. The logical end of this road is to leave decision making to some super man regardless of the fact that, according to the inexorable law that absolute power corrupts absolutely, even the wisest of men in such circumstances soon begins to display symptoms of paranoia or megalomania.

Pat Garland and Pat Whitehouse now both pick up the story as it unfolded in the early days following the Imperial Hotel meeting. Pat Garland kicks off[2]:

Pat
Garland

I knew Jim Russell who was a fellow devotee of modelling the Great Western Railway in 4 mm scale and also a client of my accountancy practice. One day he said he had a friend who lived on a narrowboat near Banbury, one L.T.C. Rolt, who wanted to know what, if anything, could be done to keep the Talyllyn Railway going. I was asked as I had a wide range of contacts in the railway enthusiasts world from my then position as Chairman of the Midland

---

2. *Extracted from tape recorded discussion with Richard Hope*

Pat Garland inspects a 7mm scale model of the Talyllyn Railway on show at the Railway's centenary exhibition in 1965 which was operated by Richard Rolt and the author as 'required' by their parents! *(Talyllyn Railway Archive)*

Pat Garland
(1913-2005),

An accountant with a passion for trains. Garland played a critical role in negotiating the transfer of the Talyllyn Railway Company – lock, stock and leaky barrel – from the executors into the control of the infant Talyllyn Railway Preservation Society. The very idea that volunteers could manage, operate and maintain a real working railway set up under its own Act of Parliament seemed barely conceivable. But on 8th February, 1951 an agreement typed on a single sheet of paper was signed by Sir Haydn's widow. With great generosity she agreed to hand over the assets free of charge.

Garland became the first Treasurer of the TRPS and accountant to the railway company. Money was tight, but with the aid of his business contacts in the West Midlands, all kinds of useful equipment, including a complete steam locomotive, found its way to Towyn at little or no cost, and generous donations.
He installed a large model railway in his loft and a steady stream of visitors arrived to admire the latest developments and puff contentedly on their pipes. His sons have vivid memories of being taken out onto the front doorstep of their house in the dead of night to hear their father come tearing through the station, whistle blowing, at the controls of the Swindon parcels train.

From The Telegraph

area of the Stephenson Locomotive Society.

At that time I had never heard of the TR, although I might have seen it in some picture postcards. It did not come into my world. However, I went to Banbury with Russell to meet Rolt and also his friend Trinder in September 1950. We all went upstairs to the holy of holies office above Trinder's shop to discuss the matter. I thought the best thing we could do was to call a meeting and to discuss it further. Sir Haydn had died the previous July which set up alarm signals as we knew he had been subsidising the railway.

I well remember the meeting. It was very well attended considering there was not a lot of chance to do any advertising.

I remember Mr. Edward Thomas telling us all that the railway only ran trains on Mondays, Wednesdays and Fridays because they did not think the engine was strong enough to run every day!

I was persuaded to become Honorary Treasurer and the only reason was because I really thought the whole scheme as put forward taking a statutory railway in a derelict condition and trying to restore it was very unlikely to succeed and it would need someone who knew how to wind it up on hand when the inevitable occurred. How wrong I was!

> The motivation for all of us was the sense of adventure and of actually being able to do something with a railway of our own

Pat Whitehouse joins in[3:]

Pat Whitehouse

I think most of us who went to the meeting at the Imperial Hotel were members of the Birmingham Loco Club as most of us knew each other and we probably did not have anything else to do on that particular evening. I don't think there was anyone there from the general public. I did not really know either Rolt or Trinder, although about that time I had gone to a model engineering exhibition in London where I recollect Jim introducing me to them and also talk of someone possibly getting hold of the Talyllyn Railway and converting it into a miniature railway. I know I was only young at the time, but I poured scorn on that proposal. However, both Pat Garland and I knew Jim Russell and this is probably another

reason why we went along. Pat had first got to know Jim during the war because neither of them were in service as I was. Jim was a photographer living in Banbury and also a great railway enthusiast. Both of them were mad about the GWR. So, Pat introduced me to Jim and the three of us became good friends and Jim used to develop my pictures. Although Jim mentioned the Talyllyn Railway only vaguely in conversation, I knew of it from my boyhood days when on family holiday. My wife and I also travelled on it in 1947 when I took some cine shots which eventually found their place at the beginning of the TR publicity film I shot in the 1950s.

At the Imperial Hotel meeting there were four people on the platform: Trinder, Rolt, Russell and Edward Thomas. Tom Rolt was without question the leading authoritative voice. It came over without any doubt as to Tom's feelings; he was quite dramatic about it as he had this big arty streak in him. There was no doubt that he felt strongly and that he also felt there was a practicability in the thing. Jim Russell added his bit because he was a former railwayman. Bill Trinder was the meeting Chairman and also full of enthusiasm. However, at the time, I don't think anyone who attended the meeting really thought anything was actually going to happen.

We were all asked to sign our name in a book and, before I knew where I was, we had our first meeting in Pat Garland's office in Waterloo Street, Birmingham. This became the first meeting of the body of people who were going to do something. We decided to form ourselves into a committee. Trinder was Chairman, Pat Garland became Treasurer. Other members included a local authority architect, a director of an engineering firm, a clerk in the Ministry of Transport and a metallurgical chemist. I took on the role of Secretary.

We said: "Oh yes, all right, we will do something," because those were the days when we were all beginning to get a bit freer, most of us having been in the services during the war and so tied up in doing things. It also seemed to be an interesting challenge and so we were enthusiastic. But I am certain that none of us, except for John Wilkins and Pat Garland, had any idea what we were likely to be taking on. But most of us had visited the railway within the past year and we knew that to put the line in order would cost more than we could afford to pay for it ourselves.

In fact, John Wilkins sat down at one of the early meetings and said:" Well, I don't think you know what you're talking about. It's going to cost £12,000

---

3. Extracted from tape recorded discussion with Richard Hope

to relay the track and where are we going to get £12,000 from?" Everyone sort of glared at him and he was almost thrown out of the room. But John knew what he was talking about as, of course, he had only recently bought and re-equipped the nearby 15" Fairbourne Railway himself.

At the second committee meeting Mr. John Wilkins very kindly presented a report on the condition of the track and the locomotives following a trip to the railway to inspect it, which ended dismally as *Dolgoch*, steamed specially derailed. A sad end to the operation of the railway under the Haydn Jones' regime. This report was extremely comprehensive and the committee minutes summarised it as follows:

(a) The track is in very poor condition, sleepers are rotten and about 50% of rails unusable.
(b) The minimum requirement for safe running would be a new sleeper under each rail joint and the replacement of the completely u/s rails; the 10 tons of Corris rail would only go a small way to help this.
(c) The locomotive *Talyllyn* is a complete write off and *Dolgoch* will need inspection before it can again have its boiler insured – this is not in good order, being 81 years old.[4]
(d) The cost of putting the track in good order would be in the region of £11,000.
(e) One of the causes of deterioration was that the fixed wheelbase of *Dolgoch* is too large for the track.

4. *It is now known that Dolgoch had been given a replacement boiler, so this was not its original*

> **I was absolutely staggered at the derelict condition of this line. It was unbelievable**

Pat Whitehouse

I don't think there was any doubt that, if it hadn't been for Rolt and Trinder's enthusiasm, the Talyllyn Railway Preservation Society would never have got off the ground, because I think that those of us who were involved in other things may well have been prepared to let the railway die. Rolt and Trinder were the people who went off and talked to the Haydn Jones family and came back saying that they thought the family would be interested in doing some sort of deal in giving the railway to us or allowing us to run it. Once that spark was there then there was a chance. Yes, occasionally, there was a bit of an undercurrent between Trinder and Rolt about who was the founder of the enterprise. Each of them liked to view themselves as the founder and say that they thought of the idea first. Actually, I suspect Tom did the initial thinking, but that it was Trinder's extra enthusiasm and his ability to connect with Sir Haydn from a church perspective which made sure the thing got off the ground. Of course, Tom volunteered to go down and oversee it because he was the only one with the time, being a freelance person and also one with an engineering background. Taking these things into account he was the only possible choice. He gained a lot of credibility and publicity of course from that in his excellent book *Railway Adventure* about his first two years being manager.

It was a feeling of adventure. It was a challenge. All of us were looking for some kind of challenge because, for years and years and years, we'd been channeled into doing things, particularly those of us who were in the services, rather than being in a situation of accepting a challenge on our own initiative. I think the motivation for all of us was the sense of adventure and of actually being able to do something with a railway of our own. The start of the TRPS came just at the right time. Everything gelled together. Without the introduction of the five day week, it would have been very difficult, because weekend working parties were key to starting the voluntary work.

Pat
Garland

The Committee was formed to organise a society to produce labour to physically restore the railway and not necessarily to own it. However, no limits were set, it was just that the question of ownership was not discussed in detail until the Machynlleth meeting in February 1951.

I think the reason we succeeded, as we did, in gathering the people around us and their support, was because of the nationalisation of the standard gauge railways which, by and large, people greatly resented and even people of all political persuasions resented it, because inside every one of us is really an engine driver trying to get out. The thought of our lovely railways being tampered with by politicians was very unpleasant and very unacceptable. So that when people heard there was a little minnow of a railway which had escaped nationalisation and which was in

was so much in advance of anything we had had up to this moment, so that we thought it might be practical joke written by some schoolboy and that, upon presentation, it might bounce. However, it proved to be the first of many acts of generosity that Eric was to show us.

Anyway, we set off from Birmingham and our first call was at the Atlas foundry in Shrewsbury which Tom wanted to visit because quite recently and, in 1947, the foundry had had *Dolgoch* in for heavy repairs and he was anxious to find out from their engineer what the engine's future was likely to be bearing in mind that the only other engine which we had, *Talyllyn*, was acting as a hencoop for local poultry.

We motored on and the rain started to come down. It was nightfall before we reached Talyllyn Lake. We put it up at the Tyn y Cornel Hotel where we were welcomed by Mr. and Mrs. Hunter and had a thoroughly enjoyable meal. Being out of season, we were the only people staying there and we ate and lived with the Hunters in their kitchen, which was a lovely thing to do; very homely and very delightful.

As it had been dark for the closing miles of the

> Nothing ventured nothing win, so we will ask if we can have the railway in exchange for undertaking to keep it alive

danger of dying, they all automatically rushed to its assistance. It was spontaneous support. Seeing what was happening to the railways in the country as a whole, they all thought, well, it must be a good thing if there is someone fighting to preserve its independence and we ought to give them all the help we can.

The next major event was the 'great negotiation' at the offices of Mr. H.M. Arthur, a solicitor practicing in Machynlleth, who was Lady Haydn Jones' solicitor. She never did anything without consulting him. He was her legal and also financial advisor. I met them both with Trinder, Rolt and Edward Thomas. I well remember this occasion as it was my first visit to the railway. I had not even seen it until I went down for this meeting.

Rolt came up to Henley in Arden, where I was then living at the time. We set off in my car and called first at my office in Birmingham. Every morning mail and hopefully money from potential members was arriving. On this particular morning we had received a cheque, the largest cheque which up to that time we had received, which was for £50 written in a very round and juvenile looking hand and signed by one E.B. Gibbons. Now we were delighted to get this cheque, but we were not sure it was not perhaps a joke because it

journey, I had no idea at all of the beauty which is surrounded this place. I had never been into the district before. So, when I woke the next morning and saw a mist across the lake, I was enchanted. That was followed by the most gloriously warm and sunny day for any month of the year, let alone February.

We set off after breakfast, motored to Abergynolwyn, left the car and walked right down the line to Towyn: 6 ¾ miles. I was absolutely staggered at the derelict condition of this line. It was unbelievable. The rails were loose and only apparently being kept in gauge by mud and grass. I had never seen such a rundown thing in all my life. I thought, well, this is going to be a problem. In some places near Towyn red and white marks had been painted on the rails, apparently by Russell who had been marking rails which were beyond use. People had been down tidying up.

The next day was the 'great negotiation' at Machynlleth. It had previously been suggested to Mr Arthur that a limited liability non profit making trust be formed to take control of the railway. It was ascertained that there were no unknown liabilities, so all money subscribed to be devoted to the running of the railway – no money having to be used for the purchasing of the railway as it

MEMORANDUM OF AGREEMENT between Lady Haydn Jones and Talyllyn Railway Preservation Society.

1. Lady Haydn Jones agrees to transfer all the shares in the Talyllyn Railway Company to a new holding company (known as Talyllyn Holdings Limited).

2. The Talyllyn Railway Preservation society agrees to raise funds by subscription to carry on the operations of the Talyllyn Railway.

3. The Directors of Talyllyn Holdings Limited and of the Talyllyn Railway Co. shall be nominated as to two by the Talyllyn Railway Preservation society together with the Chariman to be nominated by the Talyllyn Railway Preservation society

4. The present value of the railway should be determined and the value so arrived at should be taken into account as Lady Haydn's share in the event of the Railway ceasing to operate and in the event of disposal

5. The house at Pendre and the cottage Plascoch Rhydyronen shall remain the property of the railway Company and the present value shall be taken into account when assessing Lady Haydn Jones' share as set out in paragraph 4 and the net rents from those properties shall be paid to Lady Haydn Jones quarterly.

6. The house Llechfan shall be conveyed to Lady Haydn Jones

7. Letters to be sent to the tenants of the houses at Pendre and Plascoch intimating conditions of tenancy as service tenancies.

Dated this 8th day of February, 1951

G. Haydn Jones
W.G.Trinder

is to be presented to the trust; the trust to receive the railway from the Wharf to the quarries only; the railway to be operated by the trust for at least 3 years, subject to prevailing conditions; the trust to undertake not to sell the railway after transfer.

Once we had arrived we just sat down and looked at each other and I remember saying to myself, well, nothing ventured nothing win, so we will ask if we can have the railway in exchange for undertaking to keep it alive. That was really the jist of our discussion.

Lady Haydn was a fairly old lady then and, in common with the behaviour of old ladies as a type, she did not really react one way or the other. She was content. She was brought to the meeting, was content to listen and agree to anything which Mr Arthur agreed to. They were very limited in their expressions one way or another. If Mr Arthur nodded his head that was good enough for Lady Haydn. We were able to convince Mr Arthur that we were in earnest. I think they had a very quiet affection for the railway. They must have had for Sir Haydn to have kept it going for so many years after it ceased to be viable. It was an act of faith

on his part to keep it going for so long as he did. It was not serving any commercial purpose as far as he was concerned. Bear in mind that the traffic receipts for the year before we took over were £400. We only took £650 in the first year we had it.

I explained to Lady Haydn and Mr Arthur that we had no money and the prospect of being able to buy it was quite out of the question. If she would give it to us then we, on our part, would undertake to maintain it, at any rate so far as it was possible.

Mr Arthur thought it was a rather unusual request. But at the same time I think he was impressed by the sincerity of other people wishing to preserve the railway. Trinder was a man who one could not help but be convinced of his sincerity, Rolt another. Then there was the enthusiasm shown by all the other people present and Lady Haydn would naturally wish to respect the wishes of her husband. The real reason why everyone was keen to get the railway going again was that it happened to be the last one that was left. In the context of the Haydn Jones' family business: Daniels shop and the slate company, the railway was small beer and had a desperate need for money to be spent on it which the family were not prepared to do. They were probably a bit overwhelmed with the proposition and the persuasive manner in which it was presented. Perhaps they were only too glad that somebody was prepared to do something about it and pick up the bill at the end of the day. It would not be easy to abandon the railway legally as it would be necessary to get an abandonment order which would be expensive. It was probably about the easiest thing of its kind which has ever been my good fortune to take part in. It all fell into place.

You also have to bear in mind that, at that time, the Korean war was raging and none of us knew whether or not we were going to enter a third holocaust. And it was, of course, for that reason that we had to value the line and agree a value for it with Lady Haydn and Edward Thomas so that, in the event of war intervening and the railway being closed down, at a time when she had chipped in her railway and we had chipped in pounds, shillings and pence, ultimately the whole thing would have to be sold up and then of course the value attributable to the line would be repaid to her and anything that was left over would be distributed. Well, of course, fortunately nothing of that sort ever occurred. I remember that the value which we agreed was £1,320.

The Talyllyn Railway Company was a statutory company established by Act of Parliament. No changes in its constitution could be made without promoting a Private Bill which would be very costly. No one wished to change or destroy the identity of the original company. So, I came up with the idea to create Talyllyn Holdings Limited with the sole purpose of holding the shares in the Talyllyn Railway Company with a board of directors appointed by both the Society and the Haydn Jones family, but with majority control vested in the Society.

The agreement was drawn up that very morning and then it was typed up, probably the next day. It then took an extraordinarily long time to get Talyllyn Holdings Ltd formed. We gave instructions to solicitors in West Bromwich, who were chosen because one of the younger partners was a railway enthusiast and we thought we would get the company formed under the old Talyllyn system without having to pay for it. The solicitor was conscientious. The process was not easy. He could not find any precedent for a company limited by guarantee without a share capital taking over and holding the issued shares in a company incorporated by Act of Parliament, so he had to tread warily in drawing up the articles of association. Talyllyn Holdings Limited was

eventually incorporated on 3rd October 1952 from 18 months after the Machynlleth meeting, so for the first two seasons of our operation the railway was really still owned by Lady Haydn. There were 750 shares or £15 each issue in the Talyllyn Railway Company. She was only able to produce 585. It took a long time and much discovery to unearth the balance, but in the meantime we were running away as if it was ours. Lady Haydn had kept the staff between the October meeting in Birmingham and the February 1951 meeting in the Machynlleth, following which we paid the staff. For some of the early years I kept a contingent liability of wages to be refunded to Lady Haydn, but she never called for this. We wanted to see that she had all the rents which came in. She also benefited as the railway was making a trading loss, so the Schedule A on the rents were wiped out and she did not have to pay any tax.

> **No one wished to change or destroy the identity of the original company**

The original train with Tom Rolt at Dolgoch

Operating begins

No.6 *Douglas* waits at Towyn Wharf station to take a train up the valley on 21st September, 1954. One of two new carriages put together at Pendre and the first bogie carriages on the line heads the train, and a new platform and run round loop have been installed, but otherwise everything is original; a far cry from today

H aving successfully begged the railway, it really set the pattern for our activity from then on because we still had no money, although people were chipping in quite generously and so we made it our business to enlist the sympathy of industrial people as well as private individuals. From our point of view, the fact that we were going to run it meant that there would be no limit to the enthusiasm and the dedication which could be applied to it.

Pat Whitehouse

Our first task was to obtain some money. Two thousand leaflets were printed and distributed to people in the professional railway world and to those interested in railways. Anxiously, we waited for their reaction.

The first response was encouraging and, by March, 1951, we had nearly three hundred members, each of whom was charged £1 in return for a vote at the annual general meeting and free travel on the railway.

As news of what we were attempting spread, our funds improved. By the end of the first season, we had received £652 in ordinary subscriptions, £840 from life membership subscriptions and donations totaling £903. An engineering society in North America, the Newcomen Society, sent us $500!

As soon as people got to hear about what we were doing, we got a vast number of people who said they would like to help, what a wonderful idea it was and what a fascinating thought. The actual help came from a few people, as it always does, but there was tremendous enthusiasm because it was the very first time that it had ever happened.

Edward Thomas reacted well. He was happy. It was the end of his working life and he certainly wanted to see the railway continue. He did everything he could to help us. There were some initial small problems with the Jones family who did most of the work on the railway. This seemed partly an English-Welsh thing. I think probably the chemistry between Hugh Jones and Tom Rolt was not necessarily at its best and Edward Thomas did warn us that the Jones family were 'difficult people'. But it was an understandable issue; the Jones family must have wondered what on earth was going to happen. Certainly, they must have wondered if their jobs were still going to be there with all these enthusiasts muscling in from foreign lands saying this is what we're going to do: we're going to run the railway and also offering to do it for nothing. It was, after all, the livelihood of the Jones family that was at stake for them.

The reactions of people in Towyn were mixed. There was not opposition to foreign people coming in to do something and nor was there the opposition that some other people met (for example when it was suggested that the Vale of Rheidol was bought from BR). There was some scepticism, but also some encouragement. To a large degree, the locals sat back and watched what we would do.

Edward Thomas largely agreed with that. He is reported as saying it was most encouraging to see so many English friends around him, although it was dissatisfying to see so little local representation. He was afraid the residents of Towyn did not fully realise what the Railway meant to the town. He knew of many families who only came to Towyn because the Railway was operating, and Towyn would not be Towyn but for the Talyllyn Railway. He was struck by the interest of his English friends, and the sacrifices they had made when they undertook to make the railway a success. In spite of the indifference of local people he was sure it would grow in popularity and go from strength to strength. Provided there was unity of purpose the Committee had no fear of difficulties when we had the railway at heart.

Pat Garland

So we started to run the railway. For the first year, we were really on 'Cloud Nine' with a lot of hope and numerous panics.

Pat Whitehouse

It was blatantly obvious that there were two things which had to happen. One was that the track was in a terrible state. The rails were being held into gauge by the turf that grew between them, it was so bad. Also, it was painfully obvious that the only working locomotive was in a pretty bad shape.

So, first we had to put the permanent way in working order.

Our first working party was held during Easter weekend of 1951. About thirty members turned up; among them an engineer, an architect, a policeman, a printer, a timber merchant, an optician and an ex-Indian civil servant. The members' wives helped with painting and polishing up the brasswork, cleaning windows and at least making the railway look as if it was a good concern!

Hugh Jones and his son, Dai, both of whom

TRPS First Progress Report

Negotiations between the Committee and the Executors of the late Sir Henry Haydn Jones proved protracted. This was not due to any lack of co-operation by the Executors, with whom our relations have been most cordial throughout, but to the legal and financial problems involved in changing the administration of a statutory company. The Committee put forward the proposal that the share capital of the Railway should be freely transferred to a non profit making company, to be known as Talyllyn Holdings Ltd., and that both this and the railway company should be administered by a Board of Directors consisting of representatives of the Executors (two) and the Society (two and the Chairman). The Executors most generously agreed to this proposal which was ratified at a meeting held at Machynlleth on 8th February, 1951.

The Committee's aim is to make the Talyllyn Railway the epitome of the narrow gauge era at its best and a source of pride to every railway enthusiast.

Our life member Mr. R.O.Griffiths of Towyn, whose father was responsible for maintaining the locomotives circa 1902, has informed the committee that the original livery of the railway was:- locomotives dark green, lined red and gold; coaching stock: brown, lined out. The locomotives will be repainted in this livery as repairs are completed.

Above: 'Maggie' Maguire's car FJW 591 parked at Brynglas station while he works on the track single handed. *(Photo: Talyllyn Railway Archive)*

Right: An early works train for the volunteers to work on the appalling track. Note *Dolgoch* still retains the wooden door on her driver's side as a protection against inclement weather. *(Photo: John Snell)*

Top: *Dolgoch* stands outside Pendre shed alongside three slate wagons, August 1951. *(Photo: John Snell)*

Above: Rydyronen station in April 1951, just before the TRPS started operating public passenger trains. *(Photo: John Snell)*

Left: View looking up the line between Rhydyronen and Brynglas in April, 1951. *(Photo: John Snell)*

Corris Nos. 3 and 4 having just been unloaded at Wharf from their journey by BR from Machynlleth with the delivery team. Some wag has chalked '6000' on the cabside of No.3 where her number plate should be, reflecting the GWR's flagship King George V and so No.3's GWR antecedents. It seems to be a little known fact that both these Corris engines made trips to Swindon works for repairs but were the only GWR narrow gauge engines to escape being modified with standard parts.
(Photo: Talyllyn Railway Archive)

had worked on the railway for many years, had agreed to remain on the permanent staff. Under their directions, our members did the labouring, clearing the track of growth, replacing old sleepers and painting coaches and station buildings. By taking old rails from the Abergynolwyn incline we managed to repair many of the defects in the track.

We had many derailments but none were serious as all the trains ran at a very low speed. Almost every joint ahead of the train used to rise and jump when the engine put its weight on it but soon the staff became familiar with the very bad patches of track. Some really useful help was given by John Wilkins who sent his permanent way foreman, Mr. Vaughan, on a more or less open ended commitment to do what he could for our track.

We resolved that we would open as far as Rhydyronen in May and all our efforts were concentrated in getting that part of the line fit to run on.

To this end we obtained rail and sleepers and did what we could to put that part of the track right using Mr. Vaughan as the track foreman. Hugh Jones worked with him and the North West Group provided the muscle.

Pat Garland

In the Pendre workshops David Curwen very quickly sized up the position. There were only two engines. *Talyllyn* had been out of use for a long time; it needed a new boiler and a new firebox, its cylinders needed renewing and it leaked steam all over the place. The other engine, *Dolgoch* (nicknamed the 'Old Lady' was still

Three sepia postcards 1, 3 & 5 from the first issue arranged by Ken Cope for sale in 1951: re-opening, pausing at Brynglas (with John Snell oiling No.2 whilst Tom Rolt chats with Pat Whitehouse) and train returning down the valley

considered buying one but they were reputed to be in poor condition. Tom Rolt decided to visit the officials at Swindon and explain what we were trying to do. The Swindon men became so interested in our project that they let us have both engines for £25 each. It was *Dolgoch's* first duty to collect them from Wharf once they had been transported there by BR. We sent No.4 to Hunslet for repairs late in 1951 and she returned in time to be used at Whitsun in 1952.

There we had the biggest surprise of our lives because when it came back we had an itemised invoice setting out all the work that had been done to it, together with the price which totalled £650 but, say, nil! The whole of that work was donated by Hunslet or by Mr. John Alcock, the managing director.

That was a very generous act. That was followed by the large donation from the Newcomen Society in North America. With these two outstanding contributions, we really did feel we had got quite a lift.

There was a glorious re-opening at Whitsun in 1951. Once that happened, there was so much joy. Once the thing started to roll, it was going to go on rolling.

Pat Whitehouse

Prosser, the man who suggested the idea of a preservation society to Tom Rolt, described the atmosphere in Towyn the day before the first society train ran on Bank Holiday Monday, 14th May, 1951 as "Electric! We knew we were about to make history by doing something that had never been done before."

There was a fair muster of passengers who had come early to the scene to claim the distinction of having travelled on the first train of the season. When they were all aboard, Bill Trinder, as Chairman of the Society, made a short speech before ceremoniously cutting a tape, which had been stretched across the track, and declaring the line open.

His action was answered by a shrill blast of *Dolgoch's* whistle and, punctual to the minute, the first service train to run under new management drew out to the accompaniment of much excitement

serviceable, but would not stand up to much and Edward Thomas had restricted using it to three days a week. David got the 'Old Lady' into a conditon when it was able to run.

Fairly early on we made out a shopping list. We had a piece of luck. The old Corris Railway, further down the coast, had two engines lying idle since 1948, but the Western Region of British Railways had set their price at £65 each. Edward Thomas had

and acclamation.

Total sales for the day amounted to £15.0/4d (compared with £4.1/2d for the last train in Sir Haydn's management the year before). A great encouragement to the adventurers, none of whom had ever run a public train service in their lives before.

The Committee were, somewhat understandably, concerned about the condition of the track and decided that they would only approve running as far as Rhydyronen and so Pat Whitehouse was instructed to write to Rolt and tell him. Tom Rolt was aghast as he had set in motion to run trains up the whole line and could not see how he could make ends meet just running the short distance. Matters were speedily resolved at an emergency meeting at Towyn when Edward Thomas settled the matter by saying that, if Sir Haydn had instructed him to run the railway again for the 1951 season, he would have run trains up the whole of the railway. The Committee bowed to this remark and backed down.

Pat Whitehouse

On 4th June, we began to operate our five day a week service. Tom Rolt took on the job of general manager. Dai Jones drove the engine and members spent their summer holidays working in the booking office, in the refreshment room and on the track. We had to keep patching up the track at every available moment.

Initial ticket sales were not very encouraging. The morning train on 4th June brought in just 16/6d and the afternoon one £2.12/2d. Sales of guide books and packets of old tickets increased

the total sales for the fist day to £3.13/3d, but it could be said to be a disappointing start and, at times, must have tested the strength of all the pioneers to the hilt.

Keeping going was indeed a close run thing and, initially, not enough people came forward to help as Tom Rolt underlines in his first report at the end of June: "Labour is the biggest problem at the present. Regular labour is hardly adequate when things are going smoothly, and in the event of illness or any emergency it would be quite inadequate. Volunteer help has been very limited during June. Without such help, Mr. Oliver can do little more than deal with track defects as they develop and are reported to him by the train crew. No substantial track improvement work can be done without volunteers." So, without the Fairbourne Railway's help, track matters would have been even bleaker than they actually were.

> We knew we were about to make history by doing something that had never been done before

When we began operating a regular train service we soon became hardened to jibes about 'playing trains.' In fact we were from the outset fully conscious of our responsibility to the public. It was abundantly clear to us that serious blunder on our part leading to an accident might very easily put the damper on our project and on any others of a similar nature. We felt this responsibility all the more keenly in the early days because of the appalling state of disrepair and decrepitude into which locomotives, rolling stock, way and works had fallen. Such a state of affairs could not be remedied overnight and, in the meanwhile, it was a case of make do and mend.

The First Day

Ken Cope, Commercial Manager

Operating staff being few in number, I acted as booking clerk and guard and the procedure was to issue tickets from Wharf office until the train was due to leave, then lock the office and jump on the trains as guard. We ran five trains between the Wharf and Rhydyronen, most of them well loaded and, there being no loop at the latter place, the carriages had to be pushed back into the siding, the locomotive proceeding a short way down the main line, after which staff and passengers pushed the carriages out of the siding to the station platform and the locomotive was coupled to them again. This was seized on by the representative of one national daily, the subsequent report having the heading "Passengers push the train."

From the booking office 305 tickets were issued during the day and sixteen from the TR van. Train receipts came to £11 19/1d to which was added £3 1/3d from sales of old tickets, guides etc. The guides were old stock found in various drawers at the Wharf, which disgorged an amazing amount of old forms, timetables etc, most of them ruined by damp.

Details of the passengers carried were as follows:

Train No.1 - 48 returns, 25 half returns, 2 singles, 5 members **£3 1/10d**

Train No.2 - 42 returns, 6 half returns, 9 singles, 4 half singles **£2 12/4d**

Train No.3 - 38 returns, 58 half returns, 8 singles, 2 half singles, 7 members **£3 11/9d**

Train No.4 - 33 returns, 22 half returns, 3 singles, 5 half singles **£2 4/7d**

Train No.5 - 5 returns, 7 half returns, 1 single, 1 half single **8/7d**

We have come a long way since then.

The first day...

Whit Monday, 1951 and the first public passenger train in the history of the TRPS is nearly ready to leave for its historic journey to Rhydyronen. *Dolgoch* simmers in the station at Wharf, Bill Trinder stands by the white tape and Tom Rolt alongside the train.

(Photos: *Talyllyn Railway Archive*)

John Snell leans out of *Dolgoch's* cab with a crowd of people dressed in their best clothes on re-opeing day on 14th May, 1951. Edward Thomas proudly wears his three piece suit

Train returning from Rhydyronen. PBW sits on the floor of Van No.5 with his feet on the footboard.

Passengers gather around the train at Wharf on 14th May, 1951

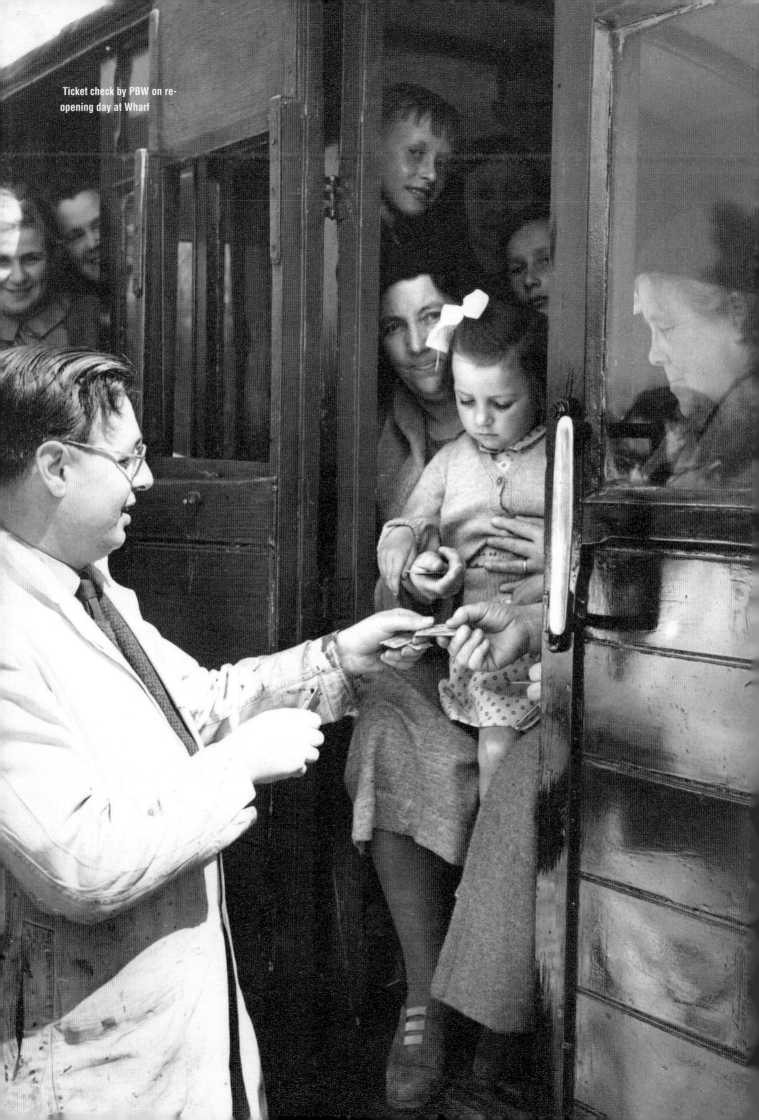

Ticket check by PBW on re-opening day at Wharf

Passengers on the re-opening day

Dolgoch leaving Wharf with one of the first trains on 14th May, 1951

David Curwen explains *Dolgoch* to interested boys at Wharf on the re-opening day

Dolgoch shunting at Wharf on 14th May, 1951.
David Curwen is driving and Tom Rolt is in the
shadows by the coaches.

David Curwen looks out
from *Dolgoch's* footplate at
Rhydyronen on 14th May, 1951

Tom Rolt happily waving a flag from the unique
brake van No.5 as *Dolgoch* leaves Wharf station
with one of the first ever preserved railway trains

Pushing the coaches
at Rhydyronen on
14th May, 1951

CHAPTER 4

A Journey up the line[1]

Dolgoch bursts through the bridge into Cynfal halt to pick up Jack Evans waiting with local farm goods

1. *Railway Adventure by L.T.C.Rolt, 1953, Chapter 4*

Picture now the scene at the Wharf station on some bright morning in the month of June 1951, and then in imagination let us ride the footplate of *Dolgoch* as she hauls the ten-thirty up the valley to Abergynolwyn. On a wooden bench sheltered by rhododendron bushes covered with pink and purple blossom three old men are comfortably ensconced. They may possibly be prospective passengers, but it is much more likely

that they have merely strolled down to watch the train go out. Not that the spectacle is any novelty to them because they have known the railway since they were boys, but it affords an excuse to enjoy the warmth of the sun, and to pass the time of day over a peaceful pipe. The murmur of their Welsh drifts lazily upon the air with the scent of their tobacco, and from where we stand they are half hidden from us by an enormous rounded boulder which lies close beside their seat. Incongruous in its isolation it might be a meteorite, but in fact it was brought down from the quarry many years ago as an impossibly weighty response to a request by a local lady for a rockery stone and here it has lain ever since. Perhaps it seemed a mere pebble to those stalwart quarrymen of Bryn Eglwys.

About the doorway of the booking office there is a more animated group and an occasional thudding sound signifies that another ticket has been issued and stamped '15JUN51' on the old dating machine. Already some passengers have taken their seats

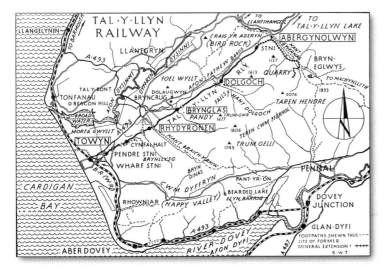

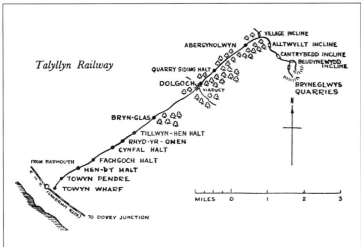

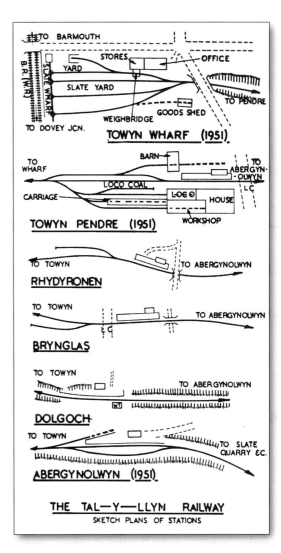

Top left: Map showing location of TR.

Bottom left: Diagram of TR.

Above: Station diagrams of track layout in 1951.

On 29th September, 1951, the 'Old Lady' *Dolgoch* adorned with brass nameplates cast at Hunt Bros. foundry to the order of the Midlands based Committee, waits to depart from Wharf with the members' train. John Snell is driving and, behind the engine to the front, Bill Trinder and Bill Harvey look on. (Photo: James Boyd)

Tom Rolt selling tickets from No.5 van

in the waiting train. A gentle salt-laden breeze is blowing in from a sea which shows blue and sparkling above the rim of the green fields beyond the Wharf. It flutters the flag over the station building and plays with the smoke and the feather of steam that is drifting from *Dolgoch's* chimney and safety valve. Her driver has been persuading some lubricant into the less accessible portions of the 'Old Lady's 'peculiar motion' with the aid of a length of pipe, while the fireman goes from coach to coach pouring oil into the axle boxes from a pint bottle which once contained fizzy lemonade. These may be what are termed 'fat boxes' in theory, but grease does not melt until the bearings run warm whereas a little oil works wonders in reducing rolling resistence. But now both the driver and fireman have climbed back on to the footplate and it is time we joined them there. For the stationmaster-cum-booking-clerk has locked up the station office and has now assumed the role of guard. He checks all carriage doors to see that they are properly shut, screws off the brake in his van and then gives the 'right away' which we acknowledge on the whistle. Our driver then moves his reversing lever into forward gear and persuasively joggles the handle of the regulator to and fro until we can hear a faint sound of steam escaping punctuated by a just audible click as the valves come up and we start to move forward. *Dolgoch* does not advertise her departure by any sharp staccato bark such as her large but youthful neighbours on the main line effect. So vigorous and vocal a display of power would be unseemly and even vulgar at her age. Instead there emerges from her tall thin chimney a decorous but slightly uneven and breathless panting sound which strengthens and deepens to a hoarse and throaty roar as she exerts her maximum effort on the steep gradient up the cutting beyond the Wharf bridge. This gradient is short, and the regulator is first eased and then closed as we enter the straight run on a slightly falling gradient into Pendre station. Ahead we can see old Peter opening the crossing gates in answer to our warning whistle, and as we run over the points which head off into the loop

and the shed roads, *Dolgoch* rolls alarmingly like a ship encountering a sudden heavy sea on the beam. So early in the season it is unlikely that there will be any passengers for this morning train at Pendre, but we make a brief routine stop, passing time of day with Peter and exchanging a word with David who, wiping his hands on a piece of cotton waste, has come out of the shed to see us go through.

The gradients on the Talyllyn Railway are deceptive. The passenger is not unnaturally led to suppose that the climbing is done on the upper section between Brynglas and Abergynolwyn where the line clings to its narrow shelf high above the valley floor. Yet in point of fact the heaviest locomotive work is performed on the first unspectacular section between Towyn and Rhydyronen where the high, overgrown hedges which brush the sides of the coaches conceal the fact that the line is rapidly gaining height. As *Dolgoch* again starts to labour heavily we learn that this ascent begins on the first curve east of Pendre, stiffens as we approach the first over bridge called Ty Mawr, and continues with unrelenting severity

Stuart Whitehouse buying tickets from No.5 van at Fach Goch halt on 18th April, 2015

> The engine rolls and snakes along on the uneven way, rough rail joints bring a series of sickening jolts and crashes, while it is disconcerting to look ahead and see an occasional loose rail leaping up as it receives our weight

Curiously enough the summit of this gradient is a bridge over the Braich-y-Rhiw stream beyond which the line falls away quite steeply for about 200 yards. This is the only favourable gradient which an up-train encounters between Pendre and Abergynolwyn, and it was here in the old days that picnic parties, bowling back to Towyn in their hired wagons, were apt to find some manual assistance necessary. From the foot of this short decline we begin to climb once more, not so steeply until we have gained the next bridge past Hendy farm. Here the 'Old Lady', a little breathless by this time as the pressure gauge shows, can be eased somewhat until she has traversed the dogleg curves beyond the gateway which is called Fach Goch halt. The second of these curves brings us onto the relaid 'Corris straight', a long climb at 1 in 60 whose summit is marked by Cynfal bridge and platform. But with this newly laid rail under her wheels, *Dolgoch* roars up this bank in fine style to demonstrate what a handsome slice she could cut from the running schedule, even at her age, if only the track was in this condition throughout. But alas, this 'galloping ground' is all too limited as yet. It is followed by a very short length which was relaid in Sir Haydn's day with rails purchased from the dismantled Glyn Valley Tramway, but then we are back on the old road again, and as we look ahead at the line of rails, wavering, tenuous, in places hardly visible in the grass, it looks scarcely capable of supporting the passage of an empty wagon let alone our eight ton locomotive. Fortunately for the average passenger's peace of mind the old coaches ride remarkably well all things considered, but no one who has ridden the footplate of *Dolgoch* can harbour any illusions about the state of the permanent way. The engine rolls and snakes along on the uneven way, rough rail joints bring a series of sickening jolts and crashes, while it is disconcerting to look ahead and see an occasional loose rail leaping up as it receives our weight. To experience this is to marvel at the fact that the old locomotive has not shaken herself to pieces irreparably years ago.

Although officially, the steepest gradient on the line is 1 in 60, it is generally believed that the short, vicious little bank out of Rhydyronen station is the worst on the railway and nearer 1 in 40 than 1 in 60. Conditions conspire to make it as awkward as can be. A stop at Rhydyronen means that it has to be tackled from a standing start; it is upon a curve, and the rail is often greasy by reason of the hedges and trees which shade the line at this point. On this occasion the guard has advised the loco crew that we have no passengers on board for Rhydyronen, and as there is no sign of life on the little platform we run through the station and, with our flying start, surmount the incline without any difficulty.

A down train halts at Rhydyronen in the pouring rain in 2015, but the guard still chats to a passenger

but steadily, all the way to Brynglas, where, after a warning whistle for the unprotected crossing, we draw up at the small ivy covered station. Maybe there are no passengers to pick up, but having run through Rhydyronen we are ahead of schedule and the pause will give *Dolgoch,* at the best of times rather a tricky steamer, a chance to recover her breath for the long pull of nearly two miles to Dolgoch.

With the needle of the pressure gauge almost back to the hundred mark we draw out of Brynglas and into the long cutting which soon became known to us as 'Tadpole' because, as a result of the choked ditches, heavy rain often floods the road bed here above rail level. From this cutting onwards the uneasy motion of our locomotive, an oscillation not merely vertical, but in every other direction, becomes more disquieting, especially as we are standing on the left-hand side of the footplate. For we have reached the spectacular part of the

"It is remarkable to stand at Dolgoch when the trees on the slopes in their high summer foliage conceal the line from view and to hear the improbable sound of a locomotive whistle, followed by an extraordinary, syncopated but quite unrhythmical, clank and clatter as our train runs over the viaduct and into the station"

"At Dolgoch our driver is at pains to bring 'the Old Lady' to a stand precisely opposite the water column, a feat which calls for no mean skill and which even after long experience sometimes fails to come off. The fireman then lifts the wooden bung out of the tank filler and lowers into position the wooden chute which, when not in use, slides back into a recess in the stone pillar beneath the wooden supply tank. The driver then pulls the wire which, via a pivoted lever, lifts the crude wooden flap and sends a torrent of water gushing down the trough, some of it to enter the tank but much more to wash the rear buffers. By now this simple operation must have been recorded in thousands of photograph albums throughout the length and breadth of Britain. For most of the passengers get out of the train at this point even if they are travelling through to Abergynolwyn, and the combination of *Dolgoch*, the water column, the work in hand and the station in its setting of rhododendron bushes and encircling mountains appears to be irresistibly photogenic. Out come the cameras, from the railway enthusiast's expensive Leica or Contax to young Johnie's box Brownie with its spool of holiday 'snaps,' and the clicking of shutters sounds like the stridulation of grasshoppers or the bursting of seed pods in a summer meadow. No film star can have been more frequently photographed than the 'Old Lady'"

journey and for almost the whole of the way from here to Abergynolwyn the ground falls away steeply on this side of the line. As we approach the Dolgoch viaduct the road ahead looks more like a grassy woodland ride than a railway, and that we should be following such a path on the footplate of a locomotive seems almost as unbelievable as a fairy story. There is indeed an element of fantasy about the Talyllyn. In any surroundings this ancient train which has travelled straight out of the mid-Victorian era would look strange enough, but its appearance in this setting of wild landscape

seems too improbable to be true. An unexpected glimpse, either from the floor of the valley below or from the heights above, of *Dolgoch* and her train of box-like four wheelers creeping along the mountain sides under a tell-tale banner of white steam, and reduced to the size of a toy by the scale of the scenery, is enough to make a stranger rub his eyes and believe that, even in this stereotyped and materialistic century, the age of miracles is not yet past. It is equally remarkable to stand at Dolgoch when the trees on the slopes in their high summer foliage conceal the line from view and to hear,

Talyllyn pauses at Dolgoch for water in exactly the same way as the 'Old Lady' opposite but in May, 2015 on the railway's 150th anniversary

Dolgoch runs up the valley near Abergynolwyn with a mixed train on 18th April, 2015. Nothing much has changed since 1865

Dolgoch and her train of box — like four wheelers creep along the mountainsides under a tall banner of white steam and is enough to make a stranger rub his eyes and believe that, even in this stereotyped and materialsistic country, the age of miracles is not yet passed

Up journey complete. *Dolgoch* stands at Abergynolwyn early in 1951 with John Snell on the footplate and Tom Rolt chatting with Pat and Thelma Whitehouse by the train

high above, the improbable sound of a locomotive whistle, followed by an extraordinary, syncopated but quite unrhythmical, clank and clatter as our train runs over the viaduct and into the station.

At Dolgoch our driver is at pains to bring the 'Old Lady' to a stand precisely opposite the water column, a feat which calls for no mean skill and which even after long experience sometimes fails to come off. The fireman then lifts the wooden bung out of the tank filler and lowers into position the wooden chute which, when not in use, slides back into a recess in the stone pillar beneath the wooden supply tank. The driver then pulls the wire which, via a pivoted lever, lifts the crude wooden flap and sends a torrent of water gushing down the trough, some of it to enter the tank but much more to wash the rear buffers. By now this simple operation must have been recorded in thousands of photograph albums throughout the length and breadth of Britain. For most of the passengers get out of the train at this point even if they are travelling through to Abergynolwyn, and the combination of *Dolgoch*, the water column, the work in hand and the station in its setting of rhododendron bushes and encircling mountains appears to be irresistibly photogenic. Out come the cameras, from the

railway enthusiast's expensive Leica or Contax to young Johnie's box Brownie with its spool of holiday 'snaps', and the clicking of shutters sounds like the stridulation of grasshoppers or the bursting of seed pods in a summer meadow. No film star can have been more frequently photographed than the 'Old Lady'. So no wonder she is inclined to be temperamental.

When the tank has been filled and the guard has told the last passenger the way to the waterfalls we start away on the last lap. Though the scenery here is wilder, this final stage of the journey is easier than what has gone before. At Quarry Siding the hard work is over, for the long straight stretches between the siding and Abergynolwyn, though still inclining upwards, are very easily graded. Leaving the bare mountainside for the shelter of a belt of stunted oak trees, the little platform of the terminus soon comes into sight ahead and in a few moments we clatter over the points of the loop and come to a stand. We are on time. The guard screws down his brake, the fireman uncouples and *Dolgoch* runs round her train. Her labours are ended for the morning, for except on that short bank near Rhydyronen she will need very little steam to take her train back to Towyn.

> The clicking of shutters sounds like the stridulation of grasshoppers or the bursting of seed pods in a summer meadow

Dolgoch runs back down the Afon Fathew valley towards Towyn within an avenue of trees and on track held together by the turf which grows between the rails

CHAPTER 5

No.4 *Edward Thomas* drifts into the idyllic setting of Rhydyronen station on 5th June, 1963 with 'the original train' bound for Abergynolwyn.

Learning to run our own railway

James Boyd recalls the start of the early working parties, particularly from the North West Area Group, which he spearheaded: "It was at the annual general meeting held at the White Hall Hotel, Towyn, in 1951, and when the appeal for practical help was made from the Chair, that I realised that, though the Chairman was asking for individuals to come forward, I knew that volunteers made up of groups of members would be necessary to tackle, for instance, the formidable state of the track. While he was speaking, my mind ranged over the existing spread of enthusiasts in the Manchester area and before I knew what I was about, or had given it considered thought, I had jumped up and said I would be happy to form a North-West Area of members from whom we might send parties of workers to Towyn, if that was agreeable. The idea was accepted by all. I went home somewhat regretting my rash promise I wondering what I had taken on.

It is difficult to convey the mood of young people of those times; our late teens had been clouded by the uncertainties of affairs in Europe and when the Second World War broke out, those anticipated years of youthful indulgence around the period of college or university were never to be. In those times, our annual holiday was a fortnight and the fact that most of us worked until noon on Saturdays made the limit of our personal wanderings to areas within easy distance of home. If medically fit, we had been called up into the forces and, those of us who were lucky enough to return after the war, found domestic life was circumscribed by shortages of every kind, including food. Private motoring was almost unknown; those who owned cars had had to lay

them up during the war years when petrol, tyres and parts were impossible to obtain. Travel was restricted, coal was rationed and train services few and subject to post-war shortages. The railway periodicals were also painfully thin and had been subject to censorship. They were printed on poor paper and were a wretched imitation of their prewar standard. However, the reader could not fail to appreciate that, following a wartime period when railways where a prime method of transport and had been worn down by overuse and limited maintenance, some of the more charming were succumbing every month.

The local railway societies provided occasions when mutual gossip might reveal the impending loss of yet another system which had always been one's object for a visit, but which the times had prevented. The late 1940s/early 1950s was therefore a fortunate time for the emergence of the first railway preservation proposal.

Waiting in the wings for an opportunity to participate in a way only dreamed of was a crowd of interested enthusiasts to whom war had denied many things. Here was a chance to become involved in something quite different, without

Sir Haydn derailed! John Snell explains: "I was driving *Sir Haydn* just below Dolgoch woods when it suddenly veered to the right and skittered along sideways facing the steep drop for some tense seconds before stopping. The passengers had a long walk. We got home much later. Investigation showed that, while the army had made a splendid job of relaying nearly all the bad length, they had forgotten to spike down two rails at the end of it, and nobody had noticed." *(Photo: Talyllyn Railway Archive)*

regimentation, coupons, queues, directions and to prevent the Talyllyn Railway succumbing like other lines. Why the Talyllyn? Was it to the forefront of our interest? Certainly not, but it had a head start on all other railways in that the initial pioneers had cleared the way for involvement.

There were several railway groups in the Manchester area and I was involved in or linked to most. Within a few weeks of the first AGM in 1950 I had sounded out those who joined the Society and, with the help of Pat Whitehouse, who possessed the members' address list, a portion of our housekeeping allowance was spent on telephoning those who I felt would play an active role, while I made personal calls on others so bringing in some who were not members of local societies.

Lunchbreak at Dolgoch whilst the North West Area Group take a break from their track repairs. "The Jones family from the hotel might bring sandwiches and a huge teapot with cups to the station where we would balance the cups of tea on the railhead while sitting on the platform edge." (Photo: Talyllyn Railway Archive)

> Why the Talyllyn? Was it to the forefront of our interest? Certainly not, but it had a head start on all other railways in that the initial pioneers had cleared the way for involvement

Our area's informal committee's first task was to call a local meeting to which all members and enquiring visitors would be welcome. The meeting was packed and some had to sit out on the stairway; it left no room for doubt that, in our district at least, the idea of preventing the Talyllyn Railway from going the ways of others would be stopped at all costs. Most involved at the start had no previous knowledge of the railway, nor even where it was situated, but the opportunity of outdoor work, a new venture and a co-operative task excited us all.

We set ourselves three main tasks: to attend exhibitions and shows in the neighbourhood, to send working parties to the railway and to work to assist the railway which could be done locally. There was no shortage of keenness but there were two obstacles, Firstly, our own personal cash limitations and, secondly, petrol was on ration; not

every person possessed a car.

During the first months of the Society, some of us had already been working at Towyn on an individual basis and it fell to the new area committee to decide how best to organise working parties and then liaise with Bill Faulkner on the work to be done. For a trial period, we arranged that working parties should be on a monthly calendar basis and that, to save petrol, cars would be shared and each would pay his whack. The Dolgoch Hotel was our chosen venue. This was a temperance and basically a bed-and-breakfast establishment with the tearoom open in the summer months. Mains electricity, room heating and all the soft options of today were unknown. It had a large room at the back, where we could all sit round the same dining table, and a small room at the front where the biggest fire that could be stoked in a small iron grate, gave evening comfort after a hard day's work on the line. There was no noise of trains in winter of course, but the river gurgled alongside and the bleat of sheep in all the fields around were sounds in the landscape which we from the suburbs of Manchester valued

so highly. The view could be uplifting after the mundane surroundings of our weekday work. The hillside reared up in front, trees and rocks sweeping aloft in colourful confusion, especially in the autumn. The sound of roaring water from the distant falls were constant.

Mrs. Jones mothered us all. After the evening meal it was difficult enough to stay awake until bedtime and the drowsiness was increased as the premises were lit by a dynamo driven off a Pelton wheel which had as its source a small dam up on the railway embankment behind the hotel. As the evening wore on the lights became more and more dim.

Mrs Jones would have prepared lunchtime sandwiches for everyone. To save time, those responsible for bringing up the work train from Pendre would have gone there before breakfast to light up. No.4 *Edward Thomas* became the usual and most reliable steed. At lunchtime, the ever helpful Jones family might bring the sandwiches and a huge teapot with cups to Dolgoch station where we would balance the cups of tea on the railhead while sitting on the platform edge.

Dolgoch **heads up the line leaving Pendre with a volunteer working party mixed train.** *(Photo: James Boyd)*

We prided ourselves on our versatility which, though not skilled, could cope with any emergency. Bound for Towyn on a Friday and loaded with shovels and so on for trackwork, it was nothing to find a message awaiting us that an engine was off the track and would we re-rail it and get it back to Pendre? Sometimes, Bill Faulkner would phone me breathlessly at my works on Friday afternoon to ask us to report to a particular place where there had been a crisis. For many years our winter works trains never left Towyn without rerailing ramps, jacks and Tilly lamps, for one never knew if return would be that day; sometimes we never returned at all. In those early days there was no

adequate supply of suitable tools. Instead, each carload brought its own tools with it; such jangled about on the floor of Land Rover or in the boots of saloons.

The conditions of many minor railways in the late 1940s is beyond the imagination of the young and difficult to recall today, even by those who were there. Photographs hardly do justice to the decrepitude. Track? Between those hedges, there was an unkempt field of grass, weeds, brambles, fallen branches, lagoons of brackish water; surrounding and entwining boscage had been left to run riot, only discouraged by a passing train or by catching fire from engine coals in

dry weather. Rails? One had to look for them in places. They meandered uncertainly among the grass and, in high summer, were almost invisible, In fact a problem with the first work trains was that between Pendre and really Rhydyronen the verdure over the rails was so thick and lush that the locomotive slipped continuously with the oily film of them its wheels compressed onto the rail tops.

The party would couple up about six open wagons to No.4 and then literally walk beside the train, pushing it to assist the engine whose wheels would turn violently to no purpose even with the most gentle driving. Once the train began moving

Above: No.4 *Edward Thomas*, newly returned from Hunslets, prepares to double head the 'Old Lady' *Dolgoch* in an unprecedented sight on the Talyllyn Railway with the inaugural train of the 1952 season on 2nd June, 1952. The new platform and run round loop are in place but, as yet, unauthorised by the Ministry of Transport as the TRPS Committee had not yet thought about seeking approval for its new works. Whilst the sight of a double headed train looks impressive, No.4's fire had not been cleaned from a trial trip the day before and so it did not steam well and No.2 had to push her as well as pull the train!

Below: The 'dream team' pose in front of newly arrived No.6 *Douglas* at Wharf including Ken Marrian, Pat Garland, Tom Rolt, Pat Whitehousse, Bill Faulkner, Tom Hunt, Earl of Northesk, Major Charles Walker, Edward Thomas, and Herbert and Hugh Jones in the cab

at a walking pace, the footplate crew were obliged to dismount and help with the pushing… the sight of a crew-less engine with following train, each side of it lined with bent figures shoving like mad, is one which seems to have escaped the camera. No wonder that, by the time the working site was reached, it was out with the tea.

It was an agreed policy to take up the old track as a first stage and renew what was essential with what was available. There were certain sites where this took so long to achieve that, after we had gone home, Hugh Jones and his men would need to come along during the week and bring the work to a standard where another work train could be run.

These remembrances are but scenes from the first decade of preservation, a time unknown before since, for there could only be one 'first' either in time or place. And the TRPS was the 'first' and we were there. It was a time of great enjoyment. We thought little that three or four decades later a very different Talyllyn would be our legacy.

And now I wonder if, by our popularising of the Talyllyn Railway, I had participated in the destruction of the very thing we had set out to preserve. Or had I? Or was the Talyllyn Railway but a place where we could indulge our interests or

> There could only be one 'first' either in time or place. And the TRPS was the 'first'

did we value it for its own sake? If by 'preservation' we were really intend on 'perpetuation', then we had succeeded.

Pat Garland

All the financial things were dealt with through my office in Waterloo Street in Birmingham. We paid the wages. We sent a cheque down. We only paid once a fortnight on a Thursday. We kept that up almost until Bill Faulkner went down there to live because there wasn't really anyone in the office at Wharf until he arrived in Towyn. It wasn't that they weren't capable of working out the wages, but that they had so many other jobs to do that this was one way that one could help from a distance.

In fact, on occasion, the Committee undoubtedly micro managed a bit too much, which was always one of Tom Rolt's gripes, especially as he was trying to run a decrepit railway with minimal resources. Two amusing Committee minute extracts perhaps underline this point:

"Mr. Garland complained that the telephone account at Towyn is excessive and asked that a suitable instruction be given to the staff that on no occasion must the telephone be used if a letter will suffice."

"There was some discussion on the provision of pencils. Mr. Boyd reported an attractive design of the train which is to be incorporated on one side of

Dolgoch approaching Pendre slowing down as sheep walk ahead with Pat Whitehouse in his white coat leaning out of Van No.5. (Photo: Talyllyn Railway Archive)

Bill Faulkner driving *Edward Thomas* exchanges the token whilst passing a down train at Brynglas, on 24th September, 1955. Ken Cope leans out of the first carriage window

The railway was run from Birmingham for the first year or so. We resolved as far as possible not to lumber Tom with any chores at all of a financial nature beyond keeping the petty cash book.

The main point was that the first season under Society auspices had been completed with no major disaster. From the outset the vital question had been whether the decrepit permanent way could stand another full season's running and so enable the Company to maintain continuity of working and earn revenue essential to the success of the whole venture.

The first report of the Directors to the Talyllyn Railway Company had this to say about the first season in 1951:

"During the period of our summer timetable, June 4th to September 22nd, and including the service operated on Whit Monday only between Wharf station and Rhydyronen, 15,628 passengers were carried in 358 booked or special trains. Gross

Initial petty cash book entries June 1951

Cash ex wages cheque:	**£10**
Stamps:	**15/-**
Basil Jones: one dozen sheets of carbon paper	
Trunk call to Boyd Carpenter's workshop:	
	3/- from a call box
Sandwiches for Adams photographer:	**2/-**
Phone to Dolgelly road surveyor	
Paid Gray Jones account re loco:	**10/9d**
Paid Gareth Jones for firing special:	**2/6d**
Reimbursed D Curwen hoseclips and Bostik:	**5/6d**
Paid Gareth Jones for firing afternoon train:	**2/6d**
Paid Peter Williams for lighting up: 8 mornings	
	2/6d: £1]

this pencil. It was suggested that when samples are available, the price be up-raised to sixpence."

The early operating was largely a partnership between Tom Rolt, David Curwen and Mr. Vaughan, John Wilkins' assistant from the Fairbourne Railway. For many years the Fairbourne was one of our largest creditors because we used to have an account with them once a year showing what they had provided us with – and it was all sorts of things including coal. They used to render this account and we used to pay off lump sums against it as and when we had got the money.

The first annual general meeting was held at the Presbyterian schoolroom in Towyn High Street on 29th September, 1951. Thirty seven members attended and the Chair was taken by Bill Trinder. By now the Society was 700 strong. Bill, in his address to the meeting, stressed that "The Society had brought with its membership not only railway enthusiasts, but also people who could appreciate the spirit of adventure and these people in their various ways have made it possible for the services to continue, this spirit had been carried beyond the seas and beyond international boundaries."

How did we plan? Well, although we can look back and say, yes, there was a thread that runs all the way through the steps we took, I think that each step which was taken was just regarded at that time as the next logical step to take rather than the fulfillment of any strategic plan. I don't think anyone really knew what they were at because no one had any previous experience of running a railway in this way. But everyone was determined that something was going to be done and full of enthusiasm to do it.

receipts totalled £704 1/4d and miscellaneous receipts, that is to say sales of postcards, obsolete tickets, books, timetables, etc., totalled £100 /-.

This was undoubtedly the reward of publicity. Even so, local publicity to attract passengers to the line was only carried out on a limited scale because we considered that expenditure on an extensive publicity campaign would not be justified unless rolling stock, locomotive power and permanent way were capable of handling traffic so created. Even so, traffic was turned away during the peak of the season. After the experience of this season we believe that with increased publicity, gross revenue per season could exceed four figures.

The fact that we have successfully weathered this first season of working gives us no ground whatever for complacency. No member should relax his efforts either to help the Company in a practical way or to recruit new members in the mistaken belief that the future of the line is now assured. On the contrary it is not possible in the foreseeable future that the railway can earn, in a short summer season, sufficient revenue to enable

> **The Society included in its membership not only railway enthusiasts but also people who could appreciate the spirit of adventure, and these people had made it possible for the railway to continue**

arrears of maintenance to be made good. If the Society's ideal of improvement is to be realised an immense amount of work must be done during the period when the railway is earning no revenue and is consequently more than ever dependent on the voluntary work of members and on the funds raised by the Society. If, and only if, this generous practical and financial assistance continues to be forthcoming, then we believe we shall be successful in our aim to make the Talyllyn Railway at once a credit to Wales and a source of pleasure and pride to every railway enthusiast in the country."

Chairman Lord Northesk hands out annual staff bonuses at the AGM. *(Photo: John Adams)*

Right: Ken Marrian (with cigarette, Bill Faulkner and Pat Whitehouse at the TRPS AGM. *(Photo: John Adams)*

Left: Pat Garland at TRPS AGM (with Tom Rolt and Ken Marrian adjacent. *(Photo: John Adams)*

Below: Lord Northesk holds up PBW's now famous Narrow Gauge Album book at a TRPS AGM.*(Photo: John Adams)*

Pat Whitehouse at the TRPS AGM. *(Photo: John Adams)*

"During the period of our summer timetable, June 4th to September 22nd, and including the service operated on Whit Monday only between Wharf station and Rhydyronen, 15,628 passengers were carried in 358 booked or special trains. Gross receipts totalled £704 1/4d and miscellaneous receipts, that is to say sales of postcards, obsolete tickets, books, timetables, etc., totalled £100 /-."

Above: Ken Cope displayes a calendar at the TRPS AGM. (Photo: John Adams)

Right: *Dolgoch* and the 'original train' in the new platform at Wharf on 11th June, 1952

Sir Haydn and *Dolgoch* passing each other at Brynglas in August 1953, probably for the first time.
(Photo: John Snell)

We believe we shall be successful in our aim to make the Talyllyn Railway at once a credit to Wales and a source of pleasure and pride to every railway enthusiast in the country

Pat Garland

Almost after the first season I felt we were going to be alright. In those first few seasons our faith in the railway was completely justified. From 15,000 in the first season, our passenger figures rose to 22,000 in 1952. The traffic, donations and membership were going up all the time. We didn't have a setback in traffic figures until 1956 when we did take a step back for a year. 1957 was the year of the BBC TV outside broadcast when traffic picked up again. All the way along we always seemed to manage to be able to persuade people to supply what we wanted, some way or another, without them breathing down our necks for settlement.

Pat Whitehouse

The following year, 1952, was one of consolidation but an important landmark was the interest taken in the railway by the Railway Inspectorate of the Ministry of Transport. The first indication of this interest occurred at the October committee meeting in 1951 when I

Dolgoch **leaving Pendre with an engineering train in April, 1952 (Easter) with Gareth Jones firing and probably John Snell driving** *(Photo: Daily Express)*

read a letter from Lt.-Col. Woodhouse, a member who had recently retired from the Railway Inspectorate. He warned that whilst the Ministry of Transport took a sympathetic view of the TR and the efforts made by the Society, it was likely that they might in future take a more active interest. The committee decided that the next move was with the Ministry.

This came in March 1952 when I received a letter from Lt.-Col. Wilson, then the Chief Inspecting Office of Railways to the Minister of Transport, asking for an interview. It was agreed that the Chairman, the general manager and myself should go to London to meet him and Lt.-Col. McMullen on 18th April which proved to be most pleasant but thorough meeting. Wilson was very avuncular and said: "Well, you have done it now. We can't stop you opening, but we really think that you ought to take our advice. We are not going to be difficult. We would like to come and have a look."

Lt.-Col. McMullen came up for his inspection on 12th June and we had a day with the trolley and went down the line from Abergynolwyn all the way to Towyn. We stopped off in various places and he looked under the rails,

> **I would remind you that the responsibility for safety of passengers is yours**

under the bridges and he looked at it all. In the event he said: "Well, if the railway had stopped running, we wouldn't have let you re-open it. But now we're here, provided that we stick to the set of basic rules that we will talk about, there will be no problems. But we do want to be kept in touch." After that, he came every year to have a look and see how things were going. That was probably the first bit of nasty heart beating we had. Fortunately his initial written advice was that "In my opinion, the line is being run without undue danger to the public."

Pat Whitehouse had to eat humble pie a couple of times on behalf of the Society when the Ministry found out that a new platform had been built at Wharf and a new loop at Brynglas. Plans and drawings had to be submitted and retrospective permission obtained, but the Ministry were really very patient with the TRPS and a considerable source of help in such matters as pointing out the local council's obligations for road over bridges and suchlike.

The first source of rail was some second hand track we bought from a Harlech scrap merchant who had dismantled the Corris Railway. After that

Abergynolwyn station in April, 1952 during relaying showing the extended platform. *Dolgoch* has brought up a works train with several of the ex Corris wagons still displaying their former GWR ownership. *(Photo: John Snell)*

Dolgoch with works train at the start of the mineral extension just beyond Abergynolwyn station platform, April, 1952. *(Photo: John Snell)*

Dolgoch with a down ballast train passes the old water tower and station of her namesake on Easter Sunday in 1952. *(Photo: John Snell)*

Dolgoch pauses at Rhydyronen in April, 1952 with the works train assisting the track relaying work at Abergynolwyn station. On the footplate are Gareth Jones and Gareth Evans, the son of the Pendre blacksmith. *(Photo: John Snell)*

Relaying track at Fach Goch with Garry, 'Pop' and another volunteer in January, 1953. *(Photo: John Snell)*

William Jones hedging at Fach Goch in January, 1953. *(Photo: John Snell)*

Bill Faulkner attending to the track at Brynglas *(Photos: Ian Faulkner collection)*

Early working party at Cynfal on 23rd March, 19551

Track Volunteers

An early working party at Cynfal with Bill Faulkner and others in a slate wagon in flood water from an overflowing stream. *(Photo; James Boyd)*

had been used up, we had to find another source. We found some rail in a Nuneaton quarry. Buying that was easy because the quarry was owned by a client of Pat Garland; and they were persuaded not to be in any hurry for payment. In relation to another batch of rail, he had to go to Ralphs and ask if they would buy the rail for us and sell it to us as and when we could pay them back. To help this, he came to an arrangement with them that they would take the old TR wrought iron rails because the material was valuable to them as they had an outlet for it making chain. At the time there were few firms making wrought iron and so they were quite glad to get those rails.

In the winter of 1952-53, we began a serious relaying programme. We used to buy sleepers from dealers who, in turn, had previously bought them from BR. We even found it was more expensive to buy them from BR direct than it was to buy them from dealers! We used to buy the grade four sleepers, identified by four white spots on the rail.

As the TR had a gauge of only two feet three inches we were able to make two sleepers from a BR one. We used to have them cut in half and take the better half of each one. Using a cross cut saw, it took us an hour to cut eight sleepers. One afternoon, a local farmer who had been watching us, walked back to his farm and returned with a petrol-driven chain saw. With this he began to cut the sleepers as fast as we could bring them to him and, in an hour he had cut fifty.

Many defects in the line were discovered by accident. On one occasion, a working party were returning to Towyn with nine wagons full of sleepers when there was a sudden jolt and three wagons came off the track, spilling a load of sleepers on the ground. On examination, it was found that the gauge at this point was two feet five inches instead of two feet three inches. Some of the sleepers had rotted away, causing the rails to slip

---

"I appreciate that a considerable amount of work has been done on the railway since my last visit two years ago, but I must say at once that I was disappointed that more work on the track has not been accomplished. The track is still undoubtedly in need of a very great deal of attention and in my opinion all your available resources should be put into improving it. The section of track between Dolgoch and Abergynolwyn is, I think, dangerous and the unrelaid sections elsewhere, particularly between Brynglas and Dolgoch are in much the same category.

Col. D. McMullen, Ministry of Transport, 1954

and slide. It was ten o'clock that night before the wagons were back on the track. Whilst the repair gang worked by the light of lamps collected from a nearby station, one of the members gave added light where needed with a blazing piece of paraffin soaked waste on a shovel.

In 1953, one of our members suggested asking the army to help us. Lord Northesk, our President, wrote to the War Office suggesting that our railway would provide an exercise in track laying and, in June, more than seven hundred soldiers from the 127 Construction Regiment, R.E. (T.A) set up camp next to our line. We provided the materials and, within a fortnight, they had relaid a mile of track and repaired a sixty foot viaduct which was bulging ominously.

Meanwhile, our volunteer working parties and permanent staff had been busy. and two new bogie coaches and a number of wagons were rebuilt in our own workshops.

> **Looking back, I can see that many of our early mishaps were more amusing than serious**

The success of our Society had been watched with interest, both in this country and abroad. Following our example, the Festiniog Railway in North Wales was re-opened for the first time since 1939. Amateur railway enthusiasts in Australia, reading of our venture, revived a narrow gauge railway in Victoria. A script writer, who visited our railway, found material for a film in it, and Ealing Studios' The *Titfield Thunderbolt* was the result.

Looking back, I can see that many of our early mishaps were more amusing than serious. On a journey from Abergynolwyn to Tywyn in July 1952, I was acting as fireman. The route was all downhill and, as we reached a particularly steep part of the track, I looked back. The three coaches were about a hundred yards behind us and travelling on their own. The coupling pin had slipped out.

Giving three sharp blasts on the whistle – a signal which we had arranged in case of emergencies – I

Dolgoch viaduct repairs

waited anxiously for the guard to look out. Finally, he did and quickly applied his brake. The engine driver put the engine into reverse and we had coupled up again and moved off before any of the passengers could realise what had happened.

On one occasion, a passenger, missing the evening train back to Tywyn, used a workmans' trolley for the return journey. Propelling the trolley like a scooter, he arrived in the station only five minutes after the train.

When one of the Corris engines, No.3, which had very narrow wheel treads, slipped between the rails one day in 1953, passengers were told that it would take several hours to put it back on the tracks. No other transport was available and they had to walk the four and a half miles back to Tywyn. On their arrival, the general manager offered to refund their money.

Instead of accepting it, twenty of them offered to join the Society and, after a quick whip round, gave £8 for track repairs.

> On examination, it was found that the gauge was 2' 5" instead of 2' 3"

It was a long hard grind to get the track safe and suitable for traffic. But, meanwhile the trains continued to run and passenger numbers steadily grew. David Smith, an early volunteers, ably describes what the track was still like even in 1954: "I remember standing by the lineside at Tynllwynhen as *Sir Haydn* came by with the afternoon train. The line dipped for two complete rail lengths as *Sir Haydn* hit the rail joint nearest me and sprung up again as the wheels of the last TR van passed into the distance. Minimum leverage with a spade head under the nearest sleeper was sufficient to lift two complete track lengths three to four inches. There and then we effected a kind of rudimentary packing, which would not pass muster in today's improved conditions."

There was still a lack of labour in 1954 with only a few stalwarts apart from weekend working parties, which were crucial to the railway's survival at that time, although somewhat frowned upon by the largely non-conformist population which, even in 1954, could support seven chapels locally. At that

Top left: *Dolgoch* **rests at Towyn Wharf on 15th August, 1953, while her crew get ready to coal her up. The train consists of two original coaches and a Penrhyn open coach, but no brake van!** *(Photo: Jim Jarvis, KRM Collection)*

Bottom left: *Sir Haydn* **shunts wagons, including the Corris van, in Pendre sidings on 5th July, 1953.** *(Photo: Jim Jarvis, KRM Collection)*

Sir Haydn and *Edward Thomas* double head in army service on 5th July, 1953 carrying men from the 127 Construction Regiment RE (TA) on the running boards whilst hauling a works train at Brynglas. *(Photo: Jim Javis, KRM Collection)*

On 5th July, 1953, *Sir Haydn* brings an army works passenger train into Brynglas station which is surrounded by second hand BR sleepers sawn in two to replace the rotten TR ones. *(Photo: Jim Jarvis, KRM Collection)*

time there were still no Sunday trains for this very reason. Pat Garland was continually exhorting members in the house magazine, *The Talyllyn News*, to help financially or physically on the track and no doubt the Committee had the words of Co. McMullen about the responsibility for the safety of passengers continually ringing in their ear. Northesk even issued a famous appeal to all members in December repeating the appeal and adding almost a threat: "I am afraid I must bring to this season of good cheer a discordant note. Unless the Society can raise an immediate and substantial sum of money, we will be unable to operate a service next year. But if every member will give something, however small, I think we shall be able to put the railway into a state where our major worries are behind us." Fortunately, many members did contribute and so the threatened disaster was avoided. The Committee always had a way with words when needed!

Pat
Garland

Pat Garland continues: We were also lucky to have the services of Chips Harrison who was a soldier at the nearby Tonfanau army camp. He had a lot of spare time. He happened to be a shipwright and a very competent workman. His commanding officer was only too pleased to think that Chips had got

something he could usefully be employed on. Chips more or less lived in Pendre for the whole of his national service and built the body for coach No.10 and most of No.9 on the W.G.Allen underframes whilst he was on National Service.

Meanwhile volunteers were scrounging the country for every possible narrow gauge vehicle that could be found and restored. We found the Corris coach and two Glyn Valley Coaches. We also found an extraordinary vehicle which became called the 'Stanton' but there is nothing really of it left any more.

Quite early on there was also the episode of *Douglas*. The Earl of Northesk, who became President in 1952, signed a series of letters written for him which were sent to everyone we could find in a trade directory which begged for money or help in other directions. And Abelsons, who must have been one of the first people to be written to, based on an alphabetical system, wrote back and said they wouldn't give us any money but they could give us an engine! It wasn't the right gauge but we sorted that with the help of Tommy Hunt. The reason why it was called *Douglas* was because it was the name of the Chairman of the company who, at that time, was in South Africa. He was not consulted about the engine being given away, so his co-directors thought that it would soften the blow a bit if they could explain to him that the engine which had been in the plant for so many years was now working on the Talyllyn wearing his name.

That meant we now had engines Nos. 2, 3, 4 & 6. No.3 was a very delicate little engine which

didn't like running on track which wasn't set to the right gauge. It had such fine scale wheel tyres and flanges that it came off at the slightest bit of uneven track. It was also high in the wheel by comparison with the others and, consequently, was a greyhound amongst the elephants.

Pat Whitehouse

As luck would have it and by good fortune, the committee was made up of people who in their walks of life had facilities to do things. Bill Trinder was Chairman because he had been chairman of the meeting at the Imperial Hotel. Pat Garland had a knowledge of financial matters. I had a knowledge of construction, civil engineering and had the facilities of a secretary and all the odds and ends one needed if taking on the committee secretary's role. Ken Cope was with the Midland Red bus company as the Traffic Manager and so was ideal to look at the basic traffic side of things. John Wilkins, who has some experience of running the Fairbourne Railway, and also had his own business, both of which were able to support us. At least there was a nucleus, purely by good luck, of people who could get together and pool their knowledge to learn how to run something. Add to that Tom Rolt's enthusiasm and also his practical engineering knowledge having been apprenticed

at Kerr, Stuarts, the team was there from the start.

The great thing about Birmingham was its "tribal" nature and that people owned their own firms. Also nobody had any thoughts of unemployment in the West Midlands as it was one of the heavy machining areas in the country. People were always busy making things. A lot of these people were also interested in railways and either belonged themselves or were connected to other people who were members of the Stephenson Locomotive Society or the Birmingham Loco Club, so there was a nucleus of people who could contribute many things in different ways. For example, Hunt Bros. in Oldbury were associated with John Wilkins on the Fairbourne Railway but also ran the Sutton Miniature Railway themselves; they gave a vast amount of help over the years. Tom Hunt was the virtual owner of Hunts Bros. and an absolute dictator in his own right, but a great friend to the railway and even chief engineer for a time between David Curwen leaving and John Bate being appointed. Effectively, he ran his own private fiefdom. If he wanted buffers cast, he had them cast.

Fortunately, it was exactly the same thing as far as I was concerned. We owned a large construction family firm. If we wanted timber to rebuild a Glyn Valley coach, we did it. In fact, we had a Glyn Valley coach into the Works and just rebuilt it. It was possible in those days to do a vast number of things as 'foreigners' which would be totally unacceptable today. There were no real independent controls in business like now. If you wanted to do something, you did it. Everyone was on the crest of a wave.

Sir Haydn with a down hill train amongst the high hedges. *(Photo: Talyllyn Railway Archive)*

Tw Andrew Barclay 'E' Class 0-4-0WTs in Ableson's yard, the front one shortly to be donated to the Talyllyn Railway and named *Douglas*

The future *Douglas* under repair and re-gauging in Hunt Bros. Griffin Foundry, Oldbury in April, 1954. *(Photo: John Snell)*

Everyone was making profits, so it didn't really matter. They were able to give things from the periphery of the businesses. The TR wouldn't have been rebuilt without all this help. Okay, sometimes I used to get it in the neck from my fellow directors on the Whitehouse company board for the amount of time I spent on railway things, but in a way they were quite proud of what we were doing, so they shut their eyes to a lot of things. We were able to

use secretaries within the firm and no cost was counted against it. If you wanted a day off to go and do something for the railway, we had a day off to go and do it. Even in those days, it was only three and a half hours to drive to Towyn and, when you are young, 28 or 30 years old, to have to drive that distance down early in the morning, do what you had to do and come back the same night was neither here nor there.

There was a certain amount of friction running the railway from Birmingham, but it was not that difficult. We in the Midlands had a different approach to life to those at Towyn which perhaps was not surprising as we had many more resources available to us and we were all used to leading our way in business and making quick decisions.

James Boyd also comments on this from his perspective leading the North-West Area: "Lest it should be thought the North-West Area activities were concentrated on working parties on the railway or that all was Sweetness and Light, how wrong that would be. The administration of the Society was based on what was then known as the committee which usually met in Garland's accountancy premises in Birmingham on a weekday evening. This suited the majority of the Committee who, perhaps because the Society had begun life at Birmingham's Imperial Hotel, found local meetings very convenient. For those who had to travel a distance, the fact that meetings were seldom held anywhere else made these events a prolonged day. For me, it meant leaving work early to reach the meeting and catching the 10.10 pm Irish boat train connection from New Street station afterwards. This train arrived in Crewe about midnight; here, I picked up my car and drove home to South Manchester in the small hours. Often it was extremely foggy and it might be 3 am before I climbed into my bed.

Lord Northesk presents a nameplate to Douglas Ableson in front of *Douglas* (named after him) at the handover of the engine to the TRPS in the company of Pat Whitehouse, Bill Faulkner and Pat Garland

Douglas on low loader outside Hunt Bros. Griffin Foundry with Tom Hunt on the right hand side who was chief engineer to the Birmingham Committee in the days when the railway was directed from Birmingham

Four engines together at Wharf for the first time ever! On 19th July, 1954 Nos.2,3,4 & 6 on the occasion of No.6's arrival and No.2's departure for Oldbury. *(Photo: Talyllyn Railway Archive)*

Douglas being prepared to come off the lowloader at Wharf on 19th July, 1954

Many Committee meetings were not always easy; apart from members of the Committee who were elected at each agm, each area was permitted to send a representative and such were not permitted to vote. Nonetheless, as an elected Committee member myself, I would often find myself the only one from the North-West Area which had strong views on working parties, liaison or lack of it while at Towyn and put forward many sensible suggestions based on its experience. Human nature being what it is, it was soon apparent that rules and regulations were being created by persons who were seldom seen at Towyn and, though allowing for the undoubtedly enthusiastic efforts which they threw into the cause, it began to rankle with the North-West Area that its voice on that few matters went largely unheeded.

The informal North-West Area committee expected me to further the Society's growth with creative thoughts at every Birmingham visit. However, it was often a hopeless task to pit our viewpoints against the overwhelming numbers at such opportunities. To drive home, tired and defeated over what we felt was a sensible scheme and, and then to explain our misfortunes at the next area meeting, made it a double disappointment."

Even amongst the Committee, the position was not always perfect, but then Boyd was not a

person who liked to feel he was subordinate to the two Pats either.

Pat Whitehouse

Relations with Bill Trinder quite quickly deteriorated. Partly that was circumstantial and partly his character and experience was so different to those of the Midlands' industrialists who were just used to getting on with things and getting them done. One example of this was when the Committee thought it would be useful to have one or two more people associated with us who knew something about narrow gauge railways. So very early on I wrote to Jimmy Boyd in Manchester because he had initially been involved in trying to revive the Festiniog Railway.

When I wrote to Jimmy, in my naiivity I said we were looking for people from outside who had some knowledge of narrow gauge railways because the majority of people then on the Committee, and certainly the people who first thought of all this, had no real experience. Jim responded and we got him on

> **Lest it should be thought that all was Sweetness and Light, how wrong that would be**

the Committee. On one of the days when Trinder was getting himself a bit uptight on the basis he took the view no one ever told him about anything, I made the mistake of saying why don't you have a look at the file and I gave him all the correspondence to read. When he saw the letter I had written to Jimmy Boyd, he was terribly upset and went into a sulk. He never really got on with me after that. I don't think he actually spoke to me for nearly a year!

The Committee were not very happy with Trinder as Chairman and there was a distinct danger of a rift which needed to be avoided. But as it so happened in the second year in 1952, I was sitting in the Talyllyn brake van with my legs over the side talking to a Mr Rogerson who ran a model shop in Reading about having somebody as our President. He said he knew the very chap: the Earl of Northesk. So we asked him if he would be interested, he was and Pat Garland and I talked it over and thought why not approach Northesk to see if he would be prepared to be both President and Chairman. He turned out to be totally acceptable to everybody and one of the best things we ever did because, when building something new, you have a challenge and you have to go out and find someone who is a leader. Northesk was a leader and a wonderful man.

> **The Committee were not very happy with Trinder as Chairman and there was a distinct danger of a rift which needed to be avoided**

Pat Garland took on the task of breaking the news to Bill Trinder: I had to write a very carefully worded letter to Trinder, pointing out what I considered to be the error of his ways with the result that he resigned as Chairman and we accepted Lord Northesk. I remember going to Banbury to see Tom Rolt about it and explaining why I had written the letter I had to Trinder. Tom was upset about it but I was convinced I was right. In the event it didn't do any harm but Tom gradually started to take a less active role. There was also an issue with Tom in relation to the original committee: John Wilkins and Tom Rolt had no time for each other, yet they were both 150% in favour of the TR. This is the most remarkable feature of the TRPS: how people from so many different walks of life sunk their differences in support of the TR. Tom was very much a one off sort of chap, an eccentric par excellence, wearing a bee keeper's hat and sandals. This was absolute anathema to John Wilkins, Chairman of Wilkins & Mitchell, a leader of industry who drove around in his Rolls Royce! Council at that time was made up basically of business men, almost all of the Chairman or Managing Director levels, except for people like Tom and a couple of others. All these people were captains of industry who were picked because of the contributions they could make and a completely different mix to

Edward Thomas stands in the original platform at Wharf with the original TR train on 24th September 1955. Thelma and young Michael Whitehouse are on the platform, 'Bunnin' included!

The Earl of Northesk

*Extract from The Australian
Woomen's Weekly 12th October, 1959:*

The earl who loves dogs

LORD NORTHESK, dog-lover and motor-racing enthusiast, at the wheel of his car with his Labrador, "Jupiter," seated happily beside him.

He is David Ludovic George Hopetoun Carnegie, 11th Earl of Northesk, one of London's most spectacular prewar playboys, who judged dogs at last month;s Victorian Royal Agricultural Show.

A lover of dogs, his lordship also breeds them. Dachshunds and Labradors are his favourites. At present he has four dachshunds at his home in Berkshire and one Labrador. He makes special pets of the little "German sausage dogs" and all four sleep on his and his wife's bed.

Before the war, the Earl earned the reputation of "live wire aristocrat of the West End and speed king of the Continental playgrounds."

His Lordship's exploits made exciting and amusing reading. One year at St. Moritz, with a friend, Prince Odescalchi, he circled a frozen lake on his skis towed by an aeroplane. The next year he and a handful of young bloods raced through London in hansom cabs, from the Devonshire Club to the Kit Kat Club via St. James's and Picadilly.

The Earl went big game huntin'. A natural sportsman, he proved himself a master shot in '32 when he sent a giant crocodile to its watery grave by a shot through the brain fired from a considerable distance.

More recently, Lord Northesk again made the front pages as a driver of the Talyllyn "Puffing Billy" in Merionethshire, North Wales. President of the Talyllyn Railway Preservation Society, his Lordship is never happier then when dressed for duty – in greasy overalls – and driving the 1921 passenger carrying train from Towyn to Abergynolwyn.

He has had a passionate interest in trains from boy-hood and has 3,000 feet of track at his home. Although he stokes the Talyllyn fires manually, at home he feeds his model engine with a teaspoon.

In 1955 Lord Northesk took up motor racing. He had a special racing head fitted to the engine of his Jaguar. His fastest pace to date is a cool 140 mph.

When I asked this man of many interests if he had hobbies other than those already mentioned, he grinned. He said that he had, but until a 48 – hour day was invented he wouldn't have the time to get round to them.

Lord Northesk was firing on one of the engines on the day of our annual general meeting in 1956. A soft dewy mist had settled on the rails, making the ascent of some of the steeper gradients a tricky task. As we got into the hills, the train began to slip violently. Finally, Lord Northesk had to sit on the front buffer beam of his engine with a sack of sand in his hand sanding the rail ahead so that the wheels could get a grip.

In his speech at the end of the meeting, he told members he felt very like the chairman of British Railways, "But if anyone has a photo of Sir Brian Robertson sitting on the buffer beam of one of his Britannias with a sack of sand in his hand, I would like to see it.'

the Council which emerged after the centenary of the railway in 1965.

Pat Whitehouse

Tom and his people on the ground at Towyn had a more difficult job to do: running a decrepit railway with inadequate facilities and encouraging a varied group of people into some sort of team just to ensure each train in the timetable ran more or less to time or at all. However, some sourness with Tom Rolt did arise towards the end of the second summer in 1952. One of the difficulties which arose in the second year was a personal one because he had left his first wife, Angela, and was living with Sonia in a caravan at Brynglas. Edward Thomas got to hear of it and, as he asked what was going on, we had to tell him because we had no option really. Thomas, being a Welsh churchman, was not very amused about all this and I rather think he then said something to Tom which tended to sour our relationships for a

We continually had to pour oil on troubled waters

Top left: Lord Northesk complete with saw by Pendre engine shed. *(Photo: Ian Faulkner collection)*

Left: The Earl of Northesk in his element driving No.4

Above: The Earl, President and Chairman shovels coal for No.3 at Wharf

short while[1]. But we got over it. Like everything else, these things are passing phases. The other thing was that Tom tended to want to run things at Towyn in his own way and did not like being told what to do, whereas we in Birmingham were also used to running things in our own way. We also took the view that we had to look at things from a commercial angle rather than just preservation and this did tend to grate a bit with Tom (although earlier it was he who had proposed the miniature <u>railway conversion and, later, was to propose</u>

---

1. *Rolt in Landscape with Figures, p38 suggests it was actually the Committee who were worried and that Edward Thomas said it was none of their business.*

several quite significant changes to motive power). Added to all this, there was all the thinking about what had to be done to get the money in and we had to dance a bit to the tune of the people putting the money in. Tom was not prepared to dance to any tune. The tourists from the Midlands expected to have facilities and services and some of the business men providing goods and services had their own views about how they would do this and what things would look like. So, we continually had to pour oil on troubled waters. Eventually, after the second year, it was agreed that Tom really was not the ideal man to run the railway on the ground and, with the Society and traffic growing in the way it was, he was big

Sir Haydn runs through the woods west of Abergynolwyn with a down train

Left: *Dolgoch* shunts her train into the Pendre carriage shed at the end of the day on 15th August, 1953. *(Photo: Jim Jarvis, KRM Collection*

Sir Haydn stands on the beginning of the mineral extension at Abergynolwyn clear of the run round loop to allow a second train to enter the station

enough to accept this. Also he could not really afford to stay in Towyn on the meagre amounts he was being paid. So we had to look for our first general manager. We advertised.

It was about this time that Bill Harvey from Norwich and Allan Garraway came along to have a look at us. Bill came to Pat Garland's office and we told him all about what we were doing. I think Bill interviewed us rather than us interviewing Bill! Whilst they went on to get involved with the Festiniog Railway, they did spend some time with Tom Rolt and David Curwen giving considerable helping hand with *Dolgoch* and getting *Sir Haydn* ready for trials first. It was interesting to reflect that if it had not been for the establishment of the TRPS it was unlikely that all the railway preservation which subsequently unfolded, particularly with the Festiniog, would have happened in the successful way it did.

Our advertisements produced Ken Marrian as our general manager. He had been a former civil engineer on the LMS. He was a very happy go lucky genial pat you on the back well met sort of chap. But he was a man of profound common sense and a man who was capable of getting on with anybody. He got on with the Welsh. He got on with the staff. He got on with the volunteers. We could not have found a better choice. He used to keep bottles of *Double Diamond* in his desk drawer in the Wharf Office, so that if anyone came in they were always sure they were going to have a Marrian

Above: *Sir Haydn* arrives at Wharf with a down train on 15th August, 1953. *(Photo: Jim Jarvis, KRM Collection)*

Right: *Edward Thomas* stands with its train in Wharf station with Trefri, Edward Thomas' house, behind on 15th August, 1953. *(Photo: Jim Jarvis, KRM Collection)*

welcome. He used to live at the White Hall Hotel. He was always in the bar there with the locals in the evening and that tended to help solidify the contacts with the local people.

Whilst sometimes we, in Birmingham, used to moan about him because we used to say he was not strong enough or he was not getting on with this or that fast enough he kept the railway together for the years that he was there. I don't think that you could ever find anyone who would hear an ill word of him.

Pat Garland

Whilst Ken Marrian was a godsend, he was a 'wicked old devil' as well. When the insurance inspectors used to come down to the railway once a year, Ken used to meet them at the BR station and take them straight into the White Hall Hotel where they then spent the day. He filled them up with beer until it was flowing out of

Douglas running over Pendre level crossing with Hugh Jones driving. *(Photo: Talyllyn Railway Archive)*

Bill Faulkner pole shunting carriages with *Edward Thomas* at Wharf *(Photo: Talyllyn Railway Archive)*

Douglas on a works train using ex BR sleepers sawn in half. *(Photo: Talyllyn Railway Archive)*

their ears and they then went back home and gave us a glowing report!

At the end of the 1954 season, Ken decided he would only be able to work part time in 1955 and so Harold Parker was appointed as his assistant. Harold was a very mild mannered man and part time farmer from up the coast. He was a very good number two but, when he was appointed general manager following Ken's death in January 1958, it was really a trial for him. From my point of view as treasurer, he was however absolutely magnificent as he was a first class book keeper; he always balanced everything and there was never any doubt about the source of any income or the disposal of anything; records were perfect.

Harold resigned at the end of the 1965 season and David Woodhouse became full time traffic manager with Bill Faulkner taking on the role of Managing Director, having been deputy general manager since 1964. Eric Gibbons, who had funded and arranged the rebuilding of both Nos. 1 & 2, became Commercial Manager

Bill had a 'sabbatical' at the Dart Valley Railway as Managing Director there between 1967-70 but then continued on the TR from 1973 until he died in 1982.

Tom Rolt became a little disillusioned under the later Eric Gibbons regime. Maybe Eric went a little bit too much the other way as he was determined that the TR was going to be commercially viable in every respect. That did not suit Tom. But Tom came back and became Chairman when Northesk died and we were looking for someone else to take the lead. Tom had the joy of leading us at the railway's Centenary in 1965 when John Betjeman came down and also at the inauguration of the Nant Gwernol extension into passenger service, something he always had a strong ambition for. Tom also came back when Ken Cope went out of it. Ken couldn't adjust to the idea of things growing on the publicity side; he just could not think big enough. But he did an enormous amount of work behind the scenes on statistics and records and getting print orders for tickets. But for a man who was a publicity director, he was not easy to communicate with either.

Tom was convinced the railway needed another two, larger engines, when the traffic was growing to around 100,000 passenger journeys a year. He thought that the original engines, Nos 1 & 2 should be retired from every day service and that Nos 4 & 6 were not up to the heavy loads. To some extent he was right, of course, as witnessed by the frequent double heading in the summer. But that problem was solved by introducing three train working so the loads were lighter for the existing engines to haul and also trains ran more frequently. So Tom and David Curwen's design

Edward Thomas heads past the caravan site at Rhydyronen, the only downhill stretch of track on the 'up' journey. The first five coaches are 'imports'. The Corris coach, the 'Stanton,' a Glyn Valley coach and two Penrhyn opens. (Photo: Jim Jarvis, KRM Collection)

ideas for larger and somewhat innovative engines were not needed, although they took up many pages of the *Talyllyn News* for the amusement of armchair members to read and comment on. Eventually, John Bate's No.7 was introduced when it looked as though *Douglas* would expire and, as this was eventually appropriately named *Tom Rolt*, particularly as it is a slightly larger engine than the others and designed to cope with the heavier trains; Tom would have warmed to that. History will probably say that the originally proposed and voted on name for No.7 of *Irish Pete* reflecting the origins of the engine working for the Irish Turf Board were well but narrowly avoided, but it took a second membership agm vote and voluminous correspondence in the house magazine to get to the right result!

Pat Garland took the view that the Birmingham Committee, probably with Garland and Whitehouse leading the pack, that they picked the best that they knew from Great Western Railway practice and applied it to the TR, including the engine colour and even requirements to fit point locks. Understandably, in the early days, even during his first two years as manager on the spot, Tom Rolt got somewhat frustrated by these requirements being handed down from Birmingham, sometimes without the wherewithal to execute them. At the time, they probably seemed ludicrous, but most are in place now!

They picked the best that they knew from Great Western Railway practice and applied it to the TR

In particular, in 1952, he was asked to sign the rules, which had been drafted by the Committee in Birmingham and Tom thought that they were simply too detailed and impractical to implement and that he was doing the best he could with scant resources and not enough people. This probably became the last straw, as evidenced by his letter to Pat Whitehouse on 12th August, probably written on a 'bad day': "I would none the less have signed my acceptance of the rules if I had felt that I enjoyed the confidence, goodwill and trust of the committee in my efforts down here. Events both last season and this have, however, made it abundantly clear to me that this is not the attitude of certain members of the committee. I am not prepared, after the end of the present running season to accept further office with the Company so long as it continues under the present administration…I would like to except from these remarks Bill Trinder, Bill Faulkner and Mr. Edward Thomas." Tom's letter was discussed at length at the next Committee meeting on 18th August and all that is recorded in the minutes was:

A bustling Towyn Wharf station with Talyllyn about to leave with a well filled train formed of coaches all new to the TR, as indeed are most of the components of the engine itself. *(Photo: Jim Jarvis, KRM Collection)*

Roy Smith waters *Edward Thomas* at Dolgoch

Talyllyn returns to Wharf with a heavy train

Talyllyn Pioneers

Talyllyn heads up the bank away from Rhydyronen in 1966

"There does not appear to be any purpose in pursuing the matter further. The Committee felt that there should be a discussion at the close of the running season."

Even when Tom Rolt had retired from his managerial position but returned to the Committee a few years later, things did not seem much improved. The minutes of the Committee meeting on 14th August, 1958 reported that:

"Mr Rolt felt that this was an appropriate time to raise the question of the relationship between the Society and the Company. He felt that several matters of policy had been decided by the Railway Company not the Society, which though understandable under the circumstances, should be avoided if possible. It was unanimously agreed that this matter should be noted." Another master of the understatement by Secretary Whitehouse.

Pat Whitehouse concludes this review of the

> It was unanimously agreed tha this matter should be noted. Another master of the understatment by Secretary Whitehouse

early Committee management of the Talyllyn Railway in the TRPS formative years with a few useful summaries from his viewpoint of the time.

Pat Whitehouse

The railway was worked on a revenue account and cash flow basis with full marks to Pat Garland as a man who got on with everybody and who was careful in watching the expenditure but did not actually upset anyone by saying they could not spend something.

The TRPS Committee was pretty much the same composition of people as the Talyllyn Railway Company's board of directors, as each of us sat on both organisations doing what we did. When we were involved, the Talyllyn Railway Company ran the railway far more than it does today.

When we were running the railway and built it up, we took the view that there was only one way to do it and that was for half a dozen people to say that is what we are going to do – it would never

Democracy begins...

*The Committee records contain a letter from a Mr. Brian Bushell to Pat Whitehouse which was openly
critical of some key individuals and also the Committee's (by then called the Council) methodology:*

"At present, the Council consists entirely of people having very little experience of actually operating the railway under present day conditions. There are a couple who visit Towyn on organized working parties, but this does not bring them into close contact with the real operational side of the railway; and granted, many of the others are members who did a lot for the railway in the early days, when the line was struggling and nobody worried much about the problems of personalities and the like. Things have changed a lot since then, though, and now we are running pretty efficiently and businesslike. Most of these members have taken to sitting back and, perhaps understandably, enjoying

the fruits of their labours; but they are getting drastically out of touch...I am convinced that the majority of volunteers at Towyn would be happier to know that their money and affairs were being controlled by people like themselves who had proved their worth at Towyn in recent months; in fact, people with whom they might even find themselves working on the trains."

Mr. Bushell was invited to meet the Council as it recognised that the letter reflected the views of a number of volunteers. The archive records then contain a copy of a letter written by Bushell to all members declaring that the explanations he was given completely satisfied him and also an

unreserved written apology for having raised them in the first place. But just maybe this sort of criticism was a factor in change as membership of Council did evolve to include more members who worked on the railway and maybe it was a subliminal message to those pioneer Committee members that their time was coming to an end. Pat Whitehouse moved on. He had recently sold B. Whitehouse & Sons to international construction giant, Cubitts, and became heavily involved on their main board also gaining an O.B.E for his contribution to building safety. However, he still found time to be involved in railway preservation but, together with his friend and colleague Pat Garland, they

had moved on to the next pioneering achievement: the founding of a public limited company to run a Devon GWR branch line on a commercial basis. As Pat Whitehouse himself commented: "There was not much democracy in the early days because there were few of us, just four or five people, who ran the railway. When you get yourself into that position, you get so used to it and it was one of the reasons that I decided it would be wrong for me to continue. I think that I felt the railway needed new blood by the early 1960s and old blood does not always mix with new blood. When you get new blood, you must let them get on with the job. If I am there, I need to be running something. If I can't, then I am better out of the way."

Council formed the Traffic and Operating Committee which first met in 1965 which gradually improved communication and the involvement of operating volunteers in what was going on. Just one example of the growing pains a developing Society had to deal with following an increase in volunteers.

The first hundred years
(Harold Vickers)

Our Victorian forefathers stated their faith in the future in the Great Exhibition of 1851, which was held 14 years before the Talyllyn was built. We stated our hopes for the future when we took over the Talyllyn, also 14 years ago. The coincidence is curious, the circumstances could hardly be more different.

On the one hand the Talyllyn brought the fruits of the industrial revolution to a remote Welsh valley. On the other the revived railway brings pleasure and interest to holidaymakers seeking recreation and change. We now know that the railway worked successfully and unobtrusively for 100 years, but we don't know what it will achieve over the next century. How far can the first hundred years guide to the second?

Our forebears built the railway because they believed it would prove a rewarding exercise. They expected an adequate return on the capital they provided. But the Victorians were also firm believers in the rightness of what they did and it was this confidence in themselves that really built the Talyllyn, and built it for the future. Those who conceived and built it thought it worthwhile doing so, and applied themselves to the job. When the Society took over in 1951, it too thought the task worthwhile and applied itself. But our motive was different. We did not expect a financial profit. We just wanted to preserve a working Victorian relic, a museum piece of 1865 vintage. But wait...! It is now 1965 and we haven't learned how to stop the clock. This is why the tasks we have set ourselves is an impossible one. The railway of 1865 cannot be kept in working order and fossilised at the same time. If it is to work it must live and if it is to live it must adjust to circumstances.

have got off the ground otherwise. So when it gets beyond that stage, it needs a change of people.

After a while, there was more management available at Towyn and the various sub committees started to work. So now everyone who is involved in the running or the railway has a chance of having a serious say. If the TR tried to get too big or to alter itself, it would die because it has got to be run by its members and the whole joy of the thing is that is what happens.

I don't think anybody thought about failure in the early days, because everything was so euphoric. Traffic kept on increasing, the Society was increasing and everyone was keen on what they were doing and enjoying themselves. We hadn't enough experience to think about what would have happened if there had been a real failure. We were presented with a complete railway with things which actually worked. The only things which were likely to fail or could cause any major problem was if either the rails or the engine collapsed. We had Rolt and Curwen on the

> ## The TR has got to be run by its members and the whole joy of the thing is that is what happens

railway and it seemed to us that the engine would not collapse and for the first two seasons that worked just about. For the second season in 1952 we had No.4 back from being overhauled free of charge by Hunslets and that engine then really kept the whole show going. We had managed to buy some Corris rail from Williams, the scrap dealer at Harlech, at a very reasonable price; it was really a question of patching up the track and relaying it slightly faster than the train knocked it to pieces. The customers turned up. The volunteers turned up. The money kept coming in very well. The amount of capital expenditure was really limited to track and minor locomotive repairs; nothing was really spent on anything else.

Ten years after the Society took over the helm, traffic had increased from 5,235 passenger journeys[2] in 1950, Sir Haydn's last season, to 67,018 by 1960 and 185,574 journeys became the all time record peak in 1973 which has never yet been equaled despite the extension to Nant Gwernol.

---

2. A passenger journey is a one way trip

Talyllyn poses on Dolgoch viaduct for a Terence Cuneo sketch

Our Experiences and Celebrations

This chapter features various events, volunteer experiences and railway celebrations from the 1950s up to date, not as a history as some of the events are outside the period of this book but are included to show how the railway has progressed under local management as it matured after the 'Birmingham Committee' handed over the reigns to Council and the various sub committees. To a greater extent than the period covered by this book, the later period is really 'current affairs' rather than history and so we will leave it to future generations to produce the sequel to this book.

Local passengers

In the narrow upper valley between Dolgoch and Abergynolwyn, road and rail run closely parallel, the road at a lower level in the valley bottom. Consequently, although these two upper stations account for at least ninety per cent of the tourist traffic, local trade is almost non existent because of the proximity of the competing bus route. But at Brynglas, Rhydyronen and the two halts the position is reversed, for below Dolgoch the road and rail take opposite sides of the broadening valley, diverging until they are a long half mile apart. So, particularly if it is a Friday, which is the most favoured shopping day, we shall be on the look out for passengers at the two lower stations, on the little platform under the hedge at Cynfal and in the gateway at Fach Goch.

Even in the early society years there was still some parcels traffic, mostly meat or groceries, saving the shopkeeper a trip up the valley when a customer on a farm requires just an odd item or is unable to come down to Towyn to do the shopping in person. Very occasionally, perhaps not more than two or three times during the season, there is a sack or two of pig or poultry food, but now that most farmers have cars this traffic has virtually ceased. British Railways' road delivery services, of course, took all the through traffic, even before the society took over.

Although from a revenue point of view this local traffic is negligible and it is upon the patronage of the holiday maker that the railway has to depend for its bread and butter, we of the small permanent staff attached the greatest importance to it and did our utmost to ensure that, whatever else might happen, we should not let our regular passengers down. For the Talyllyn Railway was not built like a miniature railway on a sea-front, as a side show for tourists, but for two practical purposes, both intimately linked with the workaday life of the district. Firstly it was built to carry slate from the quarry, secondly it was intended to serve the needs of the scattered Welsh community in its mountain valley. The first

A group of kids in a wagon by Abergynolwyn Winding House on the 'extension.'
(Photo: Talyllyn Railway Archive)

Although from a revenue point of view
this local traffic is negligible, we of the
permanent staff attached the greatest
importance to it and did our utmost to
ensure that, whatever else might happen, we
should not let our regular passengers down.
I was determined that so long as one local
passenger remained, the railway should
continue to fulfill, to the best of our ability,
the motto Ich Dien which it proudly bore
upon its crest

Miss Roberts Cynfal. We are looking out for them now on our journey back to Towyn; for the two unrelated members of the Jones clan at Brynglas and for Mrs Evans at Rhydyronen where she may be accompanied by several others including, perhaps, old Mr Pugh with his white stick and his wireless battery. Mr Pugh was a platelayer on the railway for very many years until his sight failed, and in recognition of this long service he has been rewarded with honorary membership of the Society which allows him to travel free. He is one of the few 'regulars' who sometimes travels with us to Dolgoch for he occasionally visits his married daughter there. He is a heavily built old man of nearly eighty years and he is almost totally blind; but he is very active and has known the railway for far too many years to experience any difficulty in getting in and out of the coaches or the van.

(Tom Rolt)

function had, alas, gone beyond recall, but I was determined that so long as one local passenger remained the railway should continue to fulfill, to the best of our ability, the motto *Ich Dien* which it proudly bore upon its crest.

As is natural where so few surnames are divided among so many, we soon learnt to refer to the individual members of this little band by surname coupled to that of their native place in the Welsh fashion thus: Mr Jones Pandy Mill, Mrs Jones Llwynwcws, Mrs Evans Caerffynnon,

Loading No.5 van with parcels and goods for halts up the line on 18th April in the railway's 150th year

No water

One evening in August, 1951, passengers on the railway peered anxiously from their carriages. The train had come to a sudden stop., midway between two stations and the scene on either side was one of desolation. On the right was a steep hill; to the left trees, bushes and dense undergrowth.

As the passengers watched, the engine driver and fireman leaped from their cab. The guard ran from

Pausing at Fach Goch to take on farm produce

The guard of the mixed train greets the farmer's wife at Fach Goch after she returns from Towyn market.

on steam. They discovered later that the crew had visited a farm at the top of the hill, borrowed buckets from the farmer and replenished the engine's boiler with water from a nearby stream.

Volunteers learning the ropes in high summer

The Wharf office was then the original brick building, divided inside into two rooms by a central wall containing a door and a fireplace with, usually, a blazing coal fire whatever the weather. In the other half was the weighing machine and outside the weighing platform still rail connected and the siding still in use.

The public wandered down the steep drive from Neptune Road into the office section and stood at the high counter to buy tickets: half a crown return to Abergynolwyn. The shop was a box of black & white postcards and bars of Kit Kats.

Ostensibly I was in the Towyn area to collect material for geography thesis and this gave me a marvelous opportunity to walk the valleys, study landforms and chat to farmers. However, I had told Tom Rolt, then general manager, that if you required an extra pair of hands at times of emergency, I was available.

The particular emergence, involved a consignment of ex-British Railways sleepers which had arrived at Wharf and required unloading and stacking. However, for whatever the reason I remember standing at Wharf during a break in the proceedings and seeing No.3 *Sir Haydn* emerge from under the road bridge, leave the track and proceed a short distance off the rails, across the yard. I remember even more clearly being a member of the gang deputed to follow

his van to join them. After a hurried conference they sprinted up the hillside as though the eighty six year old engine was about to explode.

This was the railway's first season under the management of the Talyllyn Railway Preservation Society. Its membership was formed of amateur enthusiasts and we had not then mastered all the primitive equipment at our disposal.

On this occasion, the large wooden water tank which was our only source of water supply at Tywyn was to blame. Although connected to the town supply, there was no valve in the tank to cut off the inflow when it was full. This meant that the supply tap had to be turned on and off as required.

On this particular evening, Dai Jones, the engine driver, had forgotten to turn on the tap in time. Rather than wait until the tank had filled, he had taken what he thought was just enough water to reach the next station. Half way there, the engine's water tank had run almost dry.

To the passengers' relief, the crew returned over the brow of the hill, and shortly afterwards they heard the reassuring sound of the engine putting

> As the passengers watched, the engine driver and fireman leaped from their cab. The guard ran from his van to join them. After a hurried conference they sprinted up the hillside as though the eighty six year old engine was about to explode.
> This was the railway's first season under the management of the Talyllyn Railway Preservation Society

No.5 *Midlander* arriving at Wharf with coach No.10 on a Friday winter's local shopping train. *(Photo: Talyllyn Railway Archive)*

the very lame *Sir Haydn* back to Pendre. My own recollection was that the locomotive was seldom entirely on the line and every few yards had to be levered back on the rails.

Incidents were fairly common that year and certainly the most interesting occurred shortly after the breakage of *Sir Haydn's* trailing wheel. At that time only *Dolgoch* was in service, but, those of us engaged in prosaic duties such as sleeper stacking where largely unaware of the moment of high drama being enacted at Pendre.

Such was the position, then, when a slightly irate Tom Rolt, complete with weatherbeaten straw hat, appeared one lunchtime and demanded a volunteer for a guard. "When?" we asked. "Now!" He replied. It must be appreciated that all of us in the sleeper moving gang were covered in sawdust and stained with creosote. I, however, had one advantage, in that my shirt was brown and did not show the stains so obviously and, in addition, Tom

was able to see the whites of my eyes. Accordingly, I found myself promoted to guard of the afternoon train with whispered instructions from Tom to "keep the passengers calm if anything goes wrong."

Suffice to say, we arrived, according to my reckoning about 31 minutes late at Pendre. Tom said "29 looks better". Then, collecting his thoughts after the panic and realising that the guard was scruffy by any standards, remarked "Hadn't you better go and have a wash?"

Train preparation started with looking for couplings in case the train became divided. The carriages were coupled with a hook and shackle and a link. The shackle was thrown over one carriage hook and a link placed over the other, the downward facing hook on the shackle then being dropped into the link. It was necessary to match

The Coronation Special

The Coronation day of Queen Elizabeth II, 1953 was celebrated by a special train in the railway, free for children under 14. Gareth Jones positions the headboard and No.4 Edward Thomas heads the flag, bedecked train up the the line

(Photos: Talyllyn Railway Archive)

Gareth Jones' railway career started on the TR and preogressed to Senior Traction Inspector for DB Shencker on the national network

Sir Haydn **returning downhill at Ty Mawr with the same train as apposite, but with the Corris brake van added**

the coupling combination with the space between the coaches, such that the buffers were held tight together on the straight – not always easy when spaces and link lengths were all different. You had to watch out for one particularly long link which, if the train braked and the coaches closed up, would ride up the coach hook and slip off. I once looked back on a train slowing down for Dolgoch and saw fifteen feet of daylight between the two halves of the train. Fortunately, in the down direction, the brake van was next to the loco and it was possible to alert the crew, so a very gradual stop reunited the two halves of the train with an acceptable bump and nobody was any the wiser.

(David Leech)

We would run into Wharf, controlled purely by the loco handbrake) and see an anxious queue of potential passengers winding up the slope in the hope of being able to travel. After booked passengers had been found seats, the guard would count up those left vacant (three a side in the TRs and, for a first class supplement, the Glyn Valleys, four a side elsewhere), give the magic number to the booking clerk, then fit the passengers in, splitting up groups as necessary. Expectations were lower in those days, time not so precious, and the TR virtually unique, so any grumblings were rare.

(John Gott)

Talyllyn Pioneers

The last task before leaving Wharf was to check you had Miss Thomas on board. Miss Thomas was the refreshment lady. Small, mild but determined, she ran up the platform at the last minute, her hair done up tightly in a bun, pink overall flying and cash box tucked firmly under her arm. It was easy to leave her behind and if you did you had to stop halfway out of the station to pick her up. Every guard I knew left he behind at some time.

(David Leech)

> **Every guard I knew left her behind at some time... It wasn't really my fault that Miss Thomas was left behind at Wharf**

It wasn't really my fault that Miss Thomas was left behind at Wharf as I had seen her board the train but not alight to go into the shop. Diminutive Miss Zella Thomas, was a determined chapel member. She was normally very quietly spoken, perhaps demure, though not averse to a quick cigarette behind the tea van when she thought nobody was looking. We had to wait for her at Pendre while she staggered up the cutting breathing more fire and brimstone than a Welsh dragon and with language that would have put a Liverpool docker to shame.

(Gordon Rhodes)

Health & Safety was then but a gleam in some youthful bureaucrat's eye. No.10 (the semi open 'Stanton van') had a small guard's compartment from which one emerged after passing under Wharf bridge, to edge down the footboard clipping tickets whilst keeping one's arm looped round the roof supports. It was, of course, critical to complete the task before arriving at Fford Cadfan bridge…

(John Gott)

As virtually all traffic originated at Towyn, the biggest problem for the guard was achieving an arrival time back at Wharf that would ensure connections were made to the British Railways trains at Towyn in both directions, as a large proportion of passengers arrived by rail. It was possible to have the BR trains held for a few minutes if necessary as Towyn station was fully staffed, complete with signal box, and the

Sir Haydn running through Pendre yard with a very full train comprising the two new bogie coaches and the new bogie coach

The view from Neptune Road looking over at Wharf station with two trains in the new platform at the same time headed by No.2 and No.3 respectively, two old Penrhyn open coach bodies lying on their side and ash wagons by the wagon turntables adjacent to the main line siding. *(Photo: Talyllyn Railway Archive)*

Both former Corris engines, *Sir Haydn* and *Edward Thomas* pass Quarry Sifing with an 'express' train

concept of service to the passenger was absolute. Conversely, Talyllyn trains were held if BR trains were delayed, the BR request being relayed to Wharf including how many passengers there were for interchange.

In the early days, the timetable consisted of one morning round trip and two trains in the afternoon: the express which carried boards stating 'Dolgoch and Abergynolwyn only', left Wharf at 2.10pm and the 'all stations' left at 3 o'clock.

On arrival at Abergynolwyn, the loco on the first afternoon train ran round and propelled the train up the extension far enough to give the 'all stations' enough room to run round. Meanwhile, the station building had been unlocked to reveal a gas fridge and gas ring for a large kettle. Miss Thomas' first task was to light the fridge. This involved kneeling in front of it and poking a lighted match in the right place. Usually, there was a soft 'pop' and all was well. Occasionally, the earth shook and Miss Thomas appeared, very annoyed and somewhat flushed. The ice cream, which had accompanied her from Wharf, was put in the freezer to be sold as soon as it had solidified again. Cups of tea were dispensed from a huge enamel teapot. There were, of course, no toilets.

The return workings of the two afternoon trains were operated on the time interval system. The 'express', Dolgoch and Wharf only, left at 4.45pm and the following 'all stations' had to wait fifteen minutes before leaving Abergynolwyn. After a hurried ticket check at Dolgoch, the guard of the 'express' would write the departure time of his train on a piece of paper and leave it under a stone on the seat in the station shelter. The guard of the 'all stations' waited until fifteen minutes after the time on the piece of paper before flagging his train away. The snags with this system are obvious and the express guard always kept a good look out to the rear, even when running normally.

(David Leech)

At Dolgoch, fun would be had trying to get passengers to relinquish their seats in favour of those with tickets for main line trains with which we made a connection and, even with the promise of an extra train, we would leave the station with quite a number of standing passengers.

(John Smallwood)

At that time, the TR was receiving all the 'operated by volunteers' glory and publicity. Traffic was growing incredibly. One day, on the last train down, I had twenty seven passengers in the brake

Talyllyn arrives at Abergynolwyn with a very mixed train of carriages. *(Photo: Jim Jarvis, KRM Collection)*

van. On other occasions, after the last arrival of the day at Wharf, the whole train would be propelled back to Dolgoch to pick up the forty or so passengers who had had to wait. It was obvious that the railway had to change to offer the growing number of passengers a safe and acceptable ride.

(David Leech)

Perhaps my most hectic day on the railway was August Bank Holiday Monday, 1966. There were no morning trains and those in the afternoon were at 1.10, 2.10, 3.10 and 4.10pm. The first set

was hauled by No.4 driven by Bill Faulkner, as usual, and being full it was banked up the cutting by No.1, driven by Dai Jones, who then backed his loco onto our carriage set at Pendre. When we arrived at Wharf, volunteers were already holding back the crowd on the platform and, as soon as we stopped, all seats were filled including the TR van, with even two passengers in the van booking office cubby hole; they only moved out when I threatened not to start the train until we had unrestricted

> **The whole train would be propelled back to Dolgoch to pick up the forty or so passengers who had had to wait**

The refreshment van in its siding at Abergynolwyn station. Miss Zella Thomas is serving from inside

access to the handbrake! For our return trip we managed to find every passenger a seat and departed for Dolgoch on time, where we found the platform heaving and it was people-packing to the limit. We abandoned ticket checking in favour of stopping at the intermediate stations. Arrival at Wharf was behind time and, with the platform still crowded even that late in the afternoon, it was a case of finding seats (including the van), setting off again this time behind No.2 and with No.6 banking as far up as Quarry Siding. The run up was much the same as our first, but clearing Abergynolwyn was interesting and we left with four a side, standing passengers and fifteen in the van, with the prospect of Dolgoch looming before us. Our train connected with the Cambrian at BR so it was a case of persuading some passengers to wait for the inevitable relief train in favour of those with main line tickets. We set off rather late and by the time we arrived at Brynglas, No.6 was ready to propel the relief train up the line. By the time

No.6 had been disposed of at the end of the day, it was quite late in the evening. We climbed in to the car for the return journey to London, devoid of motorways and with only a short section of dual carriageway, arrived at 2.45am. (Gordon Rhodes)

A life in the day of the TR

We left our bicycles at Abergynolwyn station and walked a short way down the line. When the noise of an approaching train was heard, we could hardly believe our ears, for the timetable allowed us ample time to walk to Dolgoch before the train came. A train rounded the bend hauled by No.3. We boarded the brake van. The mystery of the train was soon solved as the number of passengers arriving at Towyn warranted nearly twice as many trains as those on the timetable. The other engine steam was No.2 and trains were passing for the first time that afternoon at Brynglas.

We found seats in the open Penrhyn coach at the

Most of the scouts were sent into the train which proceeded to Brynglas to notify the staff at Towyn and summon an ambulance. A few of us stayed behind to re-rail the wagons, load them with the three injured boys and push them gently to Brynglas where the ambulance had arrived five minutes before. A bathe, a meal and a calm red sunset ended this most eventful day. (G.D. Braithwaite; Tuesday 30th July, 1953)

The 'Pop' Special

Whitsunday saw about seventeen of us leave Pendre at about 9.45 a.m. behind *Douglas* in the open four wheeler. We arrived at Quarry Siding, hand shunted the empties in the right place and the first two wagons were soon being loaded. Loading ballast which consists of a mixture of slate, shale and mud is warm work– it was really getting warm.

By and by we had four wagons loaded, which *Douglas* took with us in the coach to just below Dolgoch Viaduct for unlading and placing. After we had been on this for a time and *Douglas* had disappeared down the line someone said: "How do we get this lot back to Quarry Siding?" Said one of the Johns: "We push 'em". It was getting hot.

In due course we were back at the Quarry, the large bottle of orange pop George and I had brought was all gone and we had another two wagons to load before the lunch break. It was very hot and the bottle of beer each we had brought just went down with a "sizz" and a cloud of steam, nearly grilling our ham sandwiches.

There were still several wagons to be loaded and the main line cleared for the afternoon train due about 3:30 pm. By this time we had seven loaded but all the pop was gone and it was hot. I said to one of the Johns: "Think there'll be any pop on the Up train?" John said: "Don't know, but if not they could bring some down from Aber when they pick us up." "Good show," I said, "You stop the train and give 'em the order". But he looks worried, "Not supposed to stop the train here unless it's…." "Never mind that," I said, "You stop the train with your flag and I'll see the guard and tell him how many bottles."

Soon after, the steady beat and the whistle were heard from *Douglas*. John held at the flag, the train stopped. "Eighteen bottles of pop, please, when you come back stop" I said to the guard. "O.K. I'll see to it" and off the train went. "Come on, chaps, another three more wagons of fill,"

end of the train, save for two wagons filled with boy scouts. A short way past Dolgoch viaduct, on the army relaid section, these two wagons became derailed. Owing to the empty gaps between the sleepers, the trucks were furiously flying up and down while the panic stricken scouts and the alarmed passengers in the Penrhyn coach yelled for the train to stop. Eventually, the driver brought *Dolgoch* to a standstill and bruised scouts were helped out of the wagons. Beneath them and some sleepers used as seats, in the midst of blood, broken glass and dust, were three injured scouts– one of them very badly cut and bruised and unconscious. Water was quickly fetched from the Nant Dolgoch and wounds dressed as well as possible.

> Two wagons became derailed. The trucks were furiously flying up and down while the panic stricken passengers yelled for the train to stop

shouted at another John, So on with the job.

After a while George says, "Do I hear a loco whistle?" Someone replies, "Don't be daft, train's not due back till five and it's only just gone four." On with the shoveling but a couple of minutes later there was no mistaking it, a whistle; it was *Douglas*.

We hurry down to the mainline, in time to help unload bottles of pop off the footplate. This was a real service, service never contemplated– The "Pop" Special.

The 1957 outside live BBC TV broadcast

1957 will probably be remembered as the year of the outside broadcast by the BBC on the railway as there was little doubt that this programme was an outstanding success in developing traffic. It all started in Birmingham with the showing of the Secretary's film of the early days of the Society to BBC officials. The film then went to London and later there was a phone call to say that the railway was certainly of interest and that arrangements would be made to include it in a series of outside broadcasts in the summer. It was decided that the broadcast would go out on 22nd May with Wynford Vaughan Thomas and Huw Weldon as the commentators and Lord Northesk as our star performer. The run was from Dolgoch to Abergynolwyn on a Wednesday evening and there was another programme for childrens' hour on the following day. There was little doubt that it was this piece of publicity which pushed our traffic figures up that summer from 36,928 to 57,632!

> **This publicity pushed our traffic up from 36,928 to 57,632!**

The scene of the broadcast was necessarily confined to the Dolgoch-Abergynolwyn stretch, as the train carried its own transmitting apparatus involving a tall aerial array; there are no overbridges between Dolgoch and Aber. From the train the signals were picked up on a tall tower erected near Dolgoch water tank, thence by land line to another relay point near the Dolgoch Hotel, via another relay point down the valley to a receiver in Wharf station yard, which one member describes as looking like a Martian space port! From Warf the programme was beamed to the BBC station at Blaenplwy and from then on by normal channels.

The programme *was* delightful, everything seemed to work perfectly, locomotives included, and the two commentators, Mr Wynford Vaughan-Thomas and Mr Huw Weldon treated the whole subject with dignity and sympathy. If there was a 'star', it was surely our President, Lord Northesk, affable as ever and radiating the spirit of the

Railway and Society.

It was pleasant, too, to see some of our hard-worked officials sitting back, having a ride and enjoying themselves, watching other people do the work! Treasurer Pat Garland, jovial as usual, Secretary Pat Whitehouse clutching a copy of the *Talyllyn News*, Manager Ken Marrian, obviously thinking of postcard sales, Tom Rolt in his distinctive hat and Ken Cope probably wondering how all this wonderful publicity could be used

again in the future.

Quite a goodly number of members managed to get over to populate the show; some even formed a ballast-digging party at the Quarry, compete with No.6 and train.

The locomotives carried microphones in their headlamps in order to pick up the exhaust sound clearly.

The broadcast in the Childrens' Television programme the following day was thought by many to be the better of the two. Certainly it seemed to have more spontaneity and was notable for the most complete, comprehensible and concise description of the working of a steam locomotive I have ever heard – by Lord Northesk, of course.

William Jones and Edward Thomas hedgers featured more prominently in the second programme when their apparent refusal to precipitate a *really* dangerous emergency caused some favourable press comment.

No.6 *Douglas* with a volunteer working party at Quarry Siding. *(Photo: Talyllyn Railway Archive)*

The Talyllyn Railway can be proud to have made such an interesting and unusual programme and one which we may hope will do us a tremendous amount of good, both in the way of recruits to the Society and of increased passenger traffic. Thank you, BBC and everyone else involved.

In the aftermath of the famous TV broadcast of 1957 we were pushed seriously close to failure, if not disaster. A serious mishap could have established that amateurs were incapable of running a railway safely.

The published timetable then showed three trains a day during August: one at 10.25am, an 'express' departing at 2.10pm and a last departure up at 3pm. The safe running of these trains was ensured by the three simple divisible train staffs and tickets which, with exemplary economy, allowed trains to be crossed at Pendre, Brynglas and Abergynolwyn. The serious weakness of the system was that it was inflexible, not allowing more than two trains to run consecutively in the same direction nor could it accommodate unplanned or out of course running.

As passenger numbers increased, the morning train would often include all the available rolling stock and be double headed. As soon as it had returned at 12.35 and the stock had been reformed ready for the afternoon departures, passengers would begin to accumulate for the 2.10pm. When all the seats were filled it would be sent off regardless of time, followed similarly by the other train if necessary, when it would be hoped that the first would return in time to form the booked 3pm, if not, no matter, it would have to run late!

At the end of the afternoon the passengers we had taken up would present themselves to be taken back by the advertised two trains from Aber, with the added complication that many of them had main line connexions to make and other pressing reasons why they must not be late back to Towyn.

Again we improvised, this time under considerable pressure. Normally the second of any pair of down trains would have to wait at Brynglas if the first had to turn round at Wharf and then return back to cross it. If it were allowed to run forward to Rhydyronen and wait to cross there, half an hour or more could be saved.

There were two serious objections to this practice. First, it nullified the safety inherent in the normal method under control of the train staffs and tickets and, secondly, the necessary crossing orders were given over the telephone, except at Wharf, unconfirmed and to the driver alone.

The speed of events had left the Rule Book far behind. Casual helpers, in the absence of formal instructions could only guess what was going

Sheep are herded at Quarry siding preparatory to starring on the BBC TV's outside live broadcast in 1957

Lord Northesk
talks live to the
BBC TV cameras in
front of the crowd
at Dolgoch in 1957

on. If they guessed wrong they could cause big trouble. The conditions that prevailed during August 1967 and 1958, immediately after the television broadcast, caused feelings to run high; we just couldn't continue indefinitely as we had done. The background to these critical years is the number of passengers carried. In 1955 we had carried 25,811 and, only two years later, this figure had more than doubled to 57,132, yet the railway had remained basically unchanged and the staff inexperienced. The next doubling in numbers to 122,167, took over five times as long to 1968. This time we had hard earned experience behind us and were able to keep ahead of events.

A source of grievance had persisted for much of this time among traffic volunteers. They had been expected to work long hours with equipment that carried historic merit without regard to its suitability or otherwise to the conditions that prevailed. In some cases it was potentially unsafe yet the volunteers who had to use it had no official channel for their complaints or suggestions.

The TRPS AGM specials

Pat Whitehouse recalls the magic of the return journey from Towyn:

It was the Talyllyn Railway Preservation Society who ran the first of the 'Preservation Specials'; the idea being to take Society members along on Annual General Meeting day to see *their* railway. To start with the numbers were small and the train was only an ex-GWR diesel railcar, but it wasn't long before the numbers increased, making a steam train essential. All kinds of engines have been used for the run between London and Towyn; usually a large express engine such as a 'Star' or a 'Castle' and even a Midland Compound as far as Shrewsbury and then after that, over the winding hilly road over the mountains, two smaller engines including an ex-London & South Western Railway 'T9' 4-4-0, a South Eastern & Chatham Railway 'D' class 4-4-0, a Lancashire & Yorkshire 2-4-2T and several veteran GWR locomotives, including the last Dean Goods No. 2538 and, on many occasions, one or two 'Dukedog' outside framed 4-4-0s.

I have seen all these trains and, when the day is over at Towyn, and everyone has had his fill of the narrow gauge, the 'Special' waits at the main line station for the journey home. The first of the specials was the T9 one, and I remember that evening as we walked down the main street of Towyn in the darkness. The rain had stopped but there was a wind blowing up from the sea, and we could hear a safety valve hissing as we stepped out of the hotel onto the road. The train had been in for some time when we arrived and the lighted coaches stood alongside the up platform. At their head two locomotives glittered under the combined lights of the platform lamps and

The first TRPS Special train on the main line GWR railcars W38W, W1096W and W33W are in the bay platfrom at Ruabon

the glow from their fires, while plumes of steam rose from the safety valves and were caught by the wind to be pushed downwards towards the black shadowy figures standing in admiring groups beneath the footplates of the veterans. We joined them, men (and women too) from Portsmouth, London, Birmingham, Manchester and even Ireland, together with a few of the locals who had come to see the train depart. In the flickering light we saw the beautiful curves of the leading engine, the 'T9', and behind her the solid respectability of the 'Dukedog', her outside cranks symbolic of an age now past. The driver of the 'T9' sat waiting on the left of his footplate (contrary to good GWR practice, where they drive on the right hand side), clad in an old mackintosh with his trousers tied

round his ankles with string. Soon the key man, our old friend Headquarters Inspector George Holland, was aboard, the signal light changed from red to green, the guard's whistle blew, his lamp too showed green, and they were away, two whistles sounding in unison, arms waving from the engine cabs and from the train, detonators exploding as the wheels passed over them, to disappear into the distance, London-bound.

Inaugural run of *The Centenarian* 1st June 1965

To a casual onlooker at Penrdre, the morning of Tuesday, 1st June could have been just another ordinary day in the life of the railway. The locos

one of the ex Glyn Valley Tramway coaches, were being prepared to work the inaugural run of the *Centenarian* in conjunction with the reopening of Wharf station after its rebuild.

Nobody knew exactly what to expect; they just knew that everything must be spot on. By 1 o'clock, a rake of reasonably presentable coaches waited at Pendre for the time when it would be backed down to Wharf; one volunteer had even taken the opportunity to fit new grab handles to No. 18. By this time, the special dinner at the Corbett Arms was getting underway, and the guard left his train to look after Wharf office in the absence of Mr Parker, who was at the dinner. He returned to Pendre shortly after 2 o'clock and the

To celebrate the centenary of the railway, Tom Rolt welcomes John Betjeman, poet and railway enthusiast, to unveil the celebration plaque and then set off on board *The Centenarian* special train behind No.1 on 2nd June, 1965

gurgled quietly to themselves outside the shed, the train crews hurried to and fro, cleaning, polishing and oiling. But that day, a strange feeling of excitement and expectancy spurred everybody on to perform their tasks just that little bit better; the brasses received an extra rub, and locomotives and rolling stock unlike gradually took on a gleam of perfection.

The season was well underway, and the three trains a day service, using one stock unit, was still in operation. But on this, the morning of one of the most important days in the history of the railway, after the regular stock had been safely dispatched to Wharf to work the 10.25, there stood on the loop at Pendre and another train: the original TR coaches and van, No. 18 coach, then only recently put into service and, for good measure,

train, now with *Talyllyn* standing at its head, was propelled into Wharf just as the first of the diners returned from their meal.

The special *Centenarian* headboard was appropriated from the office whilst the guard finished off cleaning his windows, the fireman tended to the fire, Dai, the driver, made a last minute check on his engine and a considerable crowd gathered on the platform. John Betjeman, C.B.E., the guest of honour for the day and easily discernable by his now familiar hat, approach the front end of *Talyllyn*. Accompanied by a few well chosen words, the name board was positioned in front of the engine's chimney and our first regular named train stood proudly in the new Wharf platform.

The crowd's attention was taken away from the train as Mr. Betjeman crossed the platform to the side of the new office extension. Here, he became his usual self again, and filled his speech

with many of his own brand of witticisms. His sentiments where shared by all present, and as he unveiled the commemorative plaque on the station building, there was at least one spine that shivered with that inexplicable twinge of realisation that's what he had been saying refers to the likes of me. His praise for the efforts made by those who had brought the railway through from those dark days 15 years ago were echoed by many hands pounding their agreement–hands that had dug, hands that had weeded, hands that had strained to produce for us what we now take for granted; yet at the same time, hands for which this expression of approbation was but a brief respite in the struggle which we all know must go on.

The applause died away and the happy throng turned once more towards the train. Three o'clock had barely passed as *Talyllyn* strode out of Wharf and up towards the valley that has been her domain for nigh on one hundred years. She seemed

to know it too and rose well to the occasion. There must have been many on that historic train who shared the guard's emotions, the feeling that all the trials and tribulations of the past years had been worth experiencing just for this one intense moment. The whole day's events appeared to epitomise the Talyllyn; in one small inconspicuous collection of wood and steel, of fire and water, and of perfectly ordinary people, nestled in a quiet, remote corner of Wales, we seem to have the proof that in a world where dedication and devotion to duty mean little, sacrifice has its reward.

Talyllyn twenty-first

On 14th May, 1951, the world's first railway preservation society held a small ceremony at Wharf station, Towyn, to mark its taking over operation of the Talyllyn Railway. It was a simple affair at which the then society chairman, Mr. W. G. Trinder, made a brief speech, cutting white tape across the track, and declared the line open.

Sometime ago, it was felt that the 21st anniversary of this occasion should not pass unnoticed, and it was decided that, as we had the original locomotive and rolling stock restored to working order, a simple re-enactment of that first ceremony would be the most appropriate way of celebration.

14th May, 1972 was a Sunday, which was not suitable for fitting such an affair into the traffic pattern, but Monday 15th May suited well, and the original ceremony had been on a Monday also.

Arrangements were therefore made, and details worked out. First, there would be a cold buffet lunch in the museum, then the ceremony at Wharf. The inaugural train was to wait in the loop at Pendre while the press train, hauled by No.1 *Talyllyn*, overtook it and preceded it to Rhydyronen, Where the press would wait to observe the arrival of the

Once again, passengers push the train round the engine, just as they did 21 years earlier in 1951

The view from the cab window. *Dolgoch*, suitably decorated for the occasion, waits to take the first train of invited guests up the 'extension' to Nant Gwerol from Abergynolwyn

The TR today...

inaugural train, which was to be hand shunted round *Dolgoch*, as had been done in 1951. The combined trains were then to travel to Abergynolwyn, where party would visit the extension, before returning to Towyn.

Nant Gwernol Opening 22nd May

Guest of honour will be Mr. Wynford Vaughan Thomas O.B.E, and about one hundred other invited guests are expected to attend. Official proceedings should start with the invited guests leaving Wharf by special train at about 10.30 am and reaching Abergynolwyn at 11.15 am. Tywyn Silver Band should be in attendance there, to provide appropriate music ("See the Conquering Hero Comes" has been asked for) and, after speeches, Mr. Wynford Vaughan Thomas will be asked to drive in a gold plated spike to signify completion of the work. Guests will then entrain

> To have converted a moribund railway into one showing a trading profit is an achievment of which we can feel justifiably proud

for Nant Gwernol and, after a brief inspection of the site, return to Abergynolwyn where Mrs. D. Elis Thomas, wife of Member of Parliament for Merioneth, will unveil a plaque on the signal box commemorating the occasion. This plaque will be a slate and the inscription bilingual. The guests would then leave Abergynolwyn by train, arriving at Pendre about 13.15 and attend a buffet reception at Neuadd Pendre Social Club in Brook Street.

In retrospect

Bigger and more ambitious organisations than ours have foundered before reaching their fourteenth birthday. To have spanned this period and converted a moribund railway into one showing a trading profit, however modest, is an achievement of which we can feel justifiably proud.

The downhill leg of the annual 'Race the Train' with *Douglas* and *Edward Thomas* just below Brynglas. *(Photo: Barbara Fuller)*

The story of the Talyllyn preservation falls conveniently into three chapters. The first could be called "Supreme optimism and improvisation" when the tempo was leisurely (between flaps) and there were long periods between trains when the engine crews "went to ground" at Abergynolwyn or Pendre. At Abergynolwyn life could be boring to a degree if it was cold and wet, but delightful if it was fine, for while the loco simmered gently and the bees buzzed in the crew could sleep undisturbed by the hour–while the fire went out on more than one occasion. Train speeds were restricted and by the shocking track and impatient drivers often paid for there impatience, particularly with No.6 *Douglas*, when the firemen would be sent back en forward to Pendre to blurt out the sorry story while trying to get his breath back. A scratch breakdown gang would assemble, throwing sleepers, rails and jacks into whatever stock they could find and cling onto the outside of a hastily steamed loco, peering ahead and speculating on what they would find when they arrived at the scene.

The idiosyncrasies of the weighted one-way Talyllyn point levers defeated many a guard and fireman and a few of those who helped at this period escaped scot-free. The most humiliating part was explaining afterwards to the general manager how one came to put coaches or loco on the ballast. Of course you generally did it 30 minutes before booked departure from Wharf and effectively bottled up Pendre yard.

The telephone too had its moments. Much time had to be spent tracing faults and the repair gang seemed to work to a different timetable from the traffic department. In the end (they had to) the telephonists got very slick in unloading and unrailing their hand trolley from under the very buffer beam of an engine with the anchors out, although no one actually seems to have got hurt.

Those happy-go-lucky days where really ended by the television broadcasts of 1957 and gave way to what can be called the chapter of "Dangerous inadequacy". The traffic generated by the broadcast found the railway and its traffic organisation utterly inadequate for its task and in retrospect it is remarkable that nothing more serious went wrong. Special trains were run at short notice and that the timetable was frequently abandoned; train crews returned from lunch to find the trains taken from them, fireman managing to regain is loco as it sped through Pendre with a full train 45 minutes before it was due off shed. An on-time arrival with empty stock for the morning train would be converted into a 30 minute late departure by endless successive returns to Pendre for yet more stock. The all time low was reached one terrible week when the afternoon and express was twice switched into the shed road in error. The sight of *Edward Thomas* with wheels locked sliding inexorably towards the loco over the shed pit in which people were working brought cold fear to those who witnessed the incident. We learned the

Above: No.4 *Edward Thomas*, named after the company's faithful general manager and the mainstay of the service trains throughout the 1950s, takes water at Tywyn Wharf. *(Photo: Barbara Fuller)*

Top left: President David Mitchell, Chair Jane Garvey and General Manager Chris Price hold the banner as *Talyllyn* breaks through on her 15oth birthday in October, 2014. *(Photo: Barbara Fuller)*

Bottom left: *Douglas* is put to bed inside the original shed. *(Photo: Barbara Fuller)*

Edward Thomas at Wharf during the Land Rover Rally. *(Photo: Barbara Fuller).*

Edward Thomas at Wharf during the Land Rover Rally. *(Photo: Barbara Fuller).*

Below: *Talyllyn* and a single coach with the McConnel family and engine driver Bob Thomas at Nant Gwernol, the limit of steam engine working taken around 1895. Merrick is on the engine, next to the carriage is Mrs. Florence McConnel with the two girls, Muriel and Eryl and , behind them, stands the guard, probably Jacob Rowlands. The picture was taken by Mr. W.H. McConnel, the son of Mr. William McConnel, the owner and founder *(Photo: Talyllyn Railway Archive)*

hard way that running a railway is no joke, although it took several more years to digest the lesson and bring us to the third and present chapter, that of "Tolerable efficiency."

(Harold Vickers)

Heading for a Century

The celebration of our centenary next year gives me an excuse to take stock of our position. We have now poured money and physical effort into the Talyllyn Railway for thirteen years with results that none of us thought possible in 1951. The need to cater for a greatly increased traffic has absorbed some of this effort, but the greater part of it has had to be devoted to deferred maintenance and anyone who remembers what the line was like when we took over would agree that the term 'deferred maintenance' was a gross understatement. We had to cope with the back log of half a century of neglect. We are not yet out of this long tunnel yet by any means, but at least we can now see a pin point of daylight at the end of it.

(Tom Rolt)

Below: The McConnel family return to celebrate the 150th year of the railway and gather in the same place at Nant Gwernol. Third from left in front of the engine is Mr. Roger McConnel, who is the son of Mr. W.H.McConnel, the photographer of the 1980s picture. David Jones, fourth generation railway member of the Jones family stands by the front of No.1.

177

The Welsh staff

Uniquely, as the railway remained a going concern (although only just!) when the preservationists took over the Talyllyn, they also inherited the complete workforce of just three people: Edward Thomas (manager), Hugh Jones (driver and platelayer) and his son Dai.

As volunteering was then a new concept, the pioneers continued with the services of the staff. Although Edward Thomas retired as general manager, he remained on the Company board until he was 88 providing much good advice. It took some time before the Welsh and the English saw eye to eye but, as time went on, many volunteers enjoyed working with Hugh and both his sons, Dai and Herbert, and learnt much from them about how to mend track and operate the engines.

Edward Thomas[1]

Edward Thomas was a youthful 17 when he joined the staff of the company in 1897 as an assistant to his father, Hugh, who was manager at that time.

Edward Thomas was an extremely shrewd judge of character and that made him remarkably sensitive and diplomatic in his handling of human relations. I think he had a deeper understanding of the quirks of that characterful figure Sir Haydn then any other man and I firmly believe that, but for his influence, the latter would never have kept the railway running as long as he did and it was his loyalty that kept the railway alive. It is not too much to say that during this long period he was the Talyllyn Railway incarnate in one man.

From the very outset of our efforts to preserve the TR we were made aware that if there was one man in Wales who was wholeheartedly on our side it was Edward Thomas. Let me give one example. Ordinarily, it took a great deal to persuade him to leave his native heath, let alone to cross the Welsh border; yet when we asked him if he would attend the historic meeting at the Imperial Hotel, Birmingham in 1950 he needed no second bidding. Moreover, he spoke eloquently at that meeting, indeed he painted a somewhat rosy word picture of the railway and its prospects.

At that time, Sir Haydn's executors and their advisers took it for granted that the railway was no more than a load of scrap and that 1950 would be its last working season. It was Edward Thomas' influence rather than any advocacy on our part which persuaded Lady Haydn Jones to give our "crazy" scheme a trial.

When I stepped into his shoes at Towyn in 1951 I did so with much trepidation, so invidious did my position seem. After all, here was I, an ignorant English interloper, presuming to take over this particular Welsh preserve from a Welshman with years of experience behind him. I need not have worried. Admittedly the job was difficult, but without Edward Thomas' guidance, tact and unfailing support and courtesy it would have been downright impossible. He never fussed around telling me what I ought to be doing as many a man in his position might well have done under such circumstances. Indeed he stayed tactfully on the sidelines, but whenever I needed his help and advice–which was often –it was fully, freely and wisely given.

For my part I shall carry in my mind a picture of Edward Thomas starting the train away from the Wharf. Always neat and precise in his movements, I see him emerge from the office, carrying in one hand a small cloth bag containing the takings from the till. Having carefully locked the office door, he walks quickly towards the TR van waving the train away with that inimitable quick flick of the

> It is not too much to say that during this long period he was the Talyllyn Railway incarnate in one man

1. *Railway Adventure* by L.T.C Rolt

Hugh Jones on the pw trolley at Pendre. *(Photo: Talyllyn Railway Archive)*

wrist before hopping nimbly on-board. No guard's uniform, no whistle, no flag for Edward Thomas, just an old grey trilby and a mackintosh, Yet there was never any doubt as to who was in command.

The Jones family[2]

We inherited from the old regime the Welsh permanent staff, but in the event they only provided the human problem, the last straw that almost broke the camel's back. When I first arrived they had seemed to me pleasant and willing enough so that I was surprised then Edward Thomas warned me that I would find them "Very

2. *Railway Adventure* by L.T.C Rolt

3. *This might all be a little unfair as the Jones' family probably resented the '9-5' hours kept by the English trio of Rolt, Trinder and Snell who, for the first year, stayed at the Tyn y Cornel hotel at Talyllyn Lake and, as recounted by Snell later in this chapter, they returned there for dinner and chats in the hotel. John Snell admitted later in life that he didn't always chop the firewood up for lighting up the engine the next day and, eventually, Dai saw 'red' and walked out. It took a deputation led by Lord Northesk and a pay rise to get him back from the Water Board where he moved to.*

difficult people, you know, yes indeed!" I reflected gloomily that if he, a fellow Welshman who had known them all their lives, had found them difficult, what hope had I? What hope, indeed! Within weeks both walked out on me without any warning what-so-ever. David, John and I arrived at Towyn one morning to find the locomotive that was to haul the morning train cold and without a driver. David Curwen, instead of working in the shop, was compelled to act as driver while he trained his fireman, John Snell, to succeed him.

In later days it became obvious that these 'difficult people' bitterly resented our new regime and thought that by letting us down without warning they would make the Society's failure certain. But when the reaction of the stubborn English was merely to close ranks and, by a prodigious feat of improvisation, to carry on as though they had never been, resentment seemed to know no bounds. One of them, who lived in a cottage beside the railway, made a jolly practice of pouncing, like some old man of the sea, upon new and unsuspecting volunteers who had come down to work on the railway and informing them that I was mad, that my crazy attempt to run a railway which was obviously unsafe was bound to end in disaster, and the sooner they dissociated themselves from the railway and returned whence they had come the better.[3]

Hugh Jones

My father, David Jones started working on the track of the Talyllyn Railway in 1900, at which time he moved to my present house, *Plas Coch*, alongside the line near Rhydyronen station. Within two years, the engineer, Mr. Yates, made him foreman in charge of all trackwork on the railway, from Wharf station to the top of the Alltwyllt incline alongside the 'Quarrymens' Path' from Bryn Eglwys to Abergynolwyn village. In those days the foreman chose his own men, who had to be able not only to maintain the permanent way in good order, but also to cut and lay hedges, and scythe the grass and undergrowth alongside the line. It would never do for lineside grass and ferns to brush against the train.

In 1904, I was born in the little house alongside the railway– my parents' seventh son. With trains passing daily, it is no wonder I became interested in the little railway, and, with my father the foreman platelayer, I knew all the old drivers and had many footplate rides. At 14, I left school at Bryncrug, In spite of appeals by the schoolmaster for me to go for another year to the County School. I wanted a job on the railway, but my mother was against it, and I finished up at Bryn Eglwys Slate Quarry, serving a three year apprenticeship.

At the close of this, I worked slates for almost another 10 years, until the dust affected my health, and I was told by my doctor to keep away from slates for a while. I transferred to the loading slate at Wharf station, and it was here that I came in touch with Old Hugh Jones[4], the driver/fitter. I must say here that I owe all my knowledge of steam engines to this wonderful man, and credits for keeping things going up to the time Sir Haydn died is due to him more than anyone else. Although he had then left the railway, he was always ready with help and advice whenever it was asked of him.

A few years before the Second World War there was a depression in the slate industry and wages were very low. At this time, the army camp at Tonfannau was established and, one by one, my railway colleagues left for better paid jobs. Old Hugh Jones left in the early 1940's to work at the power station in the Happy Valley. I was left on my own with the slates, the track, and the locomotives to look after: at the same time I lost my wife and had three children to bring up as well, Dai, the

> **Being a wild and stubborn man, I walked out**

eldest, was then nine, and also my aged mother to look after.

I never thought then that one day Dai and Herbert would be working with me on the railway. Many a morning train ran with me as driver, fireman, and guard. Edward Thomas booked the tickets at Wharf, but then had to stay in the office, so if there were any passengers at the intermediate stations, I had to leave the engine, issue their tickets from the van, and then return to the engine. The train would be left unattended at Abergynolwyn while I took the locomotive to the foot of Alltwyllt incline for any wagons of slates there might be; These were brought down to Abergynolwyn to be coupled to the train. All this was on wages of £2 a week, With no paid holidays – if you were one minute late in the old days you'd be sent home and lose a day's pay– young people today don't know how well off they are– my first paid holiday was in 1952!

After Sir Haydn's death I had a difference of opinion with the management, and being a wild and stubborn man, I walked out. However Edward Thomas wrote asking me to come back; I replied I would only do so for £7 a week. By return of post I had a reply asking me to start as soon as possible. Then it was a race against time to get things going. Matters were bit mixed up to start with, but the railway reopened, thanks to all the enthusiasts who gave us a hand in those early days.

Dai Jones[5]

On 31st December, 1986 Dai retired ending more than one hundred years continuous service to the railway by members of the Jones' family.

However, all is not lost as his son, David Richard Jones has already followed in his father's footsteps but as a volunteer, so the tradition of service by the Jones' family will continue, albeit in a slightly different way.

One of Dai's schoolboy memories of the railway was of the day when No.2 *Dolgoch* became badly derailed at Fach Goch, ending up across the rails facing towards Aberdovey. The driver was Peter Williams and the fireman Dai's father, Hugh Jones. After the quarrymen from Bryn Eglwys had been sent for and had managed to get the engine back on the rails, *Dolgoch* was found to be unable to move under its own power, so Hugh and Dai set off for Pendre and lit up *Talyllyn* which was by then in a very decrepit state. They poured lot of oatmeal into the boiler to try and seal some of the leaks. With Hugh driving and Dai firing they set off up the line to rescue *Dolgoch* and eventually, very late that night, they managed to bring the cripple back to Pendre for repair. This was *Talyllyn's* penultimate trip before major overhaul

---

4. Referred to by James Boyd as Hugh 'Gas'
5. By Roy Smith

not realising that it was only insured for Dai to drive. The local police pounced and both Dai and Herbert had their driving licences suspended for 12 months. This was a great problem as it was a long walk from Rhydyronen to Pendre at 6 o'clock in the morning to light the engine up in time for it to work the morning train. However, the General Manager kindly allowed both Dai and Herbert to take the engine home at night and to keep it under the road bridge at Rhydyronen to light up in the morning and bring down to Pendre ready to work the train. Or perhaps the General Manager realised that this was the only way he could be absolutely certain that an engine and train would be ready at Wharf at the right time!

Dai adds a few word of his own, providing a fascinating insight into how the Talyllyn Railway was run in the last years of Sir Haydn Jones' ownership.[6]

When I was a boy I remember watching the trains go up and down the line from *Plas Coch*. There was quite a lot of slate and goods traffic moved then and Father told me that, in times past, there used to be some trains double headed, but I don't remember seeing any of those. The trains often had a dozen or more slate wagons attached to them. In between the morning and afternoon passenger trains, the engine would often go back up the line again to bring down some more slates. I remember the whole of the Wharf being stacked with slates. On fair days at Easter, there was an early morning train, about 8 o'clock, to bring people down from Abergynolwyn to Towyn for the day and another special about 6 o'clock in the evening to take them back again. There was lots of singing in the chapels in Towyn (the church people went to Aberdovey).

My first job was as a postmen but sometimes I would go on the footplate of the engine with Father, but only on the mineral extension from Abergynolwyn; I had to ride in the train up to there. I remember one run away on the incline above Nant Gwernol. The brakeman at the top dropped some slates down. They knew by experience when there would be a break in the rope. They used to say that the rope would stop for about a minute and, next, it would start again at a fast speed. The brakeman shouted to Father in Welsh: "Look out Hugh, the rope's broken." I was by his side and he just pushed me into the rock. The next minute two wagons came tearing by, hit the bottom and went right over the top of the train and down, down and down until they were all smashed in bits in the

Slate wagons in the river after running away down the Cantybredd incline after a rope break

and Dai says he still cannot understand how they managed to get it to go at all. Apparently, *Talyllyn* was steamed once more in 1947 when Dai was away on national service…

On his leaving school, a job had to be found and Hugh approached Sir Haydn with a view to Dai being employed by the railway as he (Hugh) was by then the only employee working on the engines and the track and it was becoming too great a job for one man. Sir Haydn agreed and offered Dai a job at the wage of £4 per week, which was the same as Hugh's wages in those days. Dai stuck out for £5 and, after a lot of arguing, Sir Haydn eventually agreed. Apparently, it was a while before Hugh realised this and, after he found out, relations were strained for a while.

After the Society took over in 1951, Dai became the regular driver. His best moment was on 25th November, 1982 when he was driver of *Dolgoch* when HRH The Prince of Wales rode with him on the footplate from Pendre to Rhydyronen.

His worst moment on the railway was a day in 1955 when his brother, Herbert, borrowed his scooter to go to Towyn on an urgent errand,

---

6. *These notes are taken from a tape recorded interview Richard Hope also made with Dai. As the interview was really a conversation, the text has been set out as if Dai spoke all of it in the order written but, whilst most of the words are his, some adjustments have been made to make the story easier to read.*

ravine: axles broken and wood and slate scattered all over the river bed. The wagons passed us like bullets out of a gun. It was fantastic!

Very often the rope used to snatch and break near the wagon itself and then a little bit of the rope goes with the wagon into the ravine. We would then have a chap there to hash the rope up and get things going again, rather than buying a brand new rope, which could mean that the rope was just a bit shorter than before. Sir Haydn never wanted to spend any money on a new rope.

I never saw the incident, but Father told me once that he had a difficult job hooking the rope onto the wagons once because the rope was too short on the one side nearest Abergynolwyn after a break and runaway. He shouted to the brakeman that he couldn't get the wagons onto the rope. The brakeman replied: "Oh, can't you try the engine?" So Father did. He went with *Dolgoch* and started going up the incline with the wagons to couple them up to the rope! The back end of the engine got bogged down on the rail at the foot of the incline. The engine always carried a jack in case of derailment and so Father managed to jack the back end of the engine up and, when he had done that, the whole engine then just came back down on its own!

Sir Haydn was always keen on keeping the passenger trains running, but by that time Father was the only employee (apart from Edward Thomas) and had to keep the whole railway going by himself. Sir Haydn didn't come down to the railway very much, but when he did, he always sat in the coach with the compartment in it and traveled all the way up to the first incline in it – just the engine and one coach.

Some passengers liked to come back after the last train in a slate wagon. They would be charged 2/6d for that. Just above Dolgoch station there was a little siding where the rock has been cut away just the other side of the water column. You had to put a ramp over the track to release the wagon from the siding. There were certain wagons – the red wagon was a good one – which ran more freely than others and which had good bearings and brakes. Those were used for the passengers to ride in back down the line by gravity. The wagons would usually come down all the way. You might have to push one sometimes by putting your knee on a buffer and using the other foot to push. The 'red' wagon could run all the way to Pendre gates without stopping, sometimes running down Cynfal bank at 35 mph to get over Fach Goch bank! Then it would always be necessary to put the brakes on before the crossing at Pendre.

When the engine needed some fitting attention but Father did not know what to do about it, he used to go and ask for advice from 'Old Hugh', who by then was working at the Power House in Happy Valley or, if things were bad then a fitter from the Britannia Foundry at Portmadoc would come down to help. Father would strip things down and the fitter would come over for the weekend to fix things, often working well into the evening by candle light and half drunk. The engine had to be ready for Monday. Sometimes the engine would go out without any brakes, sometimes also Van No.5 would be out of service (like when it was awaiting new tyres), so the whole train would be without brakes. It was only possible to stop it on the engine's reversing lever!

Father and I were quite pleased to hear that someone might take the railway over when Sir Haydn died, although we heard that Lady Haydn was not keen on giving the railway to the Society; but we were all in favour as the railway was more than just a job to us, it was our life.

Herbert Jones

I used to travel on the engine with Father in the school holidays, acting as his fireman, and later served in Sir Henry Haydn Jones' ironmongers

Herbert Jones on the 'Old Lady.'
(Photo: Talyllyn Railway Archive)

David and Tom Jones on the footplate of the 'Old Lady,' on the 3rd May, 2015

shop on the High Street as carrier boy, delivering customers' orders on my bicycle at wages of 5/-.

I was on No.2 *Dolgoch* when the last load of slate was brought down from the quarry in 1946 and from then to 1950 trains ran only on Tuesdays and Thursdays; on other days I'd work on Sir Haydn's farm or the TR track. From 1952 until March 1954 I did my National Service with the army coming back to the TR as an employee, for the first time under the TRPS, in 1954, working on the track and firing the engine in the season. In April 1955 I reached my 21st birthday and became a driver. At that time, no one under 21 was permitted to drive.

I lived then with Father and Dai at *Plas Coch*, Rhydyronen and used to travel to Pendre on my motor bike. When the bike wouldn't work, I'd go home on the engine, which would be left under the road bridge for the night in what came to be known as 'Rhydyronen sub-shed'.

In 1959 I married Margaret and moved into 'Railway View', the cottage that was then built onto the end of the engine shed at Pendre and is now part of the shed itself. On several mornings I have been got out of bed by early turn firemen who had forgotten the shed key, and on one morning I was tumbled out of bed by rough shunting 'next door' when an engine thudded into the far side of my bedroom wall.

Working on the engines late into the night at Pendre, Margaret would find herself pressed into

service as my 'labourer' for two-handed jobs.

The face of the railway slowly changed and three train working and volunteer drivers came onto the scene. At the same time I was made locomotive foreman.

Peter Williams and William Jones

The railway also employed Peter Williams and William Jones as hedgers in the early days of the Society. Both had retired and Peter was formerly an engine driver and quarry worker. The Society re-employed them to trim the hedges and brambles which had by then formed almost a green tunnel along the lineside completely blocking the view in places. They worked with handtools: scythes, reaphooks and shears, keeping their edges sharp with a stone they kept in their pockets. One day, Edward's daughter, June, went to Pendre to advise that her father was not well. Dai Jones was working in the pit and it was love at first sight, leading to a daughter Carol and a son David who became a volunteer in his own right and now, in turn, his son, Tom, is starting to volunteer on the railway.

Amazingly, the Talyllyn Railway has had the services of five generations of the Jones' family: Hugh's father, Hugh, Dai and Herbert and now David Jones, Dai's son as a volunteers and, also, his son, Tom, who is as keen as mustard. What a record!

Peter Williams pauses to sharpen
the cutting edge of his scythe whilst
pruning the lineside vegetaton.
(Photo: Talyllyn Railway Archive)

The 'Old Lady'

David Curwen and John Snell largely formed the locomotive department at the beginning of the TRPS. Here are their stories.

Of course, it was only possible to run the Talyllyn Railway at all if one of the original engines would still work and the credit for this success goes to David Curwen, a miniature railway engineer recommended to Tom Rolt by the famous model engineers Bassett Lowke who had converted the Ravenglass & Eskdale narrow gauge railway to a miniature line. He was helped by John Snell, a young teenage student who came along to assist in the workshop at Pendre and run the trains. David Curwen takes up the story of how they became involved and the early trials and tribulations in Pendre works:

I spent most of the war period from 1939 to 1945 working in aircraft manufacture, either for a large firm or in a government department, and I had had my fill of big organisations. One reason why was that during the war I had spent nearly a year employed by Vickers at an aircraft factory near Swindon with hardly anything to do, and I had the offer of a useful job with Dowtys nearby. But Vickers would not release me, because they had a cost-plus contract to build Spitfires and if they did, they would lose their ten percent of what I was paid. I could not wait to get back to what I had been doing before the war, working for a small engineering firm in a rural area, tackling whatever jobs came up. In partnership with one Richard Ripley, in 1946 I found myself part of such a firm located near Swindon, employing three or four fitters or handymen. One morning a Mr. Baker came to see us. He was an ex naval officer, who had not wanted to go back to the family furniture-removal firm, and therefore had set up a 10 1/4" inch gauge miniature railway at the Hillsea Lido near Portsmouth. He had hired a locomotive which was giving a lot of trouble and was not man enough for the job. Could I build him one?

"Certainly" was the only possible answer: and I started on the design after he left. I had recently spent a day as the guest of Sir John Samuel on his 7 1/4" inch gauge Greywood Central Railway (the ancestor of what is now the 'Great Cockcrow Railway near Chertsey), and one thing had

> The only person they knew of who could undertake such a task was myself

impressed me most. There was a beautiful scale model GWR 2-6-0, which was pretty hard work to manage with much of a load over any distance, while a free-lance wide-firebox machine about the same size was a doddle, and with much bigger firebox and cylinders and bearing surfaces would be a much better commercial proposition. It had been built by "Curly" Lawrence, who as L.B.S.C. wrote in every issue of the *Model Engineer*, and what he said made sense to me. My view was that as the proposed loco was to be used to earn a chap a living, all working parts and bearings must be enlarged as much as possible for long wear, and any boiler must have a wide firebox as it was much easier to manage. A long narrow firebox between the frames was too difficult. Again, the cylinders should be larger than scale so that even if pressure fell, you still had enough power to get home and take another load. I also decided to beef up the driving wheels.

So I took Curly's version of an L.N.E.R. A2 Pacific as an example and scaled it up with additional modifications. Curly had substituted Baker valve gear for the original Walschaerts, since the former was much simpler to make and maintain. One advantage of the A2 was that the rearward placing of the cylinders allowed the leading bogie plenty of room to move out on curves. We built two of these, and ran the other one ourselves on a line we built at Weymouth. There followed five 'Atlantics,' again of 10 1/4" inch gauge; only slightly shorter than the Pacifics but with fewer wheels, and man enough for most miniature railway work. Before and after my time with the Talyllyn, I built over fifty miniature locos of various designs, nearly all steam but including three or four diesels, and all but one of them still exist at the time of writing.

All these doings on the 10 1/4" inch gauge attracted some attention, and meanwhile L.T.C. Rolt, who I did not then know, was considering what might be done to perpetuate the Talyllyn Railway, which was one of the few minor lines which had not been nationalised at the beginning of 1948. Tom Rolt believed that it was important to try to keep the railway going as a memorial to the days of private ownership, though it was in such a shocking state of decrepitude that it might well be impossible to continue with the existing equipment. He therefore started by exploring the possibility of converting it to a miniature railway,

David and Barbara Curwen set up office at Dolgoch in 1951

as had been done with the Ravenglass & Eskdale mainly by the well-known firm of model engineers Bassett-Lowke Ltd. When Tom consulted them, they told him that the only person they knew of who could undertake such a task was myself.

So one morning in 1949 Tom Rolt came to see me. Would I go with him to take a good look at the railway, and give some initial estimate of the likely cost of such a conversion? "Of course" was the only possible answer. So in due course off we went, in Tom's duck-back 1922 Alvis; warm clothes and plenty of rugs, as it was mid-winter. Down from the mountains, the Alvis roared past the Tyn y Cornel Hotel at the end of Tal-y-llyn Lake, Tom shouting "This is where we will be staying, but we must go down to Towyn to check whether the train will be running tomorrow". It was getting dark; after winding down the valley road we found the Wharf office closed, and on going to the other end of town to find the engine shed, we found two men who said; "No trains tomorrow, definitely no trains tomorrow". They were working by candles and a hurricane oil lamp, struggling with the rear frames and springs of old *Dolgoch* – a fractured frame or something was getting a bodge-repair. How they

> "Of course" was the only possible answer

ever managed to tackle that kind of work I could not imagine: no welding gear, no electric drills, just hand tools.

Back to the Tyn y Cornel, then pretty basic. Captain Hunter after the war had married the farmer's daughter and was in the process of doing it all up. It had been a fisherman's pub, there were outlines of huge trout once caught carved into the slate doorstep and floor. Rumour had it that it had been a very good trout lake but had been spoilt. Captain Hunter when he took over had stopped the locals fishing for free. No doubt that was necessary, but you have to be very diplomatic with locals, who do not like newcomers telling them what to do. So they had practically cleared the lake of all fish, using otterboards by night.

The Tyn y Cornel was still very much a farmhouse-pub; no mod-cons in the bedrooms, a basin and a jug of hot water left outside the room in the morning. I had fortunately brought a hot water bottle. Downstairs there were hams hanging on hooks in the ceiling, but the food was good. One evening we observed part of the routine of the 'dry' Welsh Sunday. A knock on the door, Captain Hunter opened it a crack, a very Welsh voice said

"Oh Captain Hunter can I have a glass of beer please." "I am sorry but no, it's Sunday". "Oh Captain Hunter, Jones the Police said you would give me one". He got his pint.

The following day we spent looking over the railway, walking the length of the track. It was in the last stages of dereliction, with rails badly worn and many rail joints without fishplates but with rail ends both held in a cast iron chair with a wooden key. But many keys were missing and many rail ends close to dropping out of the chair. Locomotives and coaches were not much better, though clean.

It seemed to me that the proposed conversion to a miniature railway was possible, but much better to 15 inch gauge than 10 1/4" inch because of the length of the line, six and a half miles, and the greater protection of the passengers from the weather in the larger vehicles. I recommended this, and gave some preliminary estimates. After this visit and a mass of deliberations there were several meetings with Tom and the others involved, chiefly Bill Trinder and Jim Russell, both living in Banbury where Tom was also based, then living on his converted narrow boat *Cressy*.

During this period I married Barbara Willans. Shortly before the day, Tom telephoned to say "I hear you are going to marry my cousin Barbara." It's a small world! I had previously done various jobs for Barbara's father Kyrle Willans, connected with early crop-spraying experiments. He had converted *Cressy* well before the war from a working boat to a house boat, originally with a steam engine, which Tom had often manned on exploratory cruises. Barbara's mother Hero Willans was expert at making wonderful stews on top of the vertical boiler. Now I became one of the Cressy team too, and I remember one weekend spent on the boat at Pont Cysyllte, when we sailed across Telford's great aqueduct. I can't manage heights and this experience gave me the heebie-jeebies. Kyrle Willans had been a very versatile consulting engineer, best known perhaps for his high-speed steam engines used in many early municipal electricity supply installations.

Then in mid-1950 Sir Haydn died, and soon there was another phone call from Tom. He said that it had been decided that it was best to drop the idea of converting the railway to 15 inch gauge and instead to retain the original equipment, for its historical importance. I was a little disappointed not to be building a couple of 15 inch gauge locos and all the other bits and pieces, but I had to agree that from every point of view retaining the relics had a lot to be said for it. Tom then asked whether I would go up to Towyn as the railway's engineer, to keep the wheels turning while he dealt with the managerial side of things at Wharf. I agreed. Maybe I've always been a sucker, but the task was quite a challenge.

David Curwen drives his Lea-Francis car down the platform track at Pendre in 1951.
(Photo: John Snell)

So in mid-March 1951 I got a good tool kit together, as much as my little 1930 Morris, a very narrow open-top two-seater, could take. It had cost £100 new. Quite a lot of money then. Kyrle Willans had been Managing Director of the locomotive builders Kerr Stewart in the early 1920s and his salary then was £250 p.a. plus 5% of profits, and for that much you could live in a nice substantial house in the country. Nothing like that was available at Towyn. Tom had found accommodation for me in a cottage at Bryncrug, on the main road a couple of miles outside Towyn. The Welsh lady who lived there cooked very well for us. Among the cottage's original features was a wonderful outside loo, situated over a stream so you could see the little fishes.

At that time the main building at Pendre station contained the engine shed, with a single line just long enough for the two locos and a rather leaky wooden water tank; the original supply had been taken from the stream crossing under the railway just the other side of the road, piped to a sump under the shed, then a pump taking steam from a locomotive forced it up to the tank. But for many years water had come from the town supply, though the only tap was on the wall at shoulder height. So a hose was attached to the tap and somebody had to remember to turn it on and off to avoid either flooding or delay to trains through lack of water. The only means of washing was to fill a basin with water (hot or cold) from

the engine. A door led through the interior wall to the workshop, under the same roof but more than twice the size of the shed. The east end of the building held the house occupied by the engine driver and family. There was no electricity supply anywhere until 1952.

The workshop still contained the remains of a set of machine tools driven by line shafting and belts, powered by an old Tangye open crank paraffin engine. It all looked very tired and I thought I had better not waste my time on it. But the lathe was unique, the bed two flatbottom rails turned upside down, headstock, tailstock, and toolholder all home made. It showed how clever the old fitters were, they must have managed some heavy jobs with it. There was a good forge and some blacksmith's tools; the forge was hand-blown with a hefty bellows. But for some years little use had been made of it except boiling a kettle to make tea. The railway's only other locomotive, *Talyllyn*, was waiting patiently over a pit, and for years it been regarded as the Next Big Job. The pit trapped any exploring hedgehogs but was no danger to the hens who scratched around the dirt floor for crumbs. There had been an interruption about 1948 when the brake van's wheels needed (and exceptionally received) new tyres; otherwise the hens provided the main activity. There was also a large hand-powered screwcutting machine with a set of dies. Tom Rolt mentioned this item in his book *Railway Adventure* saying that no amount

Inside Pendre workshop with the Corris van and the TR 'original train' in the adjoining carriage shed, October 1952. (Photo: John Snell)

Talyllyn rests in endre shed after her day's work in the railway's 150th year, 2015

of ingenuity could induce it to cut a thread, but actually I made some use of it. The difficulty was simply mounting the dies correctly. There were four dies for each diameter of rod, each lettered for a particular slot in the rotating head, and years of disuse made the letters and the diameters very hard to read without a first careful cleaning, and of course the dies contained in a large wooden case had all been jumbled up.

Sir Haydn did from time to time get a written report on the condition of the engines and boilers from some qualified professional, and many years later one was found among his papers, including a damning report on the general state of *Talyllyn* in 1945, which soon led to the suspension of passenger trains and the very rare operation of freights until *Dolgoch* returned from overhaul at Shrewsbury in 1946. There was no evidence of any actual insurance. Sir Haydn said "We are always

very careful" – and beyond that, his refusals of claims were delivered in such an oracular but decisive manner nobody dared to take things further. But Tom and the new management knew that this would have to change, so my first job was to get the boiler of the one workable locomotive insured. *Talyllyn*, to my mind a better engine, was too far gone to contemplate. The enginemen who had worked under the old regime said that it could only be used in an emergency, as it had been in 1947 but not since. My view was that it should never be used at all. Several stays had failed in the firebox, and part of the sidesheet had become a sort of cone. At its point they managed to tap a standard waterpipe thread and screw in a standard bung. Oh dear.

But we were even shorter of money than Sir Haydn, and economy was very necessary to get things running at all. So to *Dolgoch*. Start with

Douglas sits in the engine shed awaiting the cleaners tomorrow

stripping off the boiler lagging and the top of the cab, give it a hydraulic pressure test, and start to deal with any problems. It did not seem too bad, so I got in touch with the Fairbourne Railway's insurance company, on the suggestion of John Wilkins, and they arranged for their boiler inspector to make the first visit any insurance company had made for some time. At this point in early April, John Snell arrived as my assistant. He had just left school, having had his nineteenth birthday a few days before the end of term, thus achieving the status of being Bryanston's Oldest Inhabitant. But he was a dedicated railway enthusiast, and having been born in Fiji was well aware of the narrow gauge variety. It was a good thing to have a willing helper in workshop like Pendre, even if inexperienced; the risks of accident if working alone were considerable. So we got on a bit faster.

John Snell introduces himself:

The 1951 the *Railway Magazine* printed news of the Talyllyn Railway Preservation Society's formation and appeal for support. This came at exactly the right time for me: I was due to leave Bryanston school finally on 3rd April and had nearly six months to fill before going up to Oxford. I was under some pressure to become a temporary junior master at a prep school near Tavistock, but I had had enough of school life: I knew the Talyllyn from an earlier visit. I wrote off to L.T.C. Rolt in Banbury as instructed, and offered my services - just like that. I showed my solicitor-guardian the favourable reply, together with an assurance on the respectability of the venture from J.I.C. Boyd, who was an old Bryanstonian and therefore acceptably respectable himself. So I was given permission to go to Talyllyn, not Tavistock – provided I could earn my keep. Thus on 9th April I took the train to Towyn, where I was met by David Curwen and stayed in his temporary lodgings at Bryncrug, a couple of miles outside Towyn. I helped David with getting *Dolgoch* through its boiler inspection, and carrying out some essential heavy repair work on its frames – in spite of being entirely untrained I must have made myself sufficiently useful to be conditionally offered a job on the railway that summer when I met Tom Rolt and Pat Whitehouse for the first time on 21st April. I stayed on as an unpaid assistant until after the reopening to Rhydyronen for Whit Monday on 14th May

David continues:

Any boiler insurance depends on regular, usually annual, inspections; and the hydraulic test is an essential element. The boiler is completely filled with water which is then pumped up to a pressure 50% higher than the normal maximum, which gives a reasonable margin of safety. Since water is incompressible, if anything breaks you simply get a leak and not the explosion which would probably result with steam. When the inspector arrived, it was therefore John's job to work away at the stirrup pump to keep the pressure gauge reading 150 psi, while I followed the inspector. There was quite a cascade coming out of the firebox from leaking tube ends, which kept John busier than he liked, but he just managed to keep the needle on the line as we looked all round, and ultimately the inspector said "well, that will take up under steam" and I happily agreed with him. In those days the typical boiler inspector was an elderly chap with a lot of experience who knew what he was doing. Provided you treated him straight and never tried to hide anything you were doubtful about, he would be very helpful.

When the pressure tests had been done, the inspector pointed to a spot in the lower part of the boiler barrel near the firebox, and asked me to drill a small hole there to that he could check the thickness of the metal, which had originally been 3/8ths of an inch. I did as he asked, and the thickness at that place proved to be 5/16ths. So he passed *Dolgoch* as fit to work at 100 psi, and we were in business. At this point let us jump forward a few years. *Dolgoch* worked reasonably happily for the three years 1951-3, and then its turn for a full overhaul came round. I heard that it would be getting a new boiler, which surprised me, so I rang Tom Rolt to ask about it. "Oh, haven't you heard?" Tom replied. "We found the smokebox tubeplate was leaking and it seemed it should be replaced, so we took the boiler off and sent it to Hunslets who had agreed to do it for us. One day I got a telephone call from them asking me to go up and have a look, as they had found more troubles.

> Perhaps fortune favours the brave

John Snell adds some detail

Dolgoch was steamed for the first time under the Society's auspices in the middle of April, 1951. She was faced with a good day's work – two Corris locomotives, which had been standing in the open at Wharf for some weeks just as they had been unloaded, had to be brought up and put under cover at Pendre. There were some twelve wagon loads of coal to bring up too. This was carried in slate wagons as the Corris rolling stock had not arrived, apart from the van. It was some time since the 'Old Lady' had had such a load on the 1 in 60 out of the station and we blasted up in fine style. No.3 was coupled up behind us and followed smoothly at first. No.4, as she came up the hill, suddenly blew out the plugs which were keeping the rainwater out of the valve chests (some souvenir hunter having bagged the displacement lubricators as she lay at Machynlleth) and started to make popping noises like a GWR cross head pump as she compressed the air in her cylinders. Her valves were obviously all right.

Corris Nos 3 and 4 stand at Pendre after *Dolgoch* has brought them up from Wharf. Four engines on shed at the same time for the first time. *(Photo: Bill Faulkner)*

Dolgoch under repair in Pendre works

So I went and found that the bottom of the barrel was corrugated by corrosion, and in the thin parts very thin indeed. We found your plugged check hole and it was just as you had said, in material 5/16ths thick: but a few inches away the barrel was only thick as a card." So, perhaps fortune favours the brave.

The next task was to investigate the trouble with the rear frames and springs which Tom and I had observed two years earlier. Whatever the problem, it had obviously got worse as we were told that after each day's work another day had to be spent on bodging things together again. So, once the boiler lagging and the upper part of the cab was back on, jack up the rear of the engine, remove the springs and have a look. The trouble dated back to 1949, when due to failure of the rear springs the frames had been broken above the rear axle on both sides by repeated impacts of the axleboxes due to the rough track. Much of that season's operation had therefore been lost while the broken frames were welded together again, but no other work done.

There were a pair of volute springs on each side, each mounted on a vertical shaft about one inch diameter, which changed at the lower end to a flat pad about 6 x 3 inches, which in turn was bolted to the frames by what had been a pair of fitted bolts

> It was then impossible to resist the temptation to go up the line,

about 3/4inch diameter. The springs were held in position on the shafts by a heavy washer and a pair of nuts. The fitted bolts were really somewhat undersized for the hammering they got, and had been worn down so that scarcely any thread was left. No wonder that the assembly was falling to bits after a day's work, and had to be dismantled. A further complication was that the central part of the footplate was held in position by the four vertical shafts, so that had to be taken out and replaced daily as well.

In principle a workmanlike repair was simple: just drill out the holes taking the eight fitted bolts and drill and tap eight new ones, preferably something more than one inch diameter. The difficulty was that there was no electricity so no powered tools could be used. An old fashioned ratchet drill held in a clamp was the only thing that would do the job, and that would be at least a week's damned hard work, especially as I would have to stand in the small space left by the removal of the area of footplate already mentioned. There was nothing much John could do to help except wipe away sweat and bring hot drinks. Tom Rolt, who had been away since before John arrived, came to have a look, sympathised, and cleared off down to the office at Wharf to tackle, as General Manager, a somewhat similar job with the mountains of paper and oddments accumulated there.

All things eventually come to an end, and finally the day arrived when all was ready to raise steam for the first time. With John as fireman and myself as driver, we carefully steamed off down to the Wharf, where the first task was to collect the two Corris locomotives, delivered by B.R. some weeks earlier, and bring them both up to Pendre. John had been commissioned by Pat Whitehouse, the Secretary of the Talyllyn Railway Preservation Society, which was now responsible for its operation, to film this happening for the 16mm silent film which Pat was making to promote the railway, and so the actual collection of the two engines was successfully recorded. Everything else went well, including

> **This time it was a case of fortune favours the foolish**

the insertion of the two new arrivals up the back siding into the repair shop at Pendre, where the track barely existed any more, and all was done by midday. No.3 suffered its first TR derailment during the shunting.

When we visited Machynlleth yard to view the two Corris engine after purchase, our first glimpse of the two engines in the searching sunlight of that March morning was not encouraging. They stood head to tail on the short length of track in the station yard which was all that now remained of the Corris Railway. They had been covered with old wagon sheets, but, as rust and broken spectacle and gauge glasses showed, these had not adequately protected them either from the weather or from those inevitable hooligans who can never see

The 'Old Lady' being prepared in Pendre shed in Haydn Jones days

**Bill Oliver and
John Snell chat
about the weather
at Easter, 1952 (So
says the caption
on the back of the
print).** *(Photo: John
Snell)*

a piece of glass without smashing it. But these first impressions were superficial and a closer examination revealed that the engines were not in such bad condition as we had been led to suppose.

It was then impossible to resist the temptation to go up the line, keeping a lookout for the platelayers who would not be expecting us. Work had started some weeks earlier with the assistance of the foreman and two men lent to us by the owner of the Fairbourne Railway, John Wilkins, and they had replaced nearly half a mile of track approaching Rhydyronen with rail and sleepers salvaged from the Corris Railway and still in the yard of the contractor, Williams of Harlech. Since the Corris was such a curvy railway not many of its rails were re-usable: most of the straight ones came from the upper section between Corris and Aberllefenni. So off we went, *Dolgoch* and the Corris van, road learning at its most basic. We got past the platelayers, who were just finishing off the relaid length, and continued: we got to

> The 'Old Lady' did one puff forward and then a hefty puff back with a terrific bang into the carriages, with much wailing and gnashing of teeth from small unnerved children

the flooded cutting above Brynglas which John had rechristened 'Tadpole Cutting' because on an exploratory walk up the line he had discovered thousands of them wriggling in it. We passed over the viaduct, but when we got to Dolgoch station we found to our dismay that the water tank, which on every previous visit we had seen to be full and overflowing, was empty.

Another crisis! There was very little water left in *Dolgoch's* tank. We must get back to Pendre without delay, so off we went backwards, pushing the Corris van rather riskily but what else could we do? Although we needed little steam on the downhill run, we did need some. As the water level fell in the gauge glass I let the fire die down, and it was effectively out and the pressure had fallen to less than 10 psi before we reached Pendre, where we stuck on the level crossing. But I had managed to avoid dropping the plug, so that was lucky. We barred the engine clear of the road and the gates, and it spent the night in the station platform. This time it was a case of fortune favours the foolish.

On our visit in 1949 Tom and I had been invited to ride on *Dolgoch* up the line beyond Abergynolwyn station, to the first incline leading up to the quarries. On the left there was a good drop through the trees into the gorge below, and if you rode on that side you could see how close to the edge the rails were, and glimpse the remains of mangled wagons in the stream. Officially the quarrymen were not supposed to ride up and down the inclines, but rules are made to be broken and we were told of one chap who ended up, luckily, in the top branches of a tree.

But what I had seen of the track during this run was instructive. We knew it was in a bad state, but now I saw it was terrible. The rails were an early steel flat-bottomed section, 21 feet long and originally weighing about 40 pounds per yard. They were partly held in cast iron chairs with a wooden key, one or two along the length of the rail and the rail ends held in a somewhat wider special joint chair, without fishplates. The sleepers were mostly rotten, often to the point of disintegration. Fortunately the ballast came up to rail level, and the strong grassy turf helped to hold the rails to gauge, more or less. At some time in the past it had been policy to replace the joint chairs with fishplates, which involved drilling holes for the fishbolts, so it was a steady job for two men for some years and never completed. At the Towyn end of the line few joint chairs remained, but as you went eastwards the proportion of joints still held in chairs steadily rose until above Dolgoch there were hardly any fishplates. On fishplated lengths, it was a common sight to see the far end of each rail rising up out of the grass as the leading wheels of the engine trod on the near end; then after shaking about a little the rail would subside back into its habitual slot in the turf. It was not very reassuring.

One little incident remains in my mind. The train was always due back past the shed at six o'clock; at 6.15 pm it was time to start worrying and if another look produced disconsolate figures trudging down the track, it was time to put some tools in a bag and keep out of sight until the Alvis roared up.

This time it was Brynglas. The train was fairly full, but on opening the regulator the 'Old Lady' did one puff forward and then a hefty puff back with a terrific bang into the carriages, with much wailing and gnashing of teeth from small unnerved children.

I had a look underneath and this resulted in a very unnerved me, for the left hand eccentric was jammed. With Tom's help somehow we managed to unbolt it and wire it up (it's wonderful what you can do with a bit of fencing wire), so that we could limp back, but lying across a rail between the two

wheels of a loco in steam is not my idea of a joke. You have to become very unimaginative for a time, rather akin to defusing a bomb.

However, having got *Dolgoch* going, my problem was to decide which engine to work on next. There was really only one choice. *Talyllyn* was much too far gone to contemplate. Of the two Corris engines, No.3 the older, which we called 'the Falcon' because it had been built at the Falcon Works in Loughborough in 1878, had been working right up to the day in 1948 when flood damage caused that railway to close. It had been looked after by the staff at Machynlleth and ought to be a runner, only needing to have the boiler inspected and insured. The newer one, the Kerr Stuart, looked not too bad mechanically, but its firebox had been condemned by the G.W.R in 1947 and that would take time and money. So John and I set about removing cab, saddletank, and boiler lagging from the Falcon. John had discovered that its wheel treads were narrower than the Kerr Stuart's, but we tried not to think about the possible implications of that.

> **By evening the rails shone more brightly than for very many years**

The insulation between the boiler itself and the steel sheets on *Dolgoch* had been many strips of well-baked wood, the two Corris engines had what the G.W.R. always used, namely asbestos plaster. In fact, the variety of blue asbestos known as crociodilite, now revealed by modern science to be the deadliest cancer-inducing asbestos of all. John and I set about breaking it up into small pieces and piling it into a wooden washtub for re-use. This process produced clouds of fine dust which I did not like, so I decided we would soak the stuff in water first, which stopped the dust and may have done some good. We realised we would need some more asbestos to re-plaster the boiler when the job was finished, so I went down to Daniel's, the ironmonger in the High Street owned by Sir Haydn, and where he used to keep the railway's supply of new dogspikes in a sack under his desk, and ordered half a hundredweight of the stuff. In due course John took the wheelbarrow down to Daniel's and brought the paper sack of crociodilite back to Pendre; anybody doing the same thing now would cause an unimaginable scandal.

On Whit Monday, 14th May, the railway ran its first public trains, though only as far as Rhydyronen to allow work to continue on track repairs further up the line. Since there was only one short siding at Rhydyronen, which had not been used for years, that meant putting *Dolgoch* into the siding very carefully, and getting passengers and volunteers to push the train past so that the engine could lead on the way back. Fortunately there were plenty of them. I drove and John fired.

Tom Rolt in his element with his Alvis after driving David Curwen and John Snell up the mountain track to Bryn Eglwys Quarry one evening. *(Photo: John Snell)*

John Snell

John Snell takes up the tale: From that time until Whitsun *Dolgoch* made only one or two more trips with track materials and we carried out a number of repairs which had been seen to be necessary. A new smokebox door was forged out of a spare wagon floorplate, and a great deal of work was done on the rear springs. The eight bolts which transmitted the load from the frames had, with the poundings from the track, stripped their threads and had needed resecuring practically every other day during 1950. Eight one inch holes had to be drilled through the frames and strengthening plates with an old ratchet hand drill and larger bolts fitted. When this work was finished Hugh Jones said that she went better than at any time since the last overhaul in 1946.

On the Saturday before Whit special trains ran right through to Abergynolwyn, and on the Monday, as history records, the line ceremonially opened as far as Rhydyronen. Five tips were made during the day, and by evening the rails shone more brightly than for very many years.

But on the footplate we had time to see (and feel) five very bad rail joints between Pendre and Rhydyronen, which we went over each time with a shattering concussion which left us in no doubt why the springs had suffered. The worst of all was cunningly sited just at the bottom of Cynfal bank. I had the bright idea of bringing slate out to mark these places for the track gang, but although this gave me some satisfaction it didn't prove much to the platelayers, as I never managed to jettison the slate by the actual joint.

I left for two or three weeks of various interviews to make arrangements for starting at Oxford at the beginning of the autumn term. I would be able to work on the railway for almost all of the coming operating season. Since I had seemed useful as a volunteer I was offered £5 a week to enable me to stay on for that time, as David's assistant to start with. So I became a temporary employee, and no longer a volunteer. But I would be able to eat.

This time it was arranged that I should stay with David Curwen, his wife Barbara, and Tom Rolt at the Dolgoch Hotel, commuting to Towyn either in Tom's Alvis or David's Lea-Francis. The next four months were a major formative experience for me.

The railway then was not what it is now. To

> **It was more important to make an individual contribution, even to stand if we could on the shoulders of giants**

start with, it was in a state of near collapse, and we were intending to run ten trips per week, Monday to Friday only, leaving weekends clear to deal with problems and maybe get some time off. In 1951 trains ran on only three days a week, six return trips in all, and more weeks than not they experienced some now reportable mishap. Working full-time in 1951 were the three of us from Dolgoch, plus Hugh and Dai Jones, father and son, who had been the only employees of the railway during 1950. In addition were Bill Oliver, a Birmingham man who had married a local girl and had been the Kleen-eze brush traveller in the district, plus Bill Maguire who had been a senior police officer in India before independence. To this base of seven paid staff were added volunteer helpers from time to time, sometimes one or none, sometimes several, often very useful, including John Bate who later joined the railway as its Chief Engineer for over forty years, continuing after retirement. But in 1951 such success was by no means guaranteed.

No telephones existed anywhere on the railway: in an up-line emergency someone had to cadge a lift, or find a phone box to ring Daniels – the ironmongers in town which had been owned by Sir Haydn - who would send a runner to the Wharf office. For long stretches the very far end of every rail would rise up out of the turf as the front wheels of the loco trod on the near end, then would quiver and settle back in the same groove (or nearly). We were pretty well stretched.

Life at Dolgoch made all the difference to the three of us. Every evening and some time at least at weekends we could unwind and talk of other things, or explore the area, and in addition there were some interesting visitors from Tom's previous lives. Tom by then had made a name for himself with his canal books, starting with *Narrow Boat*, the most interesting of these visitors came from his pre-war involvement in the Vintage Sports Car Club and the Phoenix Green Garage at Hartley Wintney, near Basingstoke. Subjects discussed of course included every aspect of engineering but ranged much wider, including political ideas, the errors and misadventures of committees and ministries and much else. One visitor I remember in particular, John Morley, who turned up at Abergynolwyn in a large open topped Packard and greeted Tom with the news "Connie Lambert's dead." Even I knew of Constant Lambert as a composer and writer, but he had been a V.S.C.C. character as well: the next day's papers included his obituary. John Morley

The view overlooking the Manager's house and the aqueduct at Bryn Eglwys quarry in July, 1951 before the vandals or the scrap men arrived. *(Photo: John Snell)*

The remains of the Cantrybedd incline winding house

stayed for a week or two, and I must say that riding in a car like his over the dramatic Mawddwy Pass for the first time added quite a lot to the experience. Especially as the Merioneth County Council still operated a fleet of steamrollers, and four or five were working that day on improving the lower stretches of that road.

I think I managed to hold my own in most of those discussions, mainly by listening and not saying very much. But it was a great education. If it is possible to sum up what that education taught me, which school could never have taught, it was that although the questions asked by politics and philosophy are vital, most argument is a pointless clash of mirror-image opinions, Tweedledum versus Tweedledee. It was more important to make an individual contribution, even to stand if we could on the shoulders of giants.

Fortunately, not every weekend was spent tidying up after some crisis at Pendre or elsewhere. One weekend Tom's mother, then in her sixties, came to stay at Dolgoch and we resolved to climb Cader Idris from the Idris Estate entrance above Talyllyn Lake. Tom and his mother shot on ahead and in due course got to the top. David and I took things a bit more gently, and when we had got as far as Llyn Cae, well on the way but only about a thousand feet up instead of three, we decided we had all the exercise we needed and turned back. I photographed the lake to prove we got that far. We were content to get a verbal account of the view from the summit.

Another Saturday we decided to explore Bryn Eglwys quarry, but by car, taking Tom's two-seater Alvis (there was a third seat under the trapdoor in the duck's arse rear end). Since the road was steeper than 1 in 3 and loose gravel, and the Alvis only had rear wheel brakes, this was perhaps a bit hazardous, but not so bad on a dry day. Anyhow, to get to the main level of the quarry the railway climbs up three inclines from the present terminus, or four above Abergynolwyn village, each rising 300 feet or so on grades varying between 1 in 2 and 1 in 1, with horse traction on the levels between. The lower of the two inclines were on the west side of the valley, but the road, starting from Abergynolwyn village, was on the east side. The road did most of its climbing in the first half mile, so David and I got out at the bottom and watched Tom charge the hill (and the bends). But the steady rasp of the Alvis exhaust did not end in any untoward noises, and Tom waited at the top while David and I climbed the hard way. From there on we rode in style. The third incline brought the railway to the east side of the valley, and for the last few hundred yards the rails lay in the middle of the road. Tom turned the car round on the level space in front of the manager's house, and I took some photos to prove we got there, with the aqueduct feeding the air compressor shed in the background.

In 1951 neither the scrap men nor the vandals had yet got to Bryn Eglwys Quarry, and everything was just as it had been left on the last day. No broken windows, no collapsed roofs: all the blacksmith's tools still lying by his hearth, chairs and table still there, some doors swinging in the wind but nothing locked. The so-called manager's house intact, but a large kitchen range in every downstairs room so it was probably the dormitory for the men who lived up there from Monday to Friday. In the small workshop near the smithy stood the only all-steel slate wagon I ever saw on the Talyllyn: just like the thousand or so on the Festiniog, but why was it there? The scrappers got it, like everything else, months later.

There were several inclines rising above that level, but none of them lead to workings with significant waste heaps, so none successful. Very obvious were the jagged ruins of the last workings in the Narrow Vein, which had collapsed after the last day's work (and been more thoroughly blown up on government instructions soon after). The history of the place was laid out before us.

We then had to get down again. The nervous part was of course the steep final length into the village. Neither David nor I much relished the

Gareth Jones cleans *Dolgoch's* headlamp at Pendre, Easter 1952. *(Photo: John Snell)*

Sir Haydn on its
first ever run on
the TR at Dolgoch.
Tom Rolt and
David Curwen are
chatting whilst the
engine is taking
water on 21st July,
1951. *(Photo: John
Snell)*

idea of riding in the car for that, but we saw the point of doing what we could to help the brakes by standing on the rear wheel springs, one of us on each side, to add weight to the adhesion of the rear wheels but so we could leap clear if things got out of hand. Tom took it very gently, and they did not, so that adventure ended well.

Tom's personal life was changing in 1951 as radically as his professional life, because he was going through the process of divorcing Angela before marrying Sonia. In those days the law insisted on a waiting period before a divorce was confirmed, during which time any evidence of contact with Another Woman was liable to send the whole process back to the starting point (except for the accumulated bills). So we never saw Sonia in 1951. The main changes during the 1952 season therefore were that Tom and Sonia lived in a rented house at Dolgoch, and Sonia helped Tom with the office work allowing him time to deal with the still frequent emergences it Pendre.

David Curwen had returned to his engineering business in the west of England, and I had only three months available instead of six. But we now had two locomotives, so it was proposed to run not ten but seventeen trips a week during the peak. Bill

Oliver and a lad from Manchester, Geoff Hayes, made up the first engine crew, while I and Gareth Jones made a second crew for the peak. Otherwise not a lot had changed. While it was too soon to say that the railway was no longer in danger of collapsing through lack of maintenance, much had been done and things were certainly improving. And there were telephones! Only the Wharf had an instrument on the main national network, but there was now a private line connecting wharf with Pendre by a wire mainly strung along the lineside bushes. Since the BBC had a local transmitter near Towyn promenade roughly in-line with that part of the railway, that telephone received the Welsh Home Service quite well, you had speak up to be heard on top of it, but it was a blessing even so.

I now lodged in Towyn, eventually with Gareth's parents, so the camaraderie of Dolgoch in 1951 had ended and I saw much less of Tom in 1952. But the foundations of a lifelong friendship had been laid. Eventually I traded on that by showing Tom the typescript of my first book, *Jennie*, and with his encouragement managed to get it published. After that, both Tom and Pat Whitehouse put various writing jobs my way and I was able to build up a certain amount of published work – much smaller in volume and variety than Tom's own output, which greatly exceeds mine, particularly with his classic engineers' biographies. I remember sitting in a train from Singapore to Kuala Lumpur with the man in seat opposite reading *Red for Danger*. No comment!

Meanwhile David continued work on No.3, which now had a name for the first time, *Sir Haydn*. He got some help from occasional enthusiast volunteers curious to discover what was going on. Tom decided that Hugh Jones, who had been the only driver employed for several years, would be better employed as foreman of the track gang, which consisted of Oliver and Maguire, since Hugh knew more than anybody about the permanent way, and that his son Dai should be driver, having learnt that job under the old regime, with myself as fireman. This arrangement did not suit Hugh, who simply ordered me to join the gang on the first Monday of the main season, and resumed his position as driver. Tom on finding out what had happened firmly enforced his ruling, which was obviously best for the railway, and from the Tuesday on the new arrangements applied. But this did not suit Hugh Jones, and after a week or two he simply walked off the job. Perhaps he thought the railway would collapse, but it did not. Dai, always the most level-headed of the family, remained for another month or so until his father's pressure forced him to resign as well. That meant that I became the railway's only driver (aged 19) for the rest of the 1951 season.

We then had to employ a new fireman, recruited from among the local youngsters several of whom seemed interested. The first proved useless, perhaps because his mother complained that he got so dirty handling coal. The second was Gareth Jones, then the butcher's delivery boy riding round town on a bicycle with parcels of meat in the front basket, arranging his movements in such a way that whenever the train passed through the town he would be watching it somewhere over or through the fence. That made him an obvious next choice. He was a big strong lad and proved an immediate success – a natural steam railwayman if ever there was one. Tom never asked his age, and was surprised later to find he was barely thirteen.

So the Talyllyn in 1951 probably had the only teenaged loco crew in the British Isles working scheduled passenger trains. Unimaginable now of course. When he was old enough, Gareth joined British Railways locomotive staff at Machynlleth, and made a career of it, continuing with steam on the main line before and after retirement as one of the small national panel of steam locomotive inspectors.

David Curwen by now had been joined by his wife Barbara, and together with Tom Rolt they were living as boarders in the small hotel at Dolgoch, and I joined them there. David had acquired a rather better second-hand car, a Lea-Francis. Most days we travelled to and from Towyn with me in the jockey seat at the duck's arse end of Tom's Alvis while David occupied the one passenger seat. The locals got used to hearing us coming several miles away.

In his book *Railway Adventure* Tom gives a good account of what it was like to operate this terribly run-down railway at the very start of its revival. Things were continuing to fall apart all the time, but we did manage to stay on the rails to start with. This began to change after *Sir Haydn* was reassembled and steamed for the first time on 18th July, its boiler having been passed by the Inspector to work at reduced pressure because of the age of the tubes. Its first tentative movements were confined to the first couple of miles of the line, which had by then had rather more attention than the rest, so those narrower treads on its wheels did not matter. On Saturday 21st July we set off with one coach and the brake van for Abergynolwyn, and *Sir Haydn's* leading wheels dropped in between the rails half a mile above Rhydyronen. It took an hour to get them back on and repair the damage, but that had been just a warning of which we took no notice. I photographed the first 'new' locomotive to take water at Dolgoch for eighty five years, and we got back to Pendre without any more trouble. A quick repaint on Sunday from Corris reddy brown into the new standard TR green was ordered by Tom Rolt, much to David Curwen's disappointment, and on Tuesday afternoon *Sir Haydn* took its first passenger train to Abergynolwyn and back with David and Dai Jones on the footplate. I followed 'on sight' with *Dolgoch* in case of trouble. Again we got away with it.

Next day we did not. *Sir Haydn* on the morning train derailed twice in Abergynolwyn station, the second time all wheels skewed across the upper points. I was guard on that train, to enable Tom to get on with the paperwork at Wharf. In those days there was no telephone anywhere on the railway and certainly no radio link. The routine in such cases was for the guard to find the nearest public telephone and contact Daniels, the Towyn

> A quick repaint on Sunday from Corris reddy brown into the new TR standard green was ordered by Tom Rolt, much to David Curwen's disappointment

ironmongers, who would send a runner to Pendre or Wharf. I did that, and then got a lift back to Pendre to light up *Dolgoch* to work the afternoon train (if possible). David motored up with tools and got *Sir Haydn* back on with Dai's help, returning the train back to Wharf only just before the afternoon train was due to leave and with only one further derailment, this time just the engine's trailing wheels which jumped back on before he could stop. After that, we abandoned trying to use *Sir Haydn* for the time being.

It was just as well because we were getting into the peak season and, every day, both morning and afternoon trains were full and more than full. We pressed the tiny Corris van into service, which with the regular brake van and all four coaches meant an official seating capacity of eighty. For 9th August my diary records one hundred and twenty one passengers in the afternoon, which was pushing things a bit, but nobody complained. And only one more derailment, when the TR van came off at the place where *Sir Haydn's* trailing wheels had jumped off and back on during its last run.

In fact that illustrates the difficulty the track gang faced. Theoretically you could check the gauge two or three times on every single rail length, and insert sufficient new sleepers so you could pull them in to correct gauge everywhere and stop worrying. But we did not have the people or the money, and anyhow it did not work like that. When we came to relay the tracks in the whole of Abergynolwyn station in January 1952, I found that in one particular place at the west end of the platform for a foot or so the gauge maxed out at two feet five and a half inches, which meant that every wheel on the railway could have dropped between the rails. But none ever did, even on *Sir Haydn*. For four days during one week while we

> ## The only way to deal with decrepit railway track properly is to renew it completely

did that job, I worked a train up to Abergynolwyn each day with *Dolgoch* to take up new materials and carry down the old, and going back down on one of those days *Dolgoch* dropped her rear wheels between the rails on the westernmost of the Five Bends a little way above Brynglas, exactly where the last train worked by the old company in October 1950 had derailed. I was driving, and this was the only time I saw the 'Old Lady' (as we called her) misbehave in this way, since her wheel treads were much wider than *Sir Haydn*. But she climbed back on before we could stop, as we had come up to the new sleepers put in after rerailing her on that occasion. We stopped and I went back, to find that in climbing back onto the rail, *Dolgoch* had sheared off from the running edge a length of steel nearly two feet long and nearly half an inch wide, still hot to the touch. Next day the gang changed that rail and inserted some more sleepers. But *Sir Haydn* had never given any trouble at that place. The lesson to my mind was, that the only way to deal with decrepit railway track properly is to renew it completely, and anything else costs more in the long run. But of course, if you haven't got enough cash, you always have to spend more.

For the rest of the season I saw comparatively little of David Curwen, who was mainly occupied with running repairs to the active equipment. The most frequent problem was how to make *Dolgoch* produce enough steam. Previous practice was to keep the blower on all the time. It was not an efficient device and used a lot of steam itself: my first experiment was to turn it off whenever the 'Old Lady' was actually pulling the train uphill, leaving it to the exhaust to draw the fire. Dai was surprised at this, but it was a successful change, proving that the blower really only produced enough extra steam to meet its own consumption. Then it was clear that a lot of air was being drawn in through the bottom of the smokebox, and cleaning that out and filling the bottom up with concrete made a great improvement and we had several days with the needle on the red line of the pressure gauge and we began to feel a lot better. But it did not last: the concrete broke up and air leaks returned, and we could see that every part was moving about separately. The right-hand cylinder moved to and fro relative to the right-hand side of the frame, a situation repeated on the left, while the blastpipe in the middle performed a slow dance of its own. More concrete, held down under a steel plate through-bolted to another plate supporting the concrete, did better. That left

---

A small boy came up to me as I got off *Dolgoch* footplate on the return to Wharf one afternoon. He had been riding in the Corris van at the rear of the train and was in quite a state, saying that it had just given a shocking lurch and crash up the line and, when he looked back, he saw that a rail was missing. "Nonsense", I said, "they were all there when I went over on the engine; you must have made a mistake." But I thought I had better go back and have a look. He was quite right. A piece of the head of the rail five feet long had broken off under the train and was lying in the ditch. It was a nervous business getting the locomotive back to the shed. That night the coaches stayed down at the Wharf.

(John Snell)

other problems: one of the front springs shattered under the pounding it got, and one of the eccentric straps of the valve gear, which we were worried about because it was such a sloppy fit on the eccentric sheave, managed to seize up and bring the train to a halt half way up the line. That meant dismantling the valve rod and bringing the train back with one cylinder only- not such an unusual situation elsewhere. More uncommon were other incidents, like the whole fire dropping out while the engine was running back to Wharf to work the afternoon train – which it did, about an hour late, after everything had been reassembled and relit; and several problems with clacks and injectors, several times causing similar delays or sometimes worse, and quite often the engine disappearing in a howling cloud of steam. But we did our best, and many days were trouble-free.

On 1st September, a Saturday, when no other train was scheduled, David and I took *Sir Haydn* out again with a load of rails and sleepers, with no trouble. The tiny wheels under the cab had been replaced with enormous wide treads, rather like flanged pastry rollers. But it was decided not to risk any more trouble, with only four weeks to go. David had done enough to No.4, the Kerr Stuart now named *Edward Thomas*, to confirm that some heavy boiler work was needed, and the Hunslet Engine company in Leeds had agreed to do this at a special price. So the boiler went away to them. Hunslet had taken over the goodwill and the parts business of Kerr Stuart when that firm failed in 1930, and indeed built several more of its standard 'Tattoo' class engines nominally standard with ours, with a final one turned out in the mid-1950s for a plantation in Java. This assistance was enough to help the Talyllyn turn the corner on the way to recovery.

David and Barbara returned to Wiltshire on 14th September, and although he remained officially the TR's engineer for a while, we saw little of him at Towyn for the next twelve months, since he was organising a new firm of engineers, Curwen & Newbery, in Devizes. During the 1952 season Tom Rolt spent quite a lot of his time in the works at Pendre, while his wife Sonia held the fort at Wharf. Some basic improvements had begun. Now there was a telephone between Wharf and Pendre, extending up the line; and electricity had arrived at last. Even some washing facilities, though the traditional advice never to eat the blackberries which grew around Pendre yard unless they were above waist height remained good a while longer.

But at the end of the 1952 season David did reappear on the Talyllyn, this time with an internal-combustion light locomotive he had built for it. This was something the railway badly needed. It was unloaded at Wharf from the supporter's lorry which had brought it up from Devizes, and immediately ran happily up the line as far as it

Dolgoch waits for her next turn of duty in Pendre shed in March, 2015

could go, to the foot of the first quarry incline, where the railway now ends, and brought down a load of re-usable rail from that incline. A small crowd of supporters came along too. It was a very basic machine, no cab, just a two-seater bench at one end. Tom had donated the engine and gearbox from his narrow boat *Cressy*, now deceased, which had replaced the earlier steam installation. In fact they came originally from a Model T Ford, which had the useful ability to go as fast in reverse as forwards, which is what locomotives are supposed to do. But it was too well-worn to survive long. It had been happy enough propelling a canal boat, but more was needed on a railway even with very light loads, and inside twelve months the first No.5 had expired, unchristened.

Dolgoch still going
strong 64 years
after David Curwen
and John Snell's
involvement with
hardly anything of
the original engine
remaining after the
Gibbons' rebuilding

In September, 1952, *Dolgoch* was dismantled
and the valves, clacks, connecting and coupling
rods and eccentrics were distributed to various
members and firms for reconditioning or renewal.
Throughout most of the winter *Edward Thomas*
worked the weekly trains and many specials and
was run almost entirely on slack coal which had
been placed on one side as useless.

In June, 1953, the bits and pieces of *Dolgoch* had
been returned and the engine was re-assembled.
The insurance engineer passed the boiler and she
was given steam trials. One of the axle boxes ran hot
and this entailed lifting the locomotive to remove
the offending box. The trouble was corrected and
another trial took place. The axle box appeared to
be fairly satisfactory, but a weep of steam from the
foundation ring of the firebox was encountered. On
inspection it was found to come from a crack which
proved to be of quite considerable dimensions. This
meant that the locomotive could not be used until a

repair had been carried out. To enable the crack to
be welded, it was again necessary to dismantle the
moving parts of the engine.

We had, therefore, only one workable engine
to run the passenger service, and when the army
arrived it would have meant the suspension of
the service for a fortnight. This was unthinkable,
so it was decided to try to get *Sir Haydn* in a
running condition. The insurance engineer was
approached and he was satisfied that if certain
work was carried out she would be serviceable as
a standby engine. Examination then revealed that
five of the boiler tubes were leaking very badly, so
ten days were spent in plugging those tubes and
checking her over. Eventually, she was tried out
under steam with the boiler pressure reduced from
160 lbs to 100 lbs per sq. inch. She put up quite a
good performance at this reduced pressure and
we now had a reserve engine. Meanwhile No.2's
boiler had been examined by welding experts and

Talyllyn Pioneers

arrangements made to carry out this work in the near future.

Through connections it was agreed that the army would assist with the track and it was arranged that No.127 Construction Unit R.E. (T.A.) would provide 160 men for 9 days. But on 14th April, a letter was received from the Adjutant saying that they had been informed that the T.U.C were opposed to the railway receiving military aid and so no assistance could be given. Fortunately, Lord Northesk was able to intervene and saw Vic Feather, the Assistant Secretary of the T.U.C. and gave him full details to put the matter in perspective which allowed the army to come and put in some useful work.

When the army arrived to work on the track, No.4 was put to work continuously throughout the day and night, whilst No.3 worked the passenger service between Wharf and Brynglas. Whilst working for the army, No.4 had a bad mishap which seriously damaged the valve gear on one side of the engine. The position was now very serious as No.3, the lame dog, was the only workable locomotive and the provision of all services depended entirely on how long her boiler tubes would hold out. Something had to be done immediately.

No.4 was therefore dismantled and the driving wheels and valve mechanisms were sent off to the foundry at Portmadoc for repair. In the meantime the foundry sent a welder to deal with No.2's cracked firebox. This was repaired and she was erected in one weekend! The insurance inspector came on the Monday to give a boiler test. The test was a failure! *Dolgoch* was again dismantled and another attempt at welding the crack was made. The engine was again re-assembled and this time the test proved satisfactory. She was steamed on the Saturday and put into service. On the Friday, apparently just to be awkward, No.3 came completely off the rails and it took from early afternoon until 11.30 at night to get her back on the road again. At that time we were still in the dark whether *Dolgoch's* boiler would stand up to the test and we were working all out to get her running. From then, Nos. 2 and 3 shared the work of running the trains.

At the end of July the foundry at Portmadoc had completed the repairs to No.4 and their fitters came to Pendre and re-erected the locomotive. The insurance engineer came to test the boiler (after several people had spent two days under and in the engine removing ashpan, blowdown cock and inspection plugs!). This test was successful. No.4 was now in much better fettle and ran and behaved as if she were new.

We now had two workable engines, so No.3 was withdrawn from service and the work of re-tubing was put in hand. There is no doubt that members owe a great deal to No.3 *Sir Haydn* which for two years had been more or less written off as useless for the Talyllyn Railway because of her continuous derailments when we first took over the line. It is proved that the track and not the locomotive was at fault and that various members and the army, who spent many hours on track work, have done a very good job indeed.

We ended the season with two good locomotives and *Dolgoch* could now take it easy and be reserved for special occasions to a large extent. There is no doubt that age was beginning to tell and it was a long way still to the centenary of the opening of the railway!

The worst of it was that decay and collapse was still getting the better of us during those first two years, particularly on the track, in spite of all our work and the fact that the restoration and repair effort had risen to a level many times higher than for several decades. We were trying to scramble back over the edge of an abyss, and we only just made it. We had a good look down the hole. In the first few years it was necessarily a case of make do and mend and it was the assistance of the army at a critical time which helped tip the scales in our favour. Although progress remained slow it was continuous until the society got on top of the situation.

But we were lucky. It was only with the last two trains of the 1952 season, each of which was derailed, that we entered a period when hardly a single train got through. All attempts to run over the worst section, three quarters of a mile through the woods below Dolgoch were finally given up that winter after several unsuccessful journeys with works trains. One load of ballast had finally to be abandoned in the woods by a volunteer working party. On restarting after about the sixth successive wagon derailment, *Edward Thomas* just fell off the line, all wheels, at the second puff.

Five years later, the scene has changed quite incredibly at Towyn and it is difficult to remember quite how rough and ready things used to be. I suppose the old state of affairs had its charm– as long as one observed from a comfortable distance– but as a fireman, and then a driver, for the whole of the first season the rusty elements of the railway rapidly lost its appeal for me. The Talyllyn Railway is a different railway now– and a better one.

> We were trying to scramble back over the edge of an abyss, and we only just made it. We had a good look down the hole

Locomotives, coaches and wagons – and the Museum

Talyllyn (Photo: John Adams)

No.1 *Talyllyn*

Talyllyn was delivered in September, 1864 while the railway was still being built. She was constructed by Fletcher Jennings & Co. of Whitehaven. She was put into service handling construction and slate traffic work but did not prove very satisfactory, suffering excessive vertical oscillation and, when *Dolgoch* arrived, *Talyllyn* was returned to the makers for a trailing wheel to be added, making her an 0-4-2ST. Thereafter, she gave good service and was reputed to be the locomotive crews preferred engine to use until she was completely

worn out by 1945. In 1957, she was sent to the Midlands Works of Gibbons Brothers Ltd. for a complete overhaul where it was found that only the frame plates, wheels and some parts of the motion could be used again. She proved to be a shy steamer and was subsequently thoroughly rebuilt under John Bate's leadership between 1968-72 and is now a reliable performer. She has been painted in green and black liveries in preservation but was repainted in red livery for the railway's 150th anniversary at least ostensibly in an original Fletcher Jennings' offered livery. No one knows

"Our life member Mr. R.O.Griffiths of Towyn, whose father was responsible for maintaining the locomotives circa 1902, has informed the Committee that the original livery of the railway[1] was: locomotives dark green, lined red and gold; coaching stock: brown, lined out. The locomotives will be repainted in this livery as repairs are completed[2]."

(First TRPS Committee's first progress report)

1. The Lowca Works livery may well have been different as it appears No. 1 was repainted soon after arrival after it suffered some damage in transit

2. But they were not. The Committee's leanings saw a shade of green akin to GWR livery being adopted instead

John Snell on No.1 in the early 1950s: *"This locomotive has been out of service since 1946 and is as near to being worn out as a steam locomotive can ever be. Perhaps the most serious of her ailments could be described as 'ulcers on the firebox.' This disease has progressed to such a degree that it is now reasonably certain that any attempt to raise steam would raise a number of other things as well, including the person rash enough to try."*

Fletcher Jennings works plate

The 1960s view – before John Bate got to grips with her design and rebuilding faults - *Talyllyn* is the problem child. She has the failings of an early model, built by rule of thumb and without subtlety, and she outlines one of the shortcomings of the preservation business. Rebuilt at a heavy cost of freely given cash and enthusiasm, at a time when her speedy return to traffic was essential if it was to be entertained at all, the importance of maintaining her historic character did not allow a critical assessment of the pros and cons of economical design. She is popular with her fans, and with the general public, but those who fire and maintain her keep their own counsel.

whether she was originally supplied in red or green, although earliest records and photographs show her in lined green but Christopher Green remembers peering through the engine shed window in 1913 to see "indubitably a massive object painted the same bright red" as the coaches.

The Return of No.1

The Committee minutes record that "there was considerable discussion on the subject of Nos. 1 & 2 and in the opinion of Messrs. Hunt, Wilkins and Weddell, No.2 was not worth rebuilding and No.1 might be a better proposition." This probably partly explains why No.2 languished at Hunt Bros. for a long time because investigations showed that more and more work needed to be done, particularly to the boiler. The amount of the work was probably too much for Hunts to swallow. However, it became the unanimous view of the Committee that *Dolgoch* should not become an operable relic, but a fully working engine and that repairs were to be organised on this basis."

Very fortunately and generously a solution appeared on the horizon which was to solve the future of No.1 (and would later do the same thing for No.2). Committee minutes record: "His Lordship informed the meeting of the most generous offer made by Councillor Gibbons and the Midland Area. This is to remove No.1 to Dudley, entirely renovate and overhaul the locomotive and return it to Towyn in working order. The Midland Area are to make themselves responsible for the cost which ,

Talyllyn leaves Eric Gibbons' works on a Caudle lorry after her complete rebuilding and handover

in order that the work may proceed apace, is being guaranteed by Councillor Gibbons and the money will be reimbursed to him in due course."

This enabled *Talyllyn,* or rather the largely replica engine, to be returned to Towyn on 14th June, 1958. The official handing over ceremony took place at Messrs. Gibbons Bros. Lenches Bridge Works. This was a very glittering occasion and a hot sun shone on a very large assembly. This was a turning point in the story of the railway and the society and it was perhaps an emotional moment when the little engine, on its trailer, slowly moved forward out of the works entrance and gradually vanished from sight on the road to Wales; on each side was the inscription *"Yr wyfy mynd adref"* (I am going home).

No.2 *Dolgoch*

Dolgoch arrived sometime during the summer of 1866 also from Fletcher Jennings, but although using the same patterns for her cylinders and wheels, to a quite different design as an 0-4-0WT. Unusually, her firebox was placed ahead of the rear axle which achieved a more balanced layout; this required an unusual valve gear which was patented. From 1946, *Dolgoch* was the railway's only useable engine and so Sir Haydn was forced to send her for repairs in 1945 to the Atlas Foundry in Shrewsbury and suspend passenger operations,

although *Talyllyn* was pressed into service when essential. David Curwen just managed to keep No.2 going during the first year of TRPS operation in 1951 but, with the arrival of the two Corris engines, she was then used less and retired by 1954 to be taken to Hunt Bros. works at Oldbury

Dolgoch

John Snell on No.2 in the early 1950s: "Built in 1866, No.2 is scarcely less ancient than her sister, but because she had a less comfortable cab, she was less popular and therefore is not yet completely worn out. From the engineman's point of view Dolgoch has some good and some bad points. For sheer ability to shift a load she is probably the most powerful engine on the line and, having plenty of adhesion weight, she rarely gives much trouble with slipping. On an uneven grass covered track in a land where rain is not unknown this can be a great problem. With her great age she has whims which must be humoured. One of these is chronic steaming trouble which we hope will be cured by a new smokebox, but which has often been the cause of delay and exasperation. Properly handled, she gives no trouble on this account and indeed sometimes steams very well indeed, but she takes a malicious delight in taking advantage of every single error in putting on more coal, or leaving the injector on five seconds too long. She needs more than her fair share of maintenance, attention and money and is definitely too old for regular service."

for repairs to start, although these were not completed there and Eric Gibbons once again came to the rescue and his works rebuilt her so she could return to service in 1963, also virtually as a new engine incorporating only cylinders, wheels, coupling rods, one buffer, some fittings of the original and the most unattractive chimney supplied by Atlas (which has now, thankfully, been replaced).

No.2, could also have been delivered in red or green. Her name changed to *Pretoria* for a short while after the Boer War,

but she was probably not then painted black as some suggest. She has been green at least since the 1920s and, like No.1, in a shade similar to LNER green. In preservation she succumbed to the new 'standard' pseudo GWR green until breaking

> She takes a malicious delight in taking advantage of every single error in putting on more coal, or leaving the injector on five seconds too long

out, first, back into earlier light green, then into red (in the mistaken belief that she was red when named *Pretoria*) and, subsequently, for the 150th anniversary a shade of red likely to have been used by Fletcher Jennings as a standard colour.

John Snell on No.3 in the early 1950s: "Built in 1878 and rebuilt in 1900, No3 is a very competent engine indeed. I have only one grave complaint against her; I am six feet plus and her cab was designed with nobody taller than 4'6" in mind. She also had one other disadvantage in her early days on the TR, because she was apt to drop between the rails, but with improvement in track maintenance and the abolition of places where the gauge is more than 2'4", this trouble no longer occurs. These two points and also a certain difficulty in getting at the motion for repair and inspection really sum up all that can be criticised on her. Her pulling power is hardly less than that of *Dolgoch* and, as an extremely good steamer, she is better able to maintain the effort. Her adhesion weight is also great and slipping is reduced to a minimum. Also, since she has been turned to work cab first up the grade (because her vacuum brake equipment effectively blocked access to her cab on her left hand side), effective and reliable sanding can be provided by leaning out of the hole in the back sheet and sprinkling sand on the rail. As there are as yet no continuous brakes on the train, her combination of the good adhesion of *Dolgoch* with the good brakes of *Edward Thomas* puts her in a class above either. Finally, she is, in my view, by a noticeable margin the most economical on coal."

No.3 Sir *Haydn*

No.3 is the only survivor of three identical 0-4-0STs built by the Hughes Locomotive and Tramway Engine Co. (subsequently, the Falcon Works of the Brush group at Loughborough) in 1878 for the nearby Corris Railway. Slightly enlarged in 1900 with a bigger boiler and the addition of a pony truck, she continued in service becoming the last engine to run on the line, thereafter lying under a tarpaulin in store at Machynlleth until purchased by the TRPS in 1951. During her ownership by the Corris Railway, the GWR, British Railways and the TR, she has retained her No.3 and, on arrival at the TR was fittingly named *Sir Haydn*. Being in better condition than No.4, David Curwen prepared her for service and she was steamed and tried out but, sadly, a combination of her narrow wheel treads and the TR's over gauge track meant that she continually derailed and had to be sidelined until the track had been brought up to a better standard by 1953. She then proved very useful until trouble with her firebox caused her to be withdrawn in 1958 and it was not until 1968 that she was returned to service with a new boiler and enlarged cab, during which time it was discovered that she contained parts from both her sisters, Corris Nos. 1 & 2. Originally delivered in murky Corris reddy brown and most probably making her initial test trip in that colour, she was quickly repainted into standard TR preservation green, but has more

John Snell on No.4 in the early 1950s: "Built in 1921, No.4 is really in a different class altogether. Unlike the others, she was not designed for 'main line' work where long distances have to be covered at relatively high speeds, but is a standard Kerr Stuart contractor's design built with quite different objects in view. The class was designed to pull fairly small loads over short distances at low speeds and it was necessary to make everything as simple as possible so that maintenance could be both slight and unskilled. Hence the absence of such things as running plates and forced lubrication enabled the whole thing to be built at a competitive price. Because low speeds were envisaged, small driving wheels were provided and, at the moderate speeds of the TR, she has to run faster than she should and is therefore heavier on maintenance than she ought to be. This is, of course, offset to some extent by the simplicity of the design. She burns more coal than so relatively a modern engine should, although more economical, naturally, then *Dolgoch*. Finally, although on paper this locomotive is the most powerful of the TR stock, in practice she is not able to handle, without considerable loss of time, the trains which *Sir Haydn* or even *Dolgoch* would find quite within their power, and this in spite of being a good steamer. The reason is, of course, that being designed for light contractor's track she is very light in weight and lacks adhesion. This has often led to troubles, not only in getting the train started, but in pulling it up the banks. On several trips *Edward Thomas* has taken as much as two and a half hours to cover the six miles to Abergynolwyn. However, under normal conditions this engine can be relied upon to deal competently with all but the heaviest of trains and is ideal for light winter work."

recently sported red livery both as a Skarloey engine and a Corris one.

No.4 *Edward Thomas*

No.4 was supplied to the Corris Railway by Kerr Stuart & Co. Ltd. in 1921 as a slight modification of that company's standard 'Tattoo' 0-4-2ST intended for industrial shunting duties. She worked satisfactorily on the Corris until taken out of service in 1947 requiring boiler repairs. She was purchased by the TRPS in 1951 at the same time as No.3 and fittingly named *Edward Thomas*, also retaining the same number throughout her

ownership changes. She was unusable when purchased but, fortunately, Tom Rolt knew John Alcock, the Managing Director of the Hunslet Engine Co.Ltd (the successors to Kerr Stuart) who generously offered to overhaul her free of charge, returning her to the TR for immediate entry into service in 1952. No.4 has proved to be a reliable and economical engine ever since.

In 1958, she became the first British engine to be fitted with a Giesl ejector supplied personally and free of charge by the inventor, Dr Giesl Gieslingen of Vienna who was interested to attract the attention of British Railways to whom he wanted

'Bill's engine':
Edward Thomas

to sell his invention. He misguidedly thought that as the TR had the Earl of Northesk as its President, he would have the ear of the Queen who would 'inform' BR of his invention. Unfortunately for Dr Giesl, the nationalisation railway only bought two of his ejectors. Despite Tom Rolt extolling the virtues of the long narrow fishtailed chimney, it did not prove any more economical than the original and so it was removed in 1968 and can now be found in the museum at Wharf.

No.4 was made famous by being painted red with blue lining and adopting the name of *Peter Sam* made famous by the Rev. Wilbert Awdry who was a guard on the TR in the early preservation days. Nos. 3 and 6 have also followed suit. In the 1950s someone ordered brunswick green paint (wrongly thinking that was GWR colours) and so, together with No.6, she spent some time running in a rather brighter shade of green than was intended; but paint is, after all, only paint. No.4 also spent a short while masquerading in pseudo GWR livery and even BR black (neither of which she ever carried at the time), but is currently in standard TR preservation green.

The first No.5

"From the time the Society took over the line in 1951 the need had been felt for a small i/c locomotive to handle works trains during the winter, to avoid the waste and time expense of raising steam, and also to run a passenger service as far as Brynglas all the year round. The Company's then Chief Mechanical Engineer, David Curwen, designed and built a small engine in his works at Devizes. The engine was of very simple construction. It was powered by a second hand 40 bhp Ford motor driving through an epicyclic gearbox with drive onto the rear axle which was coupled to the front axle by a chain.

Her trial run was on Saturday 18th October, 1952, when she hauled a set of wagons and bolsters right up to Alltwyllt to bring down rails from the recently demolished quarry incline. The most she could manage was four wagons loaded with sleepers and No.4 was still needed for anything heavier, like ballast trains. No.4 therefore worked the Friday passenger service whenever track materials also had to be taken up the line. On other occasions No.5 did this duty; then the train

Tom Rolt on the Giesl Ejector

"The Giesl Ejector is a patent blast pipe and chimney which has been evolved by Doctor Adolph Giesl, Professor of Steam Locomotive Engineering at the University of Vienna. In the Giesl arrangement there is no blast pipe in the true sense of the term at all. Instead the exhaust pipe fans out into a series of nozzles which eject the steam into a venture-shaped chimney, the narrow portion of which is extended well down into the smokebox.

Dr. Giesl was naturally anxious to try out his Ejector under operating conditions in this country but failed to rouse any interest in the project as far as the British Transport Commission was concerned. Through a mutual friend in London, Dr. Giesl was then put in communication with me, the implication being that there was at least one railway left in the country which had no intention of abandoning its steam locomotives and might well agree to give the Ejector a trial. The outcome of this was that Dr. Giesl most kindly agreed to supply an Ejector and ship it to Wales free of all charge for fitting experimentally to our locomotive No.4. The only stipulation made on our part has been that the installation must involve no permanent modification so that the original chimney and blast pipe can be restored to No.4 if desired, after a fair trial period. The Ejector has been built by Messrs. Scholler Bleckmann of Vienna, the largest steel and engineering works in Austria.

It is to the credit of the Talyllyn Railway Company that it has taken the initiative in sponsoring such a trial when British Railways failed to do so. The practical results have been most remarkable, exceeding all expectations. A marked improvement in performance has been achieved in combination with a fuel saving of nearly 40%."

On 23rd March, 1957, a beautifully sunny Saturday at Jee's quarry, Hartshill, Nuneaton, the Midland Area Chairman, Mayor C.S.N. Walker presented to Mr Pat Garland on behalf of the Talyllyn Railway Company the diesel locomotive No.5 Midlander. The locomotive was conveyed to Towyn on the same day, free of cost, on one of Messrs Caudle's low loading lorries which returned on the 24th bringing No.1 back for repair. Unloading Midlander at Wharf 23rd March, 1957. Its first job was to run to Pendre and to propel the worn out Talyllyn to Wharf where it was loaded onto the Caudle lorry with the assistance of Douglas. (John Snell)

consisted of the old first class coach and the Corris van, as the TR van was too heavy.

Although she could hardly manage to exceed 10 mph with load, No.5 proved her value very quickly. In her first month of service, whilst hauling a works train, she even managed to kill a sheep, and so was properly initiated into the Talyllyn locomotive brotherhood.

The 'new' No.5 *Midlander*
TRPS members dismantled and acquired rails from

Jee's Hartshill Quarry in Nuneaton. One of their diesel engines, Ruston & Hornsby four wheeled diesel engine No.200792 *Matron* had worked there since being delivered new in 1940. An offer was made for it, in September, 1956. It was viewed in early October by Pat Whitehouse, Pat Garland and Bill Faulkner, who gave their blessing to the project. The quarry manager is reported as asking £900 for the engine, but Pat Garland burst out laughing at this and offered £2! They settled at £150 and a deposit of £100 was paid through the generosity of two Midland Area members. The quarry company gave permission for the TRPS to use the loco shed to convert the gauge of the engine from 2′6 ½. Pursuant to a suggestion by the wife of a leading member, the name *Midlander* was adopted, after rejecting *Nuneaton* and *Lady Godiva*.

No.6 Douglas

No.6 *Douglas* ("Father's engine" usually driven by Hugh Jones, as described by Dai and Herbert)

Harvey Gray, a member of the original Committee of the TRPS tells how *Douglas* came to join the TR.

I was a member of the Birmingham Locomotive Club and happened to be travelling on the upper deck of a trolley bus on the Coventry Road in Birmingham and glanced over the wall of an engineering firm's yard to notice a locomotive chimney. This resulted in club members being invited by Messrs. Ablesons of Sheldon to visit their yard on Saturday 18th June, 1949 to see their locomotives. We were shown a pair of identical Barclay 1 ft 11 ½″ gauge 0-4-0 well tanks which had been used by the Royal Air Force for transporting torpedoes and stores around a seaplane base on Southampton Water.

I attended the famous "Save the TR" meeting in 1950 and found myself appointed to the founding committee. After a couple of years' hard work by the TRPS, I felt that we were sufficiently well established to try an appeal to industry for funds and the committee naturally gave me

the task. I sent 149 of the letters I drafted which Lord Northesk personally signed to "household names" in the Midlands. I sent letter No.150 to a much less well known name – Messrs. Ablesons, having first checked with the BLC that the firm still had at least one engine of the Barclay twins in stock and up for sale.

A day or two later, I rang up Ablesons; this was easier said than done, because I was a relatively junior member of staff of a public authority and, by some oversight, my job description did not include begging the use of a steam locomotive for a Welsh railway in the name of a Peer of the Realm. Clearly, heavier guns were needed, so I left matters to Pat Whitehouse and Pat Garland both very well known in Birmingham business circles. They did the trick and soon afterwards one of the well tanks was gifted to the TRPS and it was named *Douglas* in honour of Mr. Douglas Ableson.

Douglas was green in RAF days. In TR ownership she has been both standard and 'light' green and RAF green but is currently bright red to facilitate being called *Duncan*

No.7 Tom Rolt

After 1957's television broadcast, traffic exploded and, after 1963 it increased a further 50%. With such ever growing traffic, more engines and more reliable engines were needed. Peak summer season trains were double headed and even banked up the line. *Talyllyn* and *Dolgoch* were regarded as

Father's engine:
Douglas

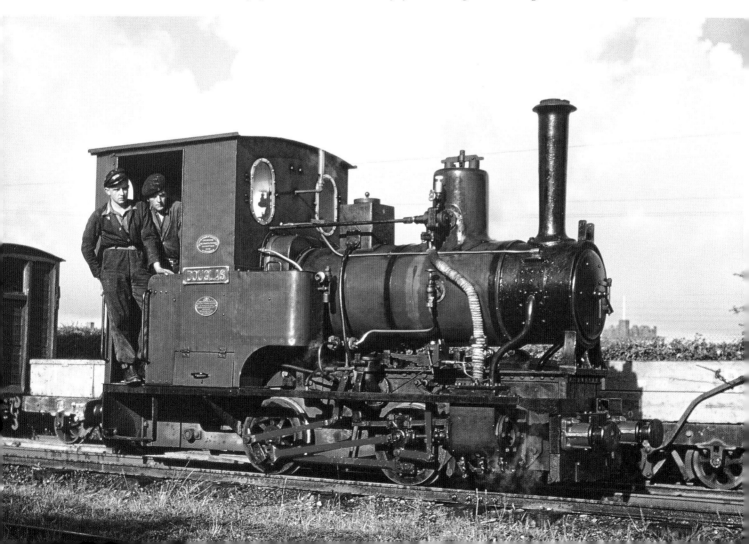

Douglas rebuilt

> John Snell on No.6 in the early 1950s: "A practical workaday locomotive with the virtues of simplicity and accessibility. The smallest of our locomotives, she has performed better than many of us expected by proving herself capable of hauling all but the very heaviest of trains. Her greatest defect is that with her short wheelbase and excessive front and rear overhang she rides badly and her speed on this account must be severely restricted."

venerable antiques (even though in fact they were nearly completely new) and *Sir Haydn* had not then been back in service for very long and its potential was then yet unclear, so *Edward Thomas* had become regarded as the mainstay of the fleet with *Douglas* a doubtful supporter. The railway hunted around for other engines, nearly bought one from Europe, could not afford a new example of an established type, such as the Hunslet 0-4-2T *Eva* design which the manufacturer offered to make for about £9,000 and so seized on this second hand engine when it became available. Rolt and Curwen had come up with all sorts of unsuitable designs generated to create a steam engine capable of hauling the longer trains then becoming common. The immediate problem was solved by two actions: introducing three train working by the creation of loops at Pendre and Quarry Siding and also John Bate carefully making both Nos. 1 and 2 useful engines by rebuilding them, so that there was more than sufficient motive power to haul the trains. Almost, simultaneously, traffic numbers took a dive when the public were provided with

Douglas' party trick is the result of a short wheelbase. As the front wheels dip into a rail joint, the footplate is given a flip, catapulting the crew upwards. Before their vertical acceleration falls off, the rear wheels are in the dip and the stars that suddenly become visible to the driver and fireman are not the result of a successful ascent into celestial orbit, but are simply the result of the steel cab roof descending smartly onto their respective skulls. Nevertheless Douglas is a game little engine with a clipped and regular exhaust beat that is a pleasure to hear.

cheap flights to summer sunshine and, suddenly, the existing engine fleet was sufficient.

As received, 2263 was a 3 foot gauge, 0-4-0 WT of Barclay's Class "E" class, slightly modified for turf burning, with an enlarged firebox and a spark arresting chimney. It was virtually an enlarged edition of *Douglas*. In its delivered form 2263 was, in John Bate's view, unsuited to purpose and so John Bate took on the task of redesigning it and using the principal components with a new frame. There was not much traffic demand to complete this work, but efforts continued by volunteers in the meantime but, once the engine got to the stage of being a running chassis, it was mothballed until *Douglas* was withdrawn needing a new boiler.

When completed, the engine was named *Tom Rolt*, fittingly by Sonia Rolt at a ceremony at

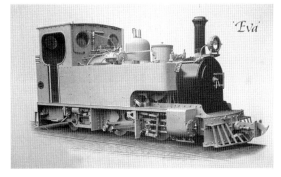

Abergynolwyn. Initially, No. 7 was named *Irish Pete* after her Irish peat bog origins and pursuant to TR humour, but this did not find universal favour, despite the name being chosen by democratic ballot. Much lobbying and whingeing persisted until a second vote was held at an AGM to choose

If No.7 had not been acquired, this neat Hunslet 0-4-2T design intended for Indian service would have been a very suitable engine, if the TR could have afforded it

Tractor No.7 at Pendre

Above: *Irish Pete* at Wharf shortly after arrival. Below: Volunters stand by No.7 as a rolling chassis at Pendre. *(Photo: Talyllyn Railway Archive)*

the present name, by a small margin. No.7 has always been painted in TR 'standard green' livery.

No.7's time in service on the TR is outside the story line of this book, but included here as it is referred to in the text. Other engines have since joined (and left) the TR fleet: all diesels. Martin Fuller has written an excellent book on TR locomotives (see bibliography) and he is preparing a second book on TR locomotives during the TRPS regime, so many engine stories are yet to come…

Coaches

The Talyllyn Railway is unique in still having all five of its original passenger train vehicles in service and largely in original condition. There are three coaches built by Brown Marshalls & Co. in Birmingham together with the brake van, having its unique ticket office added later by Yates when passenger services were extended to start from Wharf where there was then no ticket office. A fourth coach was built by the Lancaster Wagon Co. slightly later. The TRPS have numbered the coaches in a new order, but it was actually coach now numbered No.3 which was delivered first; this can be identified easily enough in a train of the original coaches as it is one foot shorter and slightly lower than its sisters and also has a separate compartment which was used by the owner of the railway, first the McConnels then Sir Haydn Jones and classified as first class. Although all these coaches were built with doors on both sides, those on the south (non platform) side were fastened out of use by agreement with Captain Tyler when he inspected the railway after construction and found the bridges too narrow for safety. He required the track through the bridges to be skewed slightly to the south and the carriage doors on the south side to taken out of use, then he was happy for the railway to operate passenger services. This set a precedent for all subsequent coaches right up to the newest bogie coaches, but the railway actually ignored the requirement to move the track which remained in the centre of the bridge line.

These five vehicles were all the railway possessed until the TRPS came on the scene. In summer months when the demand for seats outgrew the capacity of these coaches, slate wagons were simply hitched at the back of the train and passengers sat either on planks placed on the wooden bodies or on the timber sides themselves;

in good summer weather these wagons were very popular, especially as the railway allowed families and groups to gravitate back to Towyn themselves after the last train had run!

Once the TRPS began to run trains, more coaches were badly needed and, initially, some basic open coaches were sourced from the Penrhyn Railway and regauged to suit. These were lettered (and not numbered until they came to the TR) and the first to arrive were H and P, with four more bodies subsequently acquired for cannibalisation: C, D, E and G. The TR van No.5 were also pressed into use to carry passengers when needed. Two bogie frames were sourced from Tipton in 1953 (to form coaches 9 and 10) and bodies C and D were initially mounted on one of these for a season before both bogie frames had temporary softwood wooden bodies constructed on them, both gaining the nickname 'the cardboard coaches' due to the temporary construction, although they were refitted with the now standard Tisdale bodies in 1966/67.

Penrhyn coach body D was assembled on a new frame supplied from Birmingham in a single weekend over August Bank Holiday in 1956! On the Sunday morning there was a pile of steelwork on Pendre station platform, a set of axle boxes and buffers in the workshop, a Penrhyn carriage body on blocks at the end of the yard and a partly dismantled wagon down at Wharf. On Monday evening carriage No. 11 made its first trip to Abergynolwyn. These four wheelers have been variously rebuilt and reconstructed, including one

Above: Unloading a Penrhyn open coach body from a BR truck by the Wharf exchange sidings. *(Photo; J.M. Lloyd)*

Left: Brown Marshalls carriage worksplate

The original train

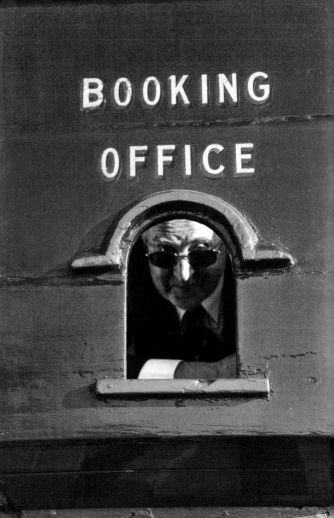

New bogie coach No10

being used as a tea van for a while. Now, Nos. 7, 8, 11, 12 and 13.

More coaches were still needed to meet the increasing passenger numbers and, following advice received from John Milner that several Glyn Valley Tramway and Corris Railway coaches were still in existence in the Ceiriog Valley and at Gobowen used as sheds and henhouses, investigations were made and four coach bodies acquired for rebuilding and reuse: two GVT coaches, one Corris coach and a former 3ft. coach body from Bodens Stone Ltd. in Stanton, Derbyshire (rebuilt as No. 16). Additionally, a Corris four wheeled van (now No.6) was acquired together with several wagons at the same time as engines Nos. 3 and 4, although the van has subsequently been completely rebodied. Like the TR van, the Corris van was also pressed into service to carry passengers.

The first of these to be rescued was No.14, the only first class coach supplied to the Glyn Valley Tramway at Chirk, built in around 1982/3 at the Shrewsbury works of the Midland Carriage and Wagon Co, Ltd. The exact date of building cannot

> His children were greatly attracted to it and it was given over to their tender mercies to be used as a play house

be ascertained as the design drawing is undated and unsigned and no order books survive. As it was the only first class carriage owned by the tramway it was more sumptuously fitted out inside than the normal third class coaches, originally being upholstered in corded blue cloth with sprung cushions and having mirrors and luggage racks on the end walls. Interior woodwork was in mahogany and roof panels were in white lincrusta wax cloth with gilt mouldings. There was a three quarter height partition between the compartments and a single roof lamp, burning colza oil, served to light both of these. The coach was finished externally in the elaborate livery adopted by the GVT in its early years. This was creamy white with deep green paneling with a very elaborate gold leaf lining on each panel and a GVT monogram on the centre waist panel. The coach bore the running number 14.

Following closure of the line, the coach was sold and when next heard of it was in the possession of a noted local resident, Mr. Moss Edwards of Llwyn-y-Cil. It was later bought by a garage proprietor at Chirk and in 1953 the vicar, the Rev.

W.C.Dickin bought it ostensibly as a hen house. This idea was destined to be still born for his children were greatly attracted to it and it was given over to their tender mercies to be used as a play house. It performed this purpose for the next three years until in the early part of 1956 John Scholes of the British Transport Commissions historical department wrote to Chirk Parish Council about the possibility of preserving it. But it was bought by a TRPS member and presented to the Society and taken to Towyn on 8th December 1956 by a B. Whitehouse & Son lorry, unloaded and gingerly taken up to Pendre by Douglas and rebuilt in the workshop by Mr. Green (senior) and his son Brian, two master coach builders from the Midlands, as far as possible in original style with the only changes being those necessary to make it compatible with the TR stock.

The restoration of the GVT 3rd class coach No.14 and Corris Railway coach No.17 are next described by the Greens themselves writing for the *Talyllyn News* under the pseudonym of 'Mallet' & 'Chisel.'

"The old T.R. van had obviously been in a very rough shunt and one end was in a "fragile" state when Bill Faulkner asked whether something could be done with it. Thus began a career of rebuild and repair of the rolling stock on the T.R. Most of this work has been associated with vehicles that did not originate on the T.R. and some people have wondered why this has been so. The reason is to be found in the fact that no passenger-carrying vehicle has been taken out of service for longer than a week. The majority of our work has been to introduce new vehicles and thus increase our passenger carrying capacity. The original T.R coaches are now in a very poor state. Their decay has been accelerated by extensive use and, of course, the very poor state of the track in

John Wilkins and Bill Faulkner stand by Glyn Valley Railway coach to be No.15

the early days of the Society, not forgetting also that they have stood outside in all weathers over these last few years. To put these vehicles back into a good state of repair would take a lot of money and a lot of time, and our personal feelings are that they should be replaced as soon as possible by new vehicles. Before the Society took possession of these vehicles they had had their roof recovered with a mixture of lead and galvanised iron sheeting.

"Just before the Christmas of 1956 word was passed around that someone had purchased for the Society an ex-G.V.T. carriage that had been found in a vicarage garden. We were again asked "could something be done with it?" So that particular Christmas was spent measuring up the remains on an extremely bleak Wharf platform. The wind was so cutting that we could only work outside for a few minutes at a time before returning to the car for a warm up.

> an excellent state of preservation, and with a coat of paint, a little polish and reglazed windows, it will be as good as the day it was made

"Early in 1958 news was heard of what is now No.15. The remains of this G.V.T coach were found on a Glyn Ceiriog farm and a Midland Area party arrived one Saturday to load it up. Unbeknown to them, the roof was covered with a layer of concrete and this, together with slimy, sodden timber, contributed to a weight that was nearly unmanageable. After a week in Mr. Hunt's works at Oldbury the floor had not even started to dry out, so a floorboard was ripped out and what a mess! Two inches of waterlogged felt and then another floor. It has always been a puzzle why this insulated floor was fitted on what had always been a 'hard class' vehicle, whilst the other, which was always a first had not got this feature. The second G.V.T. was rebuilt entirely differently from its original state. We decided on this policy as the patterns for the first coach were to hand, and by re-using them the coach was able to enter service much sooner than if the original style had been repeated.

'Someone must have had a lovely fire in the Corris Van. It burnt most of one corner away, and what with the ravishes of time it did look a sorry sight. The complete body was removed and dumped at the Quarry to be subsequently christened "Quarry Lodge." A replica was built, mostly on Pendre platform, but it was considered prudent not to put the stove back.

"Now for the Corris coach. A cutting from the *Border Counties Advertiser* says "…excellent state of preservation, and with a coat of paint, a little polish and reglazed windows, it will be as good as the day it was made." Well, be that as it may. We had by now become hardened to similar statements, so it was in February 1958 that we paid our first visit to Gobowen to see it. Oh dear! What a sight. More than a few licks of paint would be required before it ran on the T.R. metals. One compartment, internally, was completely untouched from its days on the Corris, except for a coat of horrible green paint. The other compartment had been completely stripped and turned into a green house. Work did not start on the vehicle until 1959 when the glazing and false roof were removed at the site to lighten the task of loading onto a B.R. lorry. This proved an easier task than had been expected, but during the journey to Towyn the chassis member of the coach cracked. Once at Pendre, and in the new workshops at that, the structure was completely dismantled for examination and most of it went to the furnace and scrap dealers respectively. The chassis was of composite construction and where it had cracked the metal was no thicker than paper. The chassis was a complete write off. Some of the woodwork was salvaged, the sliding doors are original so are the pillars on the far side of the coach, and both cant rails. The structure of the centre partitions is mostly original except where the oil lamps had burnt through, and the upper portions of the end bulkheads have been used.

"The coach has been restored virtually to its original condition, except for a few alterations necessary for it to run on the T.R. The vestibule seat no longer has a vacuum cylinder under it. Two panels of glass have been added in the sliding door recesses. These were originally wood panels, and this change has greatly improved the vision from both compartments and this has, we think, been ample excuse for the diversion. Foam rubber bench cushions replace what in Corris days were slats, similar to those left in the vestibule. Otherwise the bodywork is a complete reproduction. There was sufficient evidence remaining to establish the original outside painting and the elaborate gold leaf line out, which has been completely reproduced with the aid of a member professionally engaged in the business. This coach has been perhaps the most interesting re-build yet tackled, a rather intriguing design based on the old tram cars, very light yet amply strong enough for the job it had to do.

"What now of the future? It has been rightly decided that there shall be no more vehicles bought for restoration. It is always difficult to know just how far to go in replacing timber etc. and the finished article can never look so good as a completely new coach."

Corris Coach No.17. *(Photo: John Adams)*

Loading Corris coach onto low loader for transport to Pendre for reconstruction by the Greens. *(Photo: Talyllyn Railway Archive)*

The TRPS was very lucky in its early years and benefitted from having a key number of people in the right places, so enabling it to acquire and repair almost anything. Pat Whitehouse provided the transport for these coaches, the Greens rebuilt them, Tom Hunt provided facilities at his Oldbury works for the second GVT coach, No. 15, and carpenters from B.Whitehouse & Sons rebuilt it. Bill Faulkener was Works manager of Tearne & Sons in Birmingham who manufactured railway heraldic devices. A search in their store room revealed the retained stock of the original GVT monogram and garter transfers carefully wrapped in brown paper and tied up with string.

After rescuing the Penrhyn open coaches, the two GVT coaches and the Corris bogie coach and brake van, it was decided from then on to build new carriages, although it would have been possible to acquire further redundant bodies and indeed GVT van No.2 was considered but not proceeded with. In 1959 it was agreed that the future standard carriage should resemble the style of the Glyn Valley Railway carriages, although maybe perpetuating the style of the original TR Brown Marshalls carriages would have been more in keeping with the original train.

No. 18 was the first of the new design of standard bogie coaches built for the railway and was constructed at Pendre works entirely by society members. It is a six compartment first-

Talyllyn Pioneers

Above: The Greens stand proudly by their craftsmanship in front of the rebuilt Corris Coach No.17. *(Photo: Talyllyn Railway Archive)*

Below: The first of its class No.18 coach. *(Photo: Talyllyn Railway Archive)*

class vehicle with a seating capacity of 36 under normal conditions, but can carry 48 when required at peak times. Although it is a new vehicle it does incorporate some old material, for example the wheels are from a scrapped Welshpool & Llanfair Railway wagons and the door handles are ex G.W.R. The body style follows the design of the Glyn Valley coaches, but is reduced in size to conform to the Talyllyn loading gauge. It is 30 ft. 6 in. long over the head stocks and the bodywork is framed in solid oak. Sponge rubber seating is provided and every care has been taken to provide a comfortable and quiet ride. The finish internally is dark varnished wood, relieved by bands of cream vynide. External livery is standard T.R.

brown and peony, lined with green.

This coach was built to last, in the Talyllyn tradition. The bogies have Timken roller bearing axle boxes but were later modified to improve their riding. Similar coaches have been built, all with bodies from Raymond Tisdale & Co. Ltd., numbered from 19-23, with newly designed bogies built at Pendre. It was intended to build No.24 but traffic began to fall off and so it was not considered necessary.

Wagons

The TR originally owned about 120 wagons, but by the time the TRPS came into being, this position had deteriorated substantially. As there was an imperative need to have as many serviceable wagons as possible to support the track relaying work, the remaining wagons were canibalised and repaired as required without much thought to history.

John Bate summarises the wagon position in 1955 (of course, the position has developed since then)

In 1951 when the TRPS assumed control there were sixteen wagons on the working portion of the railway and, in addition, there were eight in the yard at Abergynolwyn village and a fair number up in the quarry. In 1952 the demolition contractor cut up the wagons there and those in the village were broken up at the same time. Of the surviving vehicles, ten were slate wagons and there were five steel body open wagons and one bolster. Pendre yard contained in addition a number of partially dismantled wagons, including one serviceable frame.

Of the ten slate wagons only two now remain in serviceable condition, Nos. 30 and 32. Nos. 21, 23 and 34 have been rebuilt as flat wagons, No.8 received a steel body and the other four, Nos. 31, 33, 35 and 36 were broken up as the frames were badly damaged and the timbers were rotten.

All the steel body open wagons which were taken over in 1951 have now been broken up and the three steel wagons now running, Nos. 8, 9 and 11, have been assembled from components at Pendre, No. 8 being mounted on a frame salvaged from the Wharf yard and Nos. 9 and 11 having new frames provided by the NW Area.

The sole Talyllyn bolster wagon, No.25, was badly damaged during the army relaying period in 1953 and was replaced by a slightly larger wagon built in the Pendre workshops.

Narrow Gauge Railway Museum

As the Talyllyn was the first preserved railway, it had the opportunity to acquire several artefacts from other like railways which were closing all around it as well as doing its best to keep artefacts and paperwork relating to its own history[1] and so a museum began, initially in a happenstance way.

The De Winton locomotive *George Henry* arrived from Bethesda, with a collection of track parts

---

1. *Apparently, after Sir Haydn's death, all the papers in his office relating to the quarry, the railway and the ironmongers businesses were burnt. Even Edward Thomas administered to the fire to ensure that no embers were left. Sir Haydn hadn't distinguished between any of the businesses and his own in his mind and dealings, so perhaps it was just as well the evidence was destroyed*

and engine nameplates, photographs, tickets, nameplates, lamps, and whistles. James Boyd and Pat Whitehouse initially secured other artefacts and these were placed in and around the former gunpowder store, across the tracks from Wharf station, with the De Winton inside. Previously, the building had been used by Lady Haydn Jones for storing her car and mowing machine. Grahan Vincent and John Milner also keenly became involved and started the genesis of the museum.

In the early days, there was no Museum policy as such and individual members simply made decisions of their own. In 1951, member Harold Dalston visited the Festival of Britain in London and saw a new diesel narrow gauge engine destined for the Guinness Brewery in Dublin which told him that their distinctive and diminutive steam engines would then be displaced. So he wrote to the brewery and asked for one and, somewhat to everyones' surprise, one was provided free of charge and carriage paid. The 1'11 ½ " gauge locomotive arrived at August Bank Holiday weekend in 1956.

The original Beyer Peacock Garratt, K1, rescued by its makers from Tasmania, was offered to the collection but had to be turned down due to lack of covered accommodation. When the Welshpool & Llanfair Railway closed even an engine from that railway was asked for, before it was realised that a preservation scheme for that line was in embryo. All this rather forced consideration of a Museum and, with the establishment of a Museum Committee, people started actively looking for exhibits from 1954 and finding somewhere better to house and display them.

Cambrai repainted bright red takes up much space outside the new museum building at Wharf

Meanwhile, in 1955, the former Welsh Highland Railway 2-6-2T *Russell* arrived, on loan from the Birmingham Loco Club who had rescued it from Fayle Bros. line when they had gone to seek out *Secundus* which was one of the very few steam engines built in Birmingham which went into the Science Museum's collection in the city. The looked for a home for it and initially offered it to Carnarvon but there was nowhere to house it, so it was offered to the TR and accepted at a rent of £1 per year provided it could be maintained. Later, once the Festiniog Railway became established, they sought to gain possession of it, but the TR were then only prepared to release it if Alan Pegler, then Chairman of the FR, guaranteed to restore it to working order. No such guarantee was forthcoming, so the BLC went along with the

> The FR's request letter is fairly aggressive which was not perhaps the best timing as the TR were then somewhat worried that there would not be enough volunteers to go round

TR's view as at least there was a museum of sorts at Wharf, whereas the FR's works at Boston Lodge was not formally open to the public. The FR's request letter is with the TR Committee's minutes and is fairly aggressive in its request which was perhaps not the best timing as the TR were then somewhat worried that there would not be enough volunteers to go round to resuscitate both railways. Eventually, when the WHR (1964) Co. was formed, the TR did release the engine and it is now restored to working order and, remarkably,

In the early days, there was no Museum policy as such and individual members simply made decisions of their own. In 1951, member Harold Dalston visited the Festival of Britain in London and saw a new diesel narrow gauge engine destined for the Guinness Brewery in Dublin which told him that their distinctive and diminutive steam engines would then be displaced. So he wrote to the brewery and asked for one. Here we see the Guiness engine installed behind the Wharf gunpowder shed

Talyllyn Pioneers

appeared in steam at Wharf station for the TR's 150th birthday!

In pre-society days there was a small yard close to the Neptune Road Bridge served by a siding where wagon loads of coal could be stored behind a locked gate. This was made available for conversion to a museum which was undertaken by the Midlands Area Group to a design produced by Robin Butterell. John Scholes, Curator of Historical Relics to the British Transport Commission opened the new building on the AGM day in September 1959 and a separate trust was formed to look after the museum and its exhibits in 1964.

Later acquisitions included the four foot gauge host wagon from the Dinorwic Quarry railway, *Pet*, an eighteen inch gauge 0-4-0 tank locomotive used within Crewe works, *Dot*, the works shunter at the world famous Beyer Peacock Manchester Works, *Rough Pup* from Dinorwic Quarry and *Jubilee 1897* from the Penrhyn Quarry. Other locomotives have been displayed or are on loan elsewhere from time to time.

The Museum also owns a steam sentinel engine called *Nutty* which worked on the Welshpool & Llanfair Railway for a time and also owns a Ruston petrol engine, *Indian Runner,* which can be seen working on the railway at the North Ings Farm Museum.

The museum is now a very professionally presented collection within the new and enlarged Wharf station building and a 'must see' on any trip to the railway.

Russell on display by the gunpowder shed at Wharf soon after arrival

What next?

This book has delved into the 'why', the 'how', the 'what' of saving the Talyllyn Railway in the 1950s. It sets out some of the feelings and personal views of those world pioneers who were given a statutory railway, rebuilt it against the odds and ran it for the enjoyment of around 90,000 passengers a year. Most of the text in this book comes from words either spoken or written by these pioneers themselves and so reflects their feelings and attitudes. Rarely does a railway history book delve into 'past current affairs' written by an author who knew all the relevant individuals personally and without some 'red penciling' from the current owners when history gets too close to current affairs. Mostly, such books are written by eminent authors from archive material and heresay. I have deliberately chosen text and words from those pioneers I knew well and those I have spent days hours and weeks with, who stayed with us at home or invited me into their home. I have endeavoured to portray the views, feelings and actions of these pioneers as they emerged.

After the Pioneers *(James Boyd)*

The Talyllyn, broadly speaking, has little past. As a slate quarry outlet, it did not enjoy the glamour and publicity which many other systems attracted. Since the Preservation Society was formed it has been transformed. We Society members have helped with a rebirth such as will never be known again.

We have moved from the threat of failure, through a period when the traffic was so great that it wore down our efforts and resources, to a period of comparative stability, when some say the adventure has gone from the Talyllyn.

New horizons, specific objectives, and the drive to reach them are always needed. The pioneers have completed their job; a policy for their successors will be to ensure that no one will be in doubt about the future.

> **The pioneers have completed their job; a policy for their successors will ensure that no one will be in doubt about the future**

Talyllyn shunts
slate wagons at
Nant Gwernol in the
1930s

Rule 3

TRPS Constitution and Rules: Rule 3: "the Society may not... effect any change calculated permanently to alter or destroy the original and historic character of the Talyllyn Railway."

This rule was to occasion much discussion both on the railway and in *The Talyllyn News*. The extracts which follow raise some issues which were hotly debated, together with the proposed extension to Nant Gwernol and even an extension to Talyllyn Lake. In reality, the Talyllyn Railway was only just alive in 1950 and, when the preservationists took over, as Pat Whitehouse has said in the earlier chapters; "No-one had any idea of what needed to be done as it had never been done before." There was no strategic plan, but everyone did what they thought best so that the railway could run again for current enjoyment and future benefit. Until the Society settled into its role and the railway had been pretty much completely re-equipped, it was make do and mend and work out the

next step as everyone went along. No wonder then that the railway changed. But has it fundamentally changed that much? Look at the pictures included in this book taken in the railway's 150th year and decide for yourself. Apart from the extreme change at Wharf driven by commercial considerations and the needs of 21st century passengers, the expansion at Pendre to provide the additional facilities necessary to service the additional demand and, also, the addition of passenger services along the mineral extension, the railway has, perhaps, not changed that much. It may now be a little over equipped for the service it needs to deliver today, but that is not a criticism; the additional locomotives now have a TR heritage of their own on a railway which has been owned and managed

> The Talyllyn Railway retains a delightful character of its own, with a heterogeneous collection of beautifully restored engines and vehicles, buildings added and adapted, and the whole completely changed. It is the holiday crowds which have destroyed its original character by their insistence on wanting to travel on the line, but they want comfort and efficiency in their journey, not the timeless go-as-you-please of 1950.
>
> *A.G.W.Garraway*

by the TRPS for longer than either the McConnell family or Sir Haydn's regimes. The new carriages are a fine collection and appropriate for modern day use. The 'original train' is probably in the best condition it has ever been.

Should the railway develop and, if so, in what direction? It appears to many outsiders to be a railway for its members (and, if so, so what as they own it, but now the holding company has charitable status some more thought might be given to that). Should it seek more passengers and participate even more in the economic and social community of Mid Wales? Is that practicable? Should it develop a potentially 'unique selling proposition' and market its famous alter ego as the *Skarloey Railway* more? No doubt discussions will continue, but James Boyd was right when he wrote: "The pioneers have completed their job; a policy for their successors will be to ensure that no one will be in doubt about the future."

The members wrote many letters to the *Talyllyn News* full of comment and advice.

it had managed with a very great struggle to run for 85 years, and that it travelled along one of the most picturesque valleys in Wales. In 1950 it had long ceased to be a commercial proposition, yet what a lure it was to those people who enthused over a collection of decaying timber, tottering masonry and tortured metal. I cannot see, when looking cold-bloodedly at the Talyllyn, anything outstanding in either the construction of the line or the motive power and rolling stock and we must get these facts very firmly in mind when our present position is reviewed.

I wonder now if foundations have been built for what I would like to see as a future for the Talyllyn. We now wonder what can be done to foster greater interest in diffident members and how to stimulate new support. I contend that the intended policy of preservation has never been defined; we have no idea where we are going. I really charge those associated with our foundation of not knowing just what it was they wanted to preserve.

Where are we going? *(B.J. Green)*

I feel we must be under no illusion as to the history of the railway. It is agreed by very learned writers that its existence was mundane and inauspicious. Its only claim to fame is really sentimental in that

Where are we going? *(Angus Crawshaw)*

We all support the Talyllyn as best we can, and I suppose most of us visit it as often as we can. After my visit this summer I feel critical – not so much about *what* has been done, which is colossal, but the *way* things are being done. I don't think we're being true to our inheritance; we were, but it looks as we're imperceptibly drifting away.

In the earlier Society days a water tank was put up at Pendre; the base is stonework and the tank is an old drum. The whole edifice is charming, and very Talyllyn. It melts into the yard as if it had been there always, but it fulfills its purpose. I would guess that it was designed and put up by somebody who loved the Talyllyn, who understood the spirit of the little railway, and wanted to preserve it.

That is one side of the picture. Now look at another. This summer, at Pendre, there was to be seen a mass of steel girders rising crudely into the Welsh landscape – the new carriage shed in embryo! An item in the last *News* tells us that the roof is to be corrugated asbestos, and one's worst fears are confirmed. I know the Committee has decided that we need a new carriage shed and I know that many people have given freely of their time and money that it might be built – but steel and asbestos! What's the hurry? Why not stone, timber and slate? Why such a violent break with what is Talyllyn, and with things Welsh? I think I know the answer. I think it is the old, old 'inevitability of gradualism.' First there is one thing that is not quite Talyllyn; a lot of people don't notice the difference and the others accept it. The next thing is a bit farther away, the next is a bit farther, and so on.

What started it? Was it the nameplate on *Dolgoch* - something she had never known before? Or was it the point indicators at Pendre, which made the yard look like an overgrown model railway?

> **First there is one thing that is not quite Talyllyn; a lot of people don't notice the difference and the others accept it. The next thing is a bit farther away, the next is a bit farther, and so on**

Personally, I can't spot the point of departure, but I think it is time we took stock of what we are doing. As I see it, the parting of the ways is upon us now. We can go on as we have in the last few years, and become a Talyllyn Railway that has no connection with the past - a trippers' piece over which few of us will sadly breathe 'the Talyllyn is dead; long live the Talyllyn.' Or we can ponder before we act, do our best to absorb the old Talyllyn atmosphere – there is still some to be found – and give our visitors a taste of Victorian country travel. Both can be paying propositions, but I believe that it is only the second alternative that has staying power.

Where are we going? *(Tom Rolt)*

That the columns of the *Talyllyn News* are always bursting with ideas and are often highly critical of

what has been done or what has not been done on the railway, is an excellent thing. It shows that a lot of people care deeply about the railway, and so long as they go on caring in this way the future is safe.

I must confess that I often look back nostalgically to the Talyllyn Railway as it was when the Society took over in 1951, but, let us face it, the railway could not be embalmed in that state of romantic dilapidation. It could not stand still. For years the Talyllyn tradition had been one of slow decay, and if the Society had not put that tradition smartly into reverse there would be no railway left today.

When the Society was formed, the Talyllyn was at the end of its tether, and it was our aim, not to preserve it in that state by a feat of brinkmanship, but to make it an example of what such a railway was like in the days of narrow gauge prosperity.

Abergynolwyn Winding House
(Sonia Rolt)

The democratic principle seemed more to mean having respect for that which one had the power to change. Respect arising from love, love from understanding and understanding involves everything to do with this unique form of life. Not any old railway, **this** one. Why it was there, the men who brought it about, the hard facts of slate in that one mountain and the men who got it out, worked it, built a village with it and all the artefacts belonging to the line; Who had lives intimately linked with it and whose efforts and the acretions of whose lives we inherited in this extraordinary way. Such feelings could never be satisfied by simply running a railway, however successfully. We had to celebrate it by our success and by the understanding we brought to it.

Every ounce of effort in the early years was devoted to renewal, to existing as well as we could, until we come to 1963 when, in the hideous reality of falling traffic receipts, we had to change or die.

For years the idea of Nant Gwernol has hovered, grail like, a symbol of an eventual goal where everything the railway stood for could be expressed. Due to the endless and valiant legal struggles it has not been possible to engender enthusiasm or, indeed, ever put before the members fully the great possibilities in this idea. Then we shall be near the heart of the matter, Bryn Eglwys and the collapsing mountain chambers whose riches where the reason for our living presence today. Most beautiful, secret and moving in itself, the gorge and platform above the piercingly sweet clarity of the rushing water below, are **the** place for us to make something new which does incorporate all we feel we should show to honour the past. The railway has been promised relics from the quarry, the quarry bell, the slate tablet from Bryn Eglwys saying that one John Pughe started quarrying slate there in 1847.

Clough Williams-Ellis, the greatest Welsh architect, has visited Nant Gwernol and offered to design our station. The one man imbued with the history of Wales and inspired with the sense of place to be able to give us something which would be nationally recognised and visited and which could become a little Wonder of Wales: reached by train only as the crown and end of the pilgrimage into the heart of the mountain. We should be

A mass of steel girders rising crudely into the Welsh landscape – the new carriage shed in embryo. *(Photo: Talyllyn Railway Archive)*

overwhelmed with the opportunity and be doing everything to bring it about.

The winding house has gone. It should have been kept. The ingenuity and effort required to keep it, a challenge to our engineers, to provide one of the visual pleasures of the journey and, for those who can look further, evocative evidence of the old crucial links between village, railway and mountain.

Gerald Manley Hopkins, the great religious poet, once wrote in his private notebooks: "I wish to die that I might not see the inscapes of the world destroyed any more." Let no one under estimate the power of the inscapes of this world to move and hold us and to show us something beyond themselves. The felicitous curve of wall, position of lamp, gate or eve of roof expressing organic growth and the usage of generations and generations of men.

We have a wonderfully devoted and skilled permanent staff at Towyn. The very best that could be found: but by the very nature of things their skills are in running a railway and making a profit out of it. Not one of them is a preservationist as such, nor should be. It should be the duty of the Council to see the wood for the trees and hold the overall view as a Preservation Society.

Let us never underestimate the public, as capable as any one of us of being moved by the evidences which we can leave for them to see and experience. Remove the experience, remove the evidence, and you have rated the public has no more than stupid milch cow, good only for the shillings and half crowns poured into every begging bag shaking in its face. Remove the possibility of the other and better experience and you will eventually remove the public, which is in the last count, everyone of us. Not there solely for a penny ride, on however glamorous a train, but for something deeper.

The very essence of the character of the Talyllyn Railway was its complete indifference to time. As soon as you try to develop the line, the whole essence of its character goes, and the whole railway becomes inadequate.

> **The very essence of the character of the Talyllyn Railway was its complete indifference to time**

This comment produced a whole flow of correspondence in the TR in house magazine and probably also contributed to Tom Rolt's eventual resignation as he had deeply held views about the development of the line and always foresaw Nant Gwernol being the ultimate dream, ending with the Clough Williams Ellis station design, probably with trains hauled there by the Curwen designed articulated tank engine. However, when the new Abergynolwyn station was eventually completed in the form it now stands, Sonia seemed happy with is as she went on record to say, after all, that "this is absolutely right."

A member's confession

Harvey Gray, a member of the original TRPS committee confesses:

On my first day's work as a Talyllyn Railway volunteer I did a dreadful thing. I helped dismantle the Abergynolwyn village incline. Of course, at the time, it seemed the obvious thing to do. The rails on the incline were relatively unworn and they

Rail was urgently needed to replace the life expired Talyllyn track and, as the rails on the inclines were in better condition, they were salvaged and re-used. Here Bill Faulkner, Eric Lees, Bill Oliver and 'Maggie' Maguire are at work on 25th March, 1951. *(Photo: Talyllyn Railway Archive)*

were desperately needed elsewhere. Back in Easter 1951 it never occurred to me or to any of the five chaps working with me that the day would come when many people would deplore the loss of the incline and the fan of tracks leading from its foot to the houses they served. The incline looked to be out of use for ever. Only recently has it become clear to me that the incline was unique. Nowhere else in Britain – perhaps in the world – did a railway company, and a statutory one at that, deliver goods to and take material away from individual houses *by rail*. Abergynolwyn was nearly unique in being a *planned* village, and a modular one at that, with road access to each house frontage and rail access to the very door.

The Abergynolwyn operation was one of stark simplicity. Heavy goods, sacks of produce, an occasional cottage piano, went down the incline, the weight of the train on the rope being used to haul the village's human waste products up the incline to the top, whence the material would be taken along the railway in the same wagons to the farms and market gardens adjoining the line for use as fertilizer.

We should have retained the incline, the winding house etc. just in case the world comes to its

> Three small boys, dressed in their Sunday best, came to inspect the proceedings with some solemnity. After a long silence, the smallest remarked: "You naughty men! Working on a Sunday!"

senses! If it did I'd be back relaying the track – unfortunately though my doctor has forbidden me to restore inclines.

Maybe, one day, the TR can recreate the incline and its winding house together with the fan of tracks running through the streets of Abergynolwyn. To do so would certainly recreate a unique and fascinating aspect of the TR's original purpose and also lay to rest the ghosts still poking the TR's conscience about having demolished the Abergynolwyn incline in the first place, dangerous though the building undoubtedly was.

The Talyllyn Railway, some may say, has become a worn out anachronism in this age of the jet plane and the atom bomb into which it has strayed. Surely then, so much time, money and energy could have been expended to some better purpose? To this I would reply with another question: What other and more fruitful fields has the planned state left open for individual initiative and creative enterprise to till today? Very few. With every year that passes there is less fertile ground left and it is a dreary, ill-

The team dismantling the rails from the Abergynolwyn incline on 27th March, 1951: L to R: Owen Prosser, Eric Lees, Harvey Gray, Bill Oliver, Bill Faulkner and Denis Maguire

nourished crop which sprouts in the state owned fields. False quantitative standards of equality and uniformity imposed in the name of democracy; the false equalisation of mere size with efficiency which assumes the larger the organisation the better it must be; these things run counter to the grain of human nature and lead to damnation and the dark night of the spirit.....It is against this imposed and world-levelling order that the creative individual is bound to fight, not only for standards of truth and of beauty, but for his own survival. (L.T.C.Rolt)

Nowadays the Talyllyn no longer has quite the excitement, the sense of pioneering precedent, that it had in the early 1950s. It has all been done rather often now. Of course, the early necrophiliac charm has gone; it had to. Tom Rolt was a sound practical engineer, he was too much of an artist to be entirely satisfied with what the Talyllyn had become. But that was an example of divine discontent: nothing can ever be perfect. The flame he lit back then is still burning. (John Snell)

As Tom Rolt emphasised in a passage in one of his books, it is usually mistaken to single out anyone as the 'inventor' of an innovation. More often it is the combined effort of a group working towards a given object which brings about a major breakthrough in a given field. Tom Rolt was not the first to propose a body of supporters as a means of keeping a railway in action; as far as is known, it was Mr. A.E. Rimmer in the January 1941 edition of *Modern Tramway* who did that. Neither were Mr Rolt's original ideas for saving the Talyllyn

those that were in the event adopted. Yet the fact remains that, by establishing the first contacts with Sir Haydn Jones and by calling the first meeting of our Society, he rightly took his place as the dominant figure in the railway preservation movement. His position as such is indisputable.

Hence he may be thought of as having left this country, and indeed the world, a highly original and distinctive form of epitaph of the very kind which one feels would have pleased him most: an animated and tangible tribute to his work.

Just as Sir Christopher Wren's tomb in St

Above:
Abergynolwyn
Winding House
sleeping

Below:
Abergynolwyn
Winding House
destroyed

Dolgoch passes the site of the Abergynolwyn Winding House in. *(Photo: Darren Turner)*

Clough Williams Ellis sketch of his suggested station at Nant Gwernol

Paul's says: "If you would see his monument, look around", so, if we would see Tom Rolt's, we have but to visit any of the new generation of locally constituted, independent railways which are coming to have an ever more important place in the pattern of public transport. Their gleaming locomotives, well polished rolling stock and carefully tended properties are all the direct progeny of what was started on the Talyllyn in 1950. For it was that scheme which established firmly and beyond doubt that it was realistic and practicable to keep a line in action, or secure its reinstatement, By mustering in its support those who would give unstintingly of time, money and effort to support the thing in which they believed. To have played the leading part in setting on foot so healthy, public spirited and generally constructive a movement as this was a splendid achievement and one that means, in effect, that every new line brought into action all the many others as yet another memorial to the man who so largely started it all.

The Talyllyn Railway Company is proud of its achievement. It spells three things: successful engineering achievement, increased prosperity in a remote part of Wales and, last but not least, a not inconsiderable addition to the sum of human happiness. (Owen Prosser)

Nant Gwernol Terminous, S-W. End.

A 21st century volunteer's view
(Jack Evans)

The Talyllyn Railway is a huge part of my life. Having always been local to the railway, I feel my attraction with it began because it was always there. I grew up in Corris Uchaf, and during school holidays our family would visit local steam railways in the area, with the Talyllyn being the main one; others were the Vale of Rheidol, Corris and the Fairbourne.

I began volunteering on the Railway at 13 years of age in the locomotive department winter working parties, I remember my first job on that occasion was given to me by David Jones; it was to clean *Dolgoch's* water gauge glass protectors in warm soapy water, although only a simple task to me as a 13 year old boy this was a memory that I know will stay with me forever. Since then the jobs I have undertaken in the department have become less 'clean'; my second job was to clean out the smokeboxes on a couple of the engines - this is a grubby job. In April 2012 I began my career in the loco department's operational side. It was the 11th of April, (a day after my 14th birthday!) the loco was No, 3 *Sir Haydn* with Driver Mike Davies and Fireman Marc Smith. On this day I was privileged to have two round trips on the footplate which were memorable. Since then I have undertaken many cleaning turns and shed days, with the occasional third man trip on the footplate learning the line, learning how a steam locomotive works, learning how to fire and above all learning how to work as a team. To me the volunteers on the railway are one big team, and without every one of them there would be no railway for us to work on and enjoy. Since joining the society I have made so many new friends, which is nice as I have friends on the railway and different friends away – this in itself is special to me.

My first major memory of the railway was back in May 2003, when I was five years old. My father, Richard Evans,' lorry was hired to move No.3 *Sir Haydn* from Tywyn Wharf to Maespoeth on the Corris Railway. I rode with him in the lorry on my booster seat; the view from the cab was great as we pulled out of Wharf Drive, where in the mirror I could see the steam loco following us on our trailer, with an old saucepan on top of the chimney acting as a lid to prevent the fire from drawing too much. Unloading the loco at Corris was fun, I watched from afar as the loco was gently winched down the ramp, touching Corris metals for the first time in some years.

In May 2012, 11 years after the previous occasion No. 3 *Sir Haydn* yet again made her way to the Corris Railway on the trailer of my father's lorry. This time no booster seat was needed in the lorry. When we got to Maespoeth and positioned to unload, I did not watch from afar, I was one of the many hands helping in assembling the ramp and

turfer winch and gradually helping ease the loco down to Corris metals once more.

Now at 17 years old I am a passed-cleaner within the loco department, and have progressed as far as firing solo. The first time you leave Tywyn Wharf, just you and the driver is memorable. You have no fireman standing in the middle for you to fall back on, you must think for yourself and act accordingly.

My personal aspiration on the Talyllyn is to one day fulfil my dream in becoming a steam locomotive driver. This takes several years which is why I am grateful I began my loco career at 14

Jack Evans leans out of *Talyllyn*. *(Photo: Kes Jones)*

Tom Rolt would have been delighted. *Dolgoch* and the original train at Nant Gwernol on 3rd May, 2015 in the railway's 150th year. The flame Tom Rolt lit is still burning

rather than 60. My aspiration for the railway itself is for it to be successful, and long living. In its 150th year personally I can see it lasting another 150 years. To ensure this happens the railway must move with the times which I believe it is doing. For years, from what I understand 'change' was always a swearword on the railway as no one liked change at all. None of us in 2015 are living in 1951, which to me is a good thing. The world now as a whole is more developed than ever with modernism taking over from the 'pioneering' age. I am not saying we ought to stop our place in being the preservation pioneers as a society, but I believe we, the younger generation, need to take things one step further and develop what we already have, to make it better and more fitting for the next century and a half. Write our own histories, rather than repeating others' history; who are we trying to mimic?

My association with the Talyllyn Railway has helped me mature, ready for the future. When I began I was awfully shy, but now I will almost definitely talk to anyone I stumble across. The railway has also helped me gain helpful experience for future careers, I recently got a job on the Vale of Rheidol Railway as a fireman; my dream job. Without the Talyllyn this would never have happened. I hope to eventually become a mechanical engineer, my experience with railways has contributed heavily to my knowledge of the subject.

To me and the generation I am within, the railway is a part of life. Without it, undoubtedly there would be something else to do/be associated with to pass the time. Narrow gauge railways fill a huge gap in the lives of many people I know, people coming from all sorts of backgrounds that may or may not be accepted by todays society – this is where Welsh Narrow gauge railways are unique, everyone is respected and made to feel welcome, or even 'finished off' in adolescence in becoming a mature and courteous adult.

Dyma ddiwedd ei hanes nhw, ond dyma ddechrau'r dyfodol ni.. (*Here's to the end of their history, and the beginning of our future*)

It may just be that another generation will thank them for preserving the Talyllyn, for it is a relic this railway, a piece of ornamental scrollwork lifted from the pattern of yesterday and kept as a memento

(Carl Davidson (USA) maker of the film
A Railway with a Heart of Gold)

Acknowledgments

Jackie Barnes
John Bate
Dick Blenkinsop
James Boyd
G.D. Braithwaite
Angus Crawshaw
Eddie Castellan
Ian Drummond
Jack Evans
Barbara Fuller
Martin Fuller
Pat Garland
John Gott
Harvey Gray
B.J.Green
Adam Harris
Richard Hope
Jim Jarvis
Kidderminster Railway Museum
Anthony Lambert
David Leech
David Mitchell
Don Newing
Mike Pope
David Postle
Chris Price
Owen Prosser
Gordon Rhodes
Richard Rolt
Sonia Rolt
Tim Rolt
John Snell
John Smallwood
Darren Turner
Harold Vickers
Pat Whitehouse
Stuart Whitehouse
David Williams

PHOTOGRAPHS

The photographer of the various photographs in the book is not always acknowledged by each picture. This is largely because most of the earlier pictures are in the Talyllyn Railway Archives and many of those acknowledged above have been kind in assisting providing these images. However, many of them were actually taken either by my father and John Adams and sometimes it has not been practical to decide which of them took a particular picture. This might seem strange but, in the 1950s, it was common for photographers to pass prints to one another which ended up in their own collections even if they did not take them. On other occasions, PBW and JHLA would have been standing side by side and so the image could have been taken by either of them. Some of the 1953 pictures of Dolgoch in my collection were taken by J.C.Flemmons.

BIBLIOGRAPHY

Fortunately, there are many books about the Talyllyn Railway and its various aspects for the reader to enjoy if more detailed information about the railway is sought after.

R.W. Kidner: *The Narrow Gauge Railways of North Wales* – this is probably the first booklet about the railway and long out of print

Lewis Cozens: *The Talyllyn Railway*- this is a short monograph, being one in a series of small booklets about minor railways and also long out of print

F.H. Howson: *Narrow Gauge Railways of Britain booklet*

Rolt & Whitehouse: *Lines of Character* – One of Rolt's earliest railway books about several railway by-ways and illustrated by my father; good reading

Rolt: *Railway Adventure* – Rolt's classic and autobiographical account of the first two years from his viewpoint of managing the TR in the TRPS days - a

Cleaning No.4 in Pendre
shed. The start of an
engineman's career.
(Photo: John Adams)

'must read' and some of Rolt's text from this book has been included here by kind permission of the Rolt family

Rolt: High Horse Riderless - this is a difficult book to read in which Rolt struggles with life's philosophy and the benefits and disbenefits of the industrial revolution on mankind, somewhat underpinning his views and behaviour in seeking to preserve the TR whilst all around him was changing

Rolt: *Landscape With Figures* – Rolt's final volume in his autobiographical trilogy which includes commentary looking back on his TRPS days and some of this text has also been included here, also by kind permission of the Rolt family

Talyllyn Century - a book written for the centenary of the TR in 1965 by the TRPS pioneers

Talyllyn Handbook – a guide book

Potter: *Talyllyn Railway* – the first attempt to write the history of the TRPS

Boyd: *Narrow Gauge Rails in Mid Wales* – one of Boyd's series of histories on narrow gauge railways

Boyd: *Talyllyn Railway* – Boyd's later book on the history of the TR up to but not including the TRPS days; this book has been criticized as it is sometimes difficult to know when Boyd was sure of his facts or making assumptions (some of which are clearly incorrect)

Bate: *Chronicles of Pendre Sidings* – written by the person probably serving the TRPS the longest and its Chief Engineer for a considerable period; as the title suggests, chronicles taken from his diaries written at the time

Alan Holmes: *Talyllyn Revived* - a history of the TRPS days

David Mitchell: *The Talyllyn Railway*: Sixty Years of Preservation - mainly a photographic book of pictures through the TRPS days of the railway

Lawson Little: *Carriages and Wagons of the Talyllyn Railway* - a detailed summary of all the TR's rolling stock

John Snell: *Mixed Gauge*s – an autobiographical account by John of his days on the TR and adventures elsewhere

Martin Fuller: *Talyllyn & Corris Steam Locomotives* - a detailed exposition of the TR locomotives up to TRPS days. A subsequent volume is in preparation describing the locomotives during the TRPS times

John Milnor & Beryl Williams *Rails to Glyn Ceiriog: The History of the Glyn Valley Tramway Part 2 1904-1937* – this has detailed coverage and pictures of the rescue of the two GVT coach bodies now in service on the TR

Sara Eade: *The Talyllyn Railway Men* – a study of men owning, affecting and working on the TR up to the TRPS days

THE QUOTATIONS

These have been taken from two sources: published works (which include Tom Rolt's books, the TR's house magazine, The Talyllyn News and other publications, leaflets and periodicals, but also from tape recordings recent President and former Secretary, Richard Hope, made of conversations with Pat Garland and Pat Whitehouse. I have taken the liberty to re-arrange some of these conversations where the order hopefully makes better consequential sense, although Pat Garland's reminiscences were very clearly set out and I have incorporated much verbatim; the recording with Pat Whitehouse wandered around a bit more between topics and back again and so I have taken greater liberties with sentence construction but I have nevertheless been faithful to the original feelings expressed, which has been relatively easy as, of course, I am very much familiar with the phrases often used by my father.

I have also made some grammatical improvements whilst trying to leave the quotations as original as possible, but I have made some tense changes and alterations to references to time elapsed where that will help the reader today follow text which was written over sixty years ago.

Spelling of place names are those in use at the time when they are written, so there are some divergencies, for example Towyn and Tywyn which are, of course, the same place.

Today's young Talyllyn members gather with General Manager, Chris Price, around *Tom Rolt* and *Dolgoch* in Pendre yard